P9-DML-449

FOREIGN MULTINATIONAL
INVESTMENT
IN THE UNITED STATES

FOREIGN MULTINATIONAL INVESTMENT IN THE UNITED STATES

Struggle for Industrial Supremacy

Sara L. Gordon and Francis A. Lees

 QUORUM BOOKS
New York • Westport, Connecticut • London

Library of Congress Cataloging-in-Publication Data

Gordon, Sara L.
  Foreign multinational investment in the United
States.

  Bibliography: p.
  Includes index.
  1. Investments, Foreign—United States.
  2. Investments, Foreign—United States—Case studies.
  3. International business enterprises—United States.
  4. Competition, International.   I. Lees, Francis, A.
  II. Title.
  HG4910.G67   1986   332.6'73'0973   85–20481
  ISBN: 0–89930–071–5 (lib. bdg. : alk. paper)

Library of Congress Catalog Card Number: 85–20481
ISBN: 0–89930–071–5

First published in 1986 by Quorum Books

Greenwood Press, Inc.
88 Post Road West, Westport, Connecticut 06881

Printed in the United States of America

The paper used in this book complies with the
Permanent Paper Standard issued by the National
Information Standards Organization (Z39.48–1984).

10   9   8   7   6   5   4   3   2   1

Contents

Exhibits _____

Figures

Preface

The U.S. Steel Corporation no longer exists; it has merged with a petroleum company and is now known as the USX Corporation. LTV has filed for bankruptcy, and steel industry profits have virtually evaporated in 1986. This scenario was predicted by us three years ago, as a result of faulty policies in Washington vis-à-vis American manufacturing. This volume critically analyzes the status of important sectors of American industry and considers the broad range of policies needed to rebalance the competitive position of these industries.

This volume sets out primarily to consider policy toward foreign direct investment (FDI) entering the United States. In addition, trade policy is also examined, since trade and investment issues have become inextricably interwoven.

Our motivation for writing this book was twofold. First, we sought to analyze the recent growth of FDI in the United States, focusing upon motivations for such investment, its impact on the domestic economy and the balance of payments, the substitution of inward FDI for international trade, and the relationship between FDI and U.S. international competitiveness in manufacturing in the face of heightened global competition. A significant part of this book is concerned with investment in the steel and motor vehicle industries; these are two industries in which import penetration is high and the United States is losing ground in the "struggle for industrial supremacy." Second, we make recommendations for policy approaches towards FDI in the United States. Because FDI is linked to the competitive position of U.S. manufacturing industries, some recommendations have relevance for U.S. industrial policy.

While our overall position is critical of the current administration in Washington, it is reassuring to observe the Reagan Administration adopting policy measures more in line with the position we endorse. The timeliness of this volume is borne out by the rising volume of inward FDI, from $15.2 billion in 1984 to an estimated $19.6 billion in 1985.

In this volume we have shown that the United States does not compete internationally in free and perfectly competitive markets. In part, this stems from the fact that oligopolistic firms have become more dominant in international trade, suggesting that a pure free-trade approach need not lead to an optimal outcome. Therefore, it is folly for the United States to continue in this direction in the face of growing trade imbalances. It is necessary for the United States to consider departing from its free-trade and investment ideology. As discussed in this book, specific micro policies toward trade and investment are required. As noted by Federal Reserve Board Chairman Paul Volcker (July 1986), the trade deficit cannot be adequately dealt with by changes in currency rates alone; the deficit has crippled American industry and has led to an unsustainable dependence on inflows of recycled foreign money.

In the steel industry, we basically endorse the International Trade Commission findings that call for an interim period of moderate protection while the industry is afforded time to restructure. In addition, subsidized public sector loans, loan guarantees, and investment tax credits can help the industry restructure itself and modernize. In the auto industry, we have proposed a modified domestic content requirement also aimed at facilitating industry restructuring. In addition, we have shown that moderate tariff relief responding to Japanese auto imports would have only small negative welfare effects.

Because macroeconomic policy changes have affected America's ability to compete in international markets, we have made a number of recommendations for changes in such policies. Included are recommendations for low interest rate policy, a foreign investment policy having the objective of reducing wide swings in the international value of the dollar, the adoption of a program to manage the balance of trade, and expansion of incentives for savings and investment. Writing in the summer of 1986, it is heartwarming to note that progress has been made in some of these areas. On September 22, 1985, finance ministers from the Group of Five met in New York and agreed upon the necessity of coordinating monetary policies and enhancing intervention in foreign currency markets. Since that date, the U.S. dollar has depreciated by 20 percent in effective terms, reducing relative prices of U.S. exports in world markets and increasing import prices. Real interest rates have declined significantly during the period 1985–1986. Forecasts for a slowdown in U.S. economic growth increase the possibility that real interest rates will continue to decline within the near future. Lower interest rates will help reduce the U.S. trade deficit by enhancing U.S. industrial competitiveness. Furthermore, lower interest rates will encourage domestic investment and assist in lowering federal budgetary deficits.

We wish to thank a number of individuals and organizations that assisted us by providing information and criticism while the book was being written. Among these are staff members of the U.S. International Trade Commission, American Iron and Steel Institute, Congressional Research Service, Volkswagen America, U.S. Bureau of Labor Statistics, and Charles River Associates. The following specialized libraries provided much-needed assistance: The Conference Board, Library of Congress, the Watson Library of Business and Economics of Columbia University, the Council on Foreign Relations, and the Information Library of the Canadian Consulate General. Two of our graduate assistants, Stephen Durando and Andre Petrunoff, carried out considerable information collecting. Francis Lees wishes to thank his wife, Kathryn, for valiant typing services, and Sara Gordon wishes to thank her parents for enthusiastic encouragement.

Abbreviations

AISI: American Iron and Steel Institute
AOC: Argon-oxygen decarbonization units
BEA: Bureau of Economic Analysis
BLS: Bureau of Labor Statistics
BP: British Petroleum
CBO: Congressional Budget Office
CDF: Charbonnages de France
CFIUS: Committee on Foreign Investment in the United States
CFP: Cie Françoise des Petroles
COCOM: Coordinating Committee for Multilateral Export Controls
DR: Direct reduction
DRI: Data Resources Incorporated
DRIO: Directly reduced iron ore
DSM: Dutch State Mines
ECI: Entry concentration index
EEC: European Economic Community
ENA: Experimental Negotiation Agreement
FDI: Foreign direct investment
FIRA: Foreign Investment Review Agency
FMS: Flexible manufacturing systems
GATT: General Agreement on Tariffs and Trade
GDP: Gross domestic product
GM: General Motors
GNP: Gross national product
IAE: International Aero Engines
ITC: International Trade Commission

LDC:	Less developed countries
LICIT:	Labor Industry Coalition for International Trade
MCC:	Microelectronics and Computer Technology Corporation
MITI:	Ministry of International Trade and Industry
MNC:	Multinational companies
MNE:	Multinational enterprise
NASA:	National Aeronautics Space Agency
NATO:	North Atlantic Treaty Organization
NCR:	National Cash Register
NEC:	Nippon Electric Company
NIC:	Newly industrialized countries
NTB:	Non-tariff barrier
NTT:	Nippon Telegraph and Telephone
OECD:	Organization for Economic Co-operation and Development
OMAs:	Orderly marketing agreements
OPEC:	Organization of Petroleum Exporting Countries
OTA:	Office of Technology Assessment
R & D:	Research and development
SICRSTA:	Siderugica Lazaro Cardenas-Las Truchas SA
SRC:	Semiconductor Research Cooperative
TPM:	Trigger price mechanism
UAW:	United Auto Workers
USTR:	United States Trade Representative
VER:	Voluntary export restraint
VRA:	Voluntary restraint agreements
VW:	Volkswagen

FOREIGN MULTINATIONAL INVESTMENT IN THE UNITED STATES

1

The Playing Field Is Not Level _____

Increasingly over the past four decades, American multinationals have found the rules of international trade and investment changing. These changes have tended to work against American industry. Foreign multinationals, national governments, and even the U.S. government have participated in rule revisions that are less fair from the standpoint of American companies. In this volume we look at the increasingly uneven playing field of global competition with regard mainly to direct foreign investment. Direct foreign investment inflows have quickened, representing one of the strategies available to foreign enterprises seeking to enlarge market share in the North American mass markets.

RATIONALE FOR STUDY

Over the past 40 years the United States has exerted a dominant influence in the field of foreign business investment. American dominance continues but is following a changing pattern. During the period 1955–1968 American manufacturers were building production facilities in Western Europe, in part to take advantage of the opportunities available in the Common Market. In the period 1968–1976 U.S. companies focused their attention on other parts of the world, including the Pacific Basin. Over the entire 40-year period to the present foreign business investors have been increasing their activities in the United States, and in the most recent ten-year period foreign direct investment (FDI) inflows have grown to almost tidal wave proportions. In short, American dominance as a supplier of business investment around the world has reversed to the point where American prominence is based on absorbing a major share of global business (direct) investment flows.

Table 1.1
Percentage Share of Global FDI Flows—Selected Countries, 1960–1981

Country	Pct. Share of FDI Outflows				Pct. Share of FDI Inflows			
	1960–1961	1969–1970	1978–1979	1980–1981	1960–1961	1969–1970	1978–1979	1980–1981[a]
United States	67	61	49	28	13	20	40	38
West Germany	4	7	10	9	10	8.5	6.5	3
Japan	2	2.5	6	8	1	1	nil	0.5
Netherlands	3.5	4.5	5	6	2	7	2.5	3
United Kingdom	16	12	12.5	19	20	12	12	8
France	9	2	5	8	6	6.5	13	6
Canada	1.5	3	5	10	26	11	5	-3.5

[a]In this period Brazil, Australia, Mexico, and Singapore ranked fourth through seventh, with 4.7%, 4.5%, 4.2%, and 3.7% of inflows, respectively.

Sources: United Nations, Centre on Transnational Corporations, *Salient Features and Trends in Foreign Direct Investment* (New York, 1983), pp. 40–43. U.S. Department of Commerce, International Trade Administration, *International Direct Investment*, August 1984, pp. 46–47.

This changing pattern is evident in Table 1.1, which contains summary data on shares of FDI inflows and outflows. Twenty-five years ago U.S. investors provided two-thirds of total FDI outflows, but the U.S. share has declined to less than 30%. Investors in West Germany, Japan, the Netherlands, the United Kingdom, and Canada have increased their shares of FDI outflows. Twenty-five years ago the most important host countries for FDI inflows were Canada, the United Kingdom, the United States, and West Germany. More recently, the United States has become the chief recipient of such inflows, taking 38% of global flows in 1980–1981. Canada, the largest recipient of FDI inflows 25 years ago, has dropped to seventh position as a recipient (host) country. In the same period the United Kingdom has jumped to second position, followed by France and West Germany.

The focus of this work is on the United States as a recipient of FDI and on the implication of large-scale inflows to the United States in its role as an economic superpower. Specifically, we examine the factors that account for the increased volume of FDI inflows to the United States; how this inflow affects the status of the United States as an economic superpower; and the mix of policies that is most appropriate for the United States to adopt vis-à-vis FDI inflows in order to facilitate the United States' continuing role as a major economic force in the world economy.

Our interest in these problems was stimulated by research initiated over six years ago, starting with an examination of the Volkswagen (VW) investment in a U.S. production facility. In that study, published in 1982,[1] we considered the theoretical issues involved in multinational enterprise investment and the specific capital budgeting aspects of the VW decision. In the Volkswagen case it was possible to assess and evaluate the net present value of the investment from the point of view of the parent multinational enterprise (MNE), as well as the value of the government subsidies provided by the state of Pennsylvania in attracting this investment.

The VW investment was prompted by a weakened competitive position and a declining share in the U.S. market for motor vehicles. As we note in this volume, more recent U.S. investments by other foreign motor vehicle producers have been prompted by their own increasing share of the U.S. market and concern over possible import cutbacks and threatened domestic content legislation. In either case, the massive domestic American market has operated as a magnet attracting foreign investors.

Creeping Expropriation

Our interest in foreign investment in the United States broadened across a larger number of industrial fronts as we came to understand that the change in international competitive position that led to large FDI inflows by foreign auto producers was only one part of an unfolding pattern. In this unfolding pattern various manufacturing sectors in the United States have experienced severe competition from foreign producers, taking the form of import penetration, acquisitions of U.S. companies by foreign investors, and establishment of North American production facilities by non-U.S. multinationals. The total impact of this foreign competition has been minimized because different American industries have been subjected to this new competition at different times. In effect, there has been a "creeping expropriation" of American industry and industrial product markets by foreign firms since the early 1960s.[2] Some of the first sectors to be taken over (1962–1972) were radios, television sets, and related consumer electronic products (Table 1.2). At this stage, there was little in the way of an effective U.S. policy response. Subsequently, other American industries have been challenged (steel, textiles, and motor vehicles). U.S. policy responses were directed to the later challenges somewhat more effectively than in the previous ten-year period. A variety of policy approaches were taken, including orderly marketing agreements (OMAs) in the case of textiles, a voluntary import quota in the case of motor vehicles, and a voluntary restraint agreement (VRA) in the case of steel. In the late 1980s high-technology industries such as computers, telecommunications, as well as aerospace industries are being challenged by non-U.S. multinationals. Overall, since 1960 this foreign competition has contributed to a relative decline of the American industrial base.[3] Unless an appropriate foreign investment and trade policy approach is taken, the U.S. industrial base will become inadequate for its needs.

America's industrial base is an essential part of the economy, despite pronouncements to the effect that the U.S. economy can shift to a service-oriented base.[4] There are several reasons for maintaining, and even reinforcing, the industrial base:

1. As a superpower it is necessary that the United States be able to produce its own industrial and military hardware.

2. The size of the U.S. internal market suggests that balance-of-payments deficits will grow to staggering amounts if it cannot produce a *very high percentage* of its manufacturing products at home. In the past the strength of the U.S. balance of payments has come from a large merchandise export surplus, coupled with substantial foreign investment outflows generating a large foreign investment income. The influx of FDI and the targeting of U.S. domestic markets by foreign producers is contributing to a reversal in the balance-of-payments position, a situation the United States can ill afford to permit to continue.

3. Technology leadership is required of a superpower. Continued leadership is not possible unless America properly blends together research and development (R & D), industrial investment, and policies on international trade and investment.

4. Basic industries such as steel and motor vehicles provide an income for a large part of the population. The replacement of these industries with lower paid employment opportunities would lead to a serious reduction in the U.S. standard of living.[5]

The preceding should not be interpreted to mean that the authors subscribe to the Reich-Rohatyn-Thurow deindustrialization thesis.[6] We do not. Rather, it is our contention that the targeted attacks on America's industries are selective and require specific and prompt responses from a streamlined federal government administrative apparatus.

The United States must be able to respond properly to the new global competitive realities. This requires the following approach toward FDI inflows:

• Establishing government machinery that is more responsive to the needs of this country where international competition and FDI inflows threaten the U.S. industrial base.

• Determining what industries are essential, how large a capacity for production is needed at home, and how much foreign investment and ownership is tolerable.

• Finding a set of policies that is appropriate to the status of each essential American industry, considering world competitive conditions.

This does not mean that the United States should adopt a strong industrial policy. Rather, the United States needs a strong FDI policy with regard to investment inflows, coupled with a forceful trade policy that will insure that key American industries retain their competitive balance and financial stability. In addition, there is need for a weak version of an industrial policy that lays out a loose framework for "safeguarded industry sectors." These safeguarded sectors should include industries which, by broad consensus between the executive and legislative divisions of government, must be mainly U.S. owned (to protect technology investment) and must supply at least 80 to 90% of U.S. domestic requirements.

Table 1.2
Phases in Foreign Competitive Inroads on U.S. Industrial Markets, 1962–1990

	Phase I 1962–1972	Phase II 1972–1982	Phase III 1982–1990
Industry facing severe foreign competitive inroad	Radio

Television | Steel Motor vehicles Textiles | Computers Telecommunications Aerospace |
| U.S. policy response | None

None | International Tariff Commission Hearings Quotas[a] Domestic Content OMAs[b] | None None None |

[a]Refers to voluntary quotas imposed by Japanese producers of motor vehicles.
[b]Refers to orderly marketing agreements negotiated with U.S. and foreign government cooperation.

U.S. POLICY ON FDI

The United States has not as yet developed a clear policy on FDI inflows. The federal government has not espoused any policy except to give strong vocal support to the free flow of business investment to and from this country. It has enacted no comprehensive legislation concerning foreign investment inflows, and any legislation applying to foreign business investment applies uniformly to domestic investors as well. Only at the state level has there been a conscious effort to influence FDI inflows, and in this case the overall approach has been parochially stimulative, incorporating generous tax relief and subsidies. State policy does not reflect national economic policy; rather, it resembles a system of regional incentives that influence the locational pattern more than the total amount and composition of inflows.

America's lack of policy on FDI inflows is unfortunate. Foreign investment in the United States is one part of the global competition that is taking place for industrial power and industrial supremacy. Industrial companies from each nation are striving to gain a larger share of world output and world markets. The industrial and manufacturing leadership long enjoyed by the United States has been narrowed, and manufacturers from foreign countries are increasing their share of world markets for industrial products, often at the expense of American producers.

Foreign producers have gained in global market power and competitive position as a result of four major developments, all of which indicate that American companies are not competing on a "level playing field." First, natural economic forces have allowed local markets for industrial products to expand more rapidly in the European Economic Community (EEC) (in the early years of the Common Market) and in emerging less developed countries (LDC) (South Korea, Malaysia, Singapore, Brazil). Second, certain foreign government policies have assisted local companies in expanding domestic and international market share. Among these policies are government subsidies to industry (low interest loans, R & D funding, and special tax incentives), protection of the home market, restriction of foreign investment inflows, and integration of the national economic plan with the needs and capabilities of local industries (the Ministry of International Trade and Industry (MITI) and indicative planning in Japan). Third, industrial companies in Europe and other regions are implementing industrial targeting policies aimed at capturing a larger share of the U.S. market. These policies may take the form of dumping, investment in the United States coupled with sourcing and transfer pricing strategies, and other anticompetitive practices. Fourth, state-owned enterprises have become an important factor in world business. These enterprises enjoy competitive advantages over private sector firms in that they are not required to generate profits and are able to obtain capital from the financial markets at lower rates of interest than private sector firms that are not backed up by the central government treasury.[7]

Foreign Government Policies

Foreign governments have kept American multinationals at bay, keeping their own sovereignty secure. Foreign governments have utilized industrial subsidies and trade investment policies in supporting their own industries in the competitive struggle for world market share.

Industrial subsidies offer foreign governments a direct and simple approach to supporting local producers. What has been the magnitude of such industrial subsidy programs? In a study published in 1983, B. Carlsson indicated that in the late 1970s industrial subsidies ranged from 1% to 3.5% of gross domestic product (GDP) in the sample of countries covered (Table 1.3). Relative to value added in mining and manufacturing, subsidies represented 3.6% to 16.0% of value added. In the case of Sweden, Carlsson found that between 1977 and 1979 subsidies represented 72% of value added in shipbuilding, 36% in steel, and 11% in textiles and apparel.

Table 1.3
Industrial Subsidies in Selected Countries, 1978–1980 (in percentages)

Industrial Subsidies	Great Britain (1979–1980)	Italy (1978)	Norway (1979)	Sweden (1979)	West Germany (1980)
As percentage of GDP	1.0	2.6	2.0	3.5	1.6
As percentage of value added in mining and manufacturing	3.6	7.1	7.6	16.0	4.0

Source: Bo Carlsson, "Industrial Subsidies in Sweden," *Journal of Industrial Economics* (September 1983): 8.

One of the best summaries of the extent to which foreign government policies give their own companies a global competitive advantage and leave U.S. firms defenseless is that provided by the Labor Industry Coalition for International Trade (LICIT) in congressional hearings held in 1982.[8] The LICIT data focused on the incidence and impact of trade-related performance requirements, which have not received as much attention as trade barriers. Foreign governments have made increasing use of performance requirements, including export levels, local content, employment, and financial performance, as a means of dictating to American and other multinational firms. The American motor vehicle industry has been particularly hard hit by this practice, with over 40 foreign governments imposing local content rules or other trade-related requirements. These requirements shift economic activity to the country imposing the requirements.

Trade distorting performance requirements . . . result in a direct transfer of investment, jobs and production to the country which imposes them—and away from other countries. The international shifts in investment, employment, production, and trade which they cause are not a response to market forces. . . . Such government directed economic decisions not only injure other countries, they also result in the misallocation of resources internationally.[9]

The United States should not hesitate to challenge these discriminatory practices through remedies available under international agreements. More importantly, the U.S. government should not wait for specific complaints to be filed by American firms, for in many cases American companies decide that access to the markets of a given country under less favorable circumstances is better than the uncertainties generated by seeking relief via government-to-government administrative procedures.

There are many examples of foreign government performance requirements. Tables 1.4 and 1.5 present detailed information concerning performance requirements in countries in which American investors have substantial interests. Table 1.4 lists 21 different types of requirements as well as the countries imposing these requirements. Table 1.5 ranks principal host countries for U.S. investment according to the amount of direct investment flow to these countries in 1972–1979. France, Brazil, Belgium, and Mexico appear to offer substantial problems for U.S. direct investors.

The Mexican Decree for Development of the Automotive Industry offers an excellent example of the distorting effects of performance requirements. Promulgated in 1977, the decree has two objectives: accelerated growth of the domestic auto industry, and generation of foreign exchange. The auto decree discriminates against foreign-owned firms and products through the following regulations:

1. Foreign exchange authorizations favor national over foreign firms. This is based on the degree of Mexican equity ownership.
2. Motor vehicle assemblers were given until 1982 to cover 100% of all foreign exchange costs through their own net exports. Net exports is defined as products sales value less imported content of all vehicles and components exported. The decree stipulates that automotive manufacturers are required to generate 50% of their net foreign exchange requirements through exports of parts or components. The remaining 50% can be obtained by means of export of vehicles and parts and components manufactured by their own plants.
3. The decree will gradually increase the percentage of local content required in production of vehicles for both Mexican and foreign-owned firms.

The decree will exert several influences on Mexico's foreign trade. First, it will reduce sales of U.S. auto parts in Mexico. Second, it will reduce U.S. sales of vehicles to Mexican free-zone areas. Finally, it will promote sales of Mexican automobiles and parts to the United States. Estimates of the shift in trade between the United States and Mexico vary, depending on various assumptions made. However, by the late 1980s exports of Mexican auto parts to the United States could exceed $2 billion annually. Chrysler de Mexico made an early decision to build an engine plant in Mexico with an annual production capacity of 200,000 engine units, and other U.S. manufacturers have been close behind Chrysler in planning to shift production to Mexico.

The top 25 host country recipients of global foreign investment have imposed a variety of trade-related performance requirements. These countries (Table 1.5) have resorted to this policy approach at the expense of American industry.

The impact of performance requirements warrants analysis. The 17 major host countries that impose "import limiting" requirements (Table 1.5) accounted for nearly one-half of U.S. exports in the late 1970s. The nine major host countries applying "export expanding" requirements accounted for nearly 40% of U.S. imports from non-OPEC (Organization of Petroleum Exporting Countries) areas. We may therefore conclude that "the incidence of trade distorting performance requirements among the world's major host countries for direct investment affects a significant proportion of U.S. foreign trade and is likely to be related to adverse trends in both imports and exports of the United States."[10]

Tactics and Strategies of Multinational Companies

Multinational companies (MNCs) must employ a variety of tactics and strategies in their efforts to enlarge their market share in the United States because they are in a different competitive position and so must adapt to the requirements of the situation at hand. As already noted, different industry sectors in the United States have been exposed to more intense foreign competition at different time periods (Table 1.2). The consumer electronics (television and radio) industry was one of the first to face the onslaught of import competition, closely followed by establishment of U.S. production facilities. Currently, the motor vehicle, steel, and textile industries are facing these competitive pressures.

The following discussion presents two distinct examples of foreign multinationals adapting their tactics and strategies to fit the situation and opportunities presented to them: the VW investment in a U.S. production facility in the late 1970s; and the Japanese auto producers over the past two decades.

Volkswagen Comes to America

Volkswagen was the largest foreign supplier of autos to the North American market until the currency crises of 1971–1973 and the devaluation of the dollar. In the period 1968–1971 annual export sales to the United States were in excess of 500,000 units. The VW market share was based on a strong export position, an overvalued dollar, and the unwillingness of American automobile producers to expand aggressively into small car manufacture. The disintegration of VW's North American market position in the early 1970s brought annual sales down to 267,000 units in 1975 and led to a reappraisal of corporate strategy. By 1975

Table 1.4
Performance Requirements for Foreign Direct Investment in Selected Countries[a]

Economic Performance Requirements

Location in Development Areas	Local Content Requirement	Technology Transfer Considerations	Restriction of Foreign Investment in Certain Areas	Encouragement of Foreign Investment in Priority Sectors	Limitations of Foreign Acquisition of Domestic firms	Limitations on Size of New Investment Projects
Austria	Algeria	Belgium	Argentina	Brazil	United Kingdom	Spain
Belgium	Argentina	Brazil	Austria	Belgium	France	Taiwan
Brazil	Australia	Canada	Denmark	Finland		
Denmark	Bolivia	India	Japan	West Germany		
Finland	Brazil	Israel	Korea	Israel		
France	Canada	Portugal	Nigeria	Italy		
West Germany	Chile		Sweden	Mexico		
Israel	Colombia		Switzerland	Malaysia		
Italy	Egypt			Philippines		
Korea	France			Switzerland		
Malaysia	West Germany					
Netherlands	Greece					
Philippines	India					
Sweden	Indonesia					
Switzerland	Israel					
United Kingdom	Kenya					
	Korea					
	Malaysia					
	Mexico					
	Netherlands					
	Nigeria					
	Norway					
	Peru					

10

Philippines
Portugal
Singapore
Spain
Taiwan
Tunisia
Turkey
Uruguay
Venezuela

Financial Performance Requirements

Foreign Firm Required to Put Up Certain Amount of Own Capital	Local Equity Participation Requirements	Limitations on Borrowing	Limitations on Remittances Abroad
Argentina	Canada	Denmark	Egypt
Belgium	Egypt	Ireland	Finland
Brazil	Greece	Italy	France
France	India	New Zealand	Greece
Netherlands	Indonesia	Peru	Mexico
Portugal	Ivory Coast	Spain	Peru
Turkey	Japan		Portugal
	Korea		Taiwan
	Malaysia		Turkey
	Mexico		
	New Zealand		
	Nigeria		
	Norway		
	Peru		
	Philippines		
	Turkey		

11

Table 1.4 (continued)

Manpower Performance Requirements

Job Retention	Registration and/or Limitation of Foreign Employees	Training of Local Employees	Management Participation
Belgium	Brazil	Belgium	Denmark
Brazil	France	Ivory Coast	Switzerland
Canada	Finland	Portugal	
Denmark	Indonesia		
W. Germany	Mexico		
India	Netherlands		
Italy	Nigeria		
Ivory Coast	Peru		
Malaysia	Switzerland		
Mexico	United Kingdom		
Philippines			
Portugal			
Sweden			

Balance-of-Payments Requirements

Level of Exports	Import Substitution Considerations	General Effect on Balance of Payments
Belgium	Brazil	Mexico
Brazil		Portugal
Canada		
Greece		
India		
Israel		
Italy		

12

Korea
Malaysia
Mexico
New Zealand
Philippines
Portugal
Singapore
Spain
Taiwan
Turkey

Other Performance Requirements

Language	Health Safety Environment	Real Estate and Construction Requirements
Canada	Canada	Finland
	Denmark	France
	Greece	W. Germany
	Israel	Greece
		Korea
		Switzerland
		United Kingdom

*These performance requirements vary in severity from country to country. They may apply to all investment or to specific industries.

Source: U.S. Department of Commerce, *Incentives and Performance Requirements for Foreign Direct Investment in Selected Countries, 1978,* and *Overseas Business Reports* for selected countries.

Table 1.5
Incidence of Performance Requirements Among Principal Host Countries for Foreign Direct Investment, Ranked by Annual Average Direct Investment Inflows, 1972–1979

Rank Country	Import Limiting	Export Expanding	Other Performance Requirements
1 United States			
2 West Germany	•		• • • •
3 United Kingdom			• • • •
4 France	•		• • • • • • •
5 Brazil	•	•	• • • • • • • •
6 Belgium		•	• • • • • • •
7 Australia	•		
8 Italy		•	• • • •
9 Netherlands	•		• • •
10 Mexico	•	•	• • • • • • •
11 Singapore	•	•	
12 Canada	•	•	• • • • • •
13 Malaysia	•	•	• • • •
14 Norway	•		•
15 Nigeria	•		• • •
16 Spain	•	•	• •
17 Indonesia	•		• •
18 Algeria	•		
19 S. Africa	•		
20 Uruguay	•		
21 Austria			• •
22 Japan			• •
23 New Zealand		•	•
24 Peru	•		• • • •
25 Ireland			•

Source: U.S. Congress, Senate, Hearings Before the Subcommittee on International Economic Policy of the Committee on Foreign Relations, *U.S. Policy Toward International Investment*, 97th Cong., July 30, September 28, and October 28, 1982 (Washington, D.C.: Government Printing Office, 1982), p. 69.

the VW parent company was working on plans to establish a U.S. production facility. A substantial part of the Volkswagen investment in this facility was made in 1977. From the point of competitiveness, Volkswagen enjoyed several advantages over domestic (U.S.) auto manufacturers.

1. Volkswagen is partly government owned and is therefore under less pressure to operate profitably than firms fully responsible to private sector investors.

2. Volkswagen received considerable investment incentives from the Commonwealth of Pennsylvania and its local government units. In an earlier study we estimated that from the point of view of Pennsylvania and its localities the value of these public sector subsidies was $68.3 million, the value of repayments $179.5 million, and the net present value $111.2 million. The subsidy benefits raised the estimated internal rate of return of the Volkswagen investment project in the United States from 18% to 23.5%.[11]

3. As a multinational corporation, Volkswagen is able to engage in a range of financial and other activities that provide substantial cash flow and profitability benefits. These include various internalization-transfer pricing transactions. Profit tax relationships suggest advantages from transfer pricing that shift earnings from the United States to the West German parent. In addition, in the late 1970s there were specific currency relationships that afforded opportunities for advantageous transfer pricing practices.

According to the Gordon-Lees study:

Since Volkswagen America uses automobile components manufactured in West Germany and several Latin American countries, there exists the opportunity to transfer profits between these units. If we rank Volkswagen manufacturing units in descending order relative to the degree of hardness of their local currencies, we get the following sequence: West Germany, U.S., and Latin America. Clearly, transfer pricing designed to shift profitability might be expected to move in the reverse order.[12]

In the VW case transfer pricing opportunities include sale and servicing of components between parent and overseas subsidiaries, loan interest and repayment of loan principal to the West German parent, sale of used capital equipment to Volkswagen America, and management fees charged the U.S. affiliate related to installation of used equipment.

The decision of the Volkswagen Corporation to invest in a U.S. production facility was influenced by the firm's ownership advantages, its ability to internalize these advantages by transfer pricing, and the locational advantages offered by the United States. Because the host country provided investment incentives, we have a case of foreign investment under subsidy. The subsidy element enhanced the profitability of the investment, but capital budgeting analysis suggests that even without subsidy the return on investment would have been fairly high.

The Japanese Invasion: From Imports to Local Content

Twenty-five years ago Japanese motor vehicle producers established a strategy for gaining a substantial share of the American market. In 1960 Japanese producers had no position in the North American market, which at that time absorbed 6 million new passenger automobiles per year.

To achieve market penetration, increase market share, and subsequently retain a strong position, Japanese producers have varied their tactics and strategies over time. At least three distinct stages can be observed: (1) low market share, policy of downward transfer pricing to build U.S. market share (before 1976); (2)

growing market share, policy of level and upward transfer pricing (1977–1981); and (3) high market share, policy of upward transfer pricing and model upgrading (1982–1988). The employment of these strategies permitted Japanese and other foreign automobile producers to achieve an impressive increase in market share at a time when domestic producers (U.S. factory sales) were on a flat plateau (Figure 1.1). In the early 1960s Japanese automobile producers sought to achieve a toehold in the formidable U.S. market. At that time Japan's total import share was almost 6 percent of the American market (Figure 1.1), and two-thirds of all auto imports came from West Germany. Downward transfer pricing and generous advertising were important tactics. Low profit in North America was offset by high profit margins in the growing and well-protected home market. Not until 1968 did Japanese producers achieve a sales level exceeding 100,000 units per year, which represented less than two % of the American market. Beginning in 1971 Japanese producers were matching and surpassing West German automobile imports entering the U.S. market, and, with their ability to use transfer prices freely, held a high (six to eight %) market share through 1975 (Table 1.6).

Table 1.6
Japanese Automobile Imports into the United States, 1964–1982

Year	Number of Imports (000)	Japanese Imports as Percent of Consumption
1964	16.0	0.20
1965	25.5	0.26
1966	56.0	0.60
1967	70.3	0.86
1968	169.8	1.68
1969	260.0	2.67
1970	381.3	4.61
1971	703.6	6.54
1972	697.7	6.40
1973	624.8	5.39
1974	791.7	8.53
1975	695.5	8.50
1976	1,128.9	10.90
1977	1,341.5	11.88
1978	1,563.0	13.61
1979	1,617.3	15.20
1980	1,991.5	22.36
1981	1,911.5	22.31
1982	1,801.1	23.70

Source: U.S. International Trade Administration, *The U.S. Auto Industry*, Publication 1419, August 1983, p. 4.

Figure 1.1
U.S. Auto Market—Import Share, 1961–1983

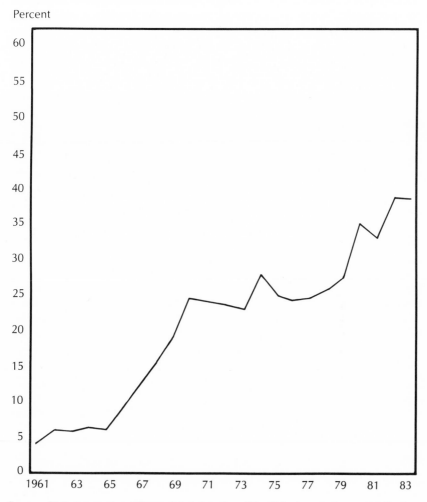

Percent

Source: U.S. International Trade Administration, *The U.S. Auto Industry*, Publication
No. 1419, August 1983, pp. 2–4.

During 1976–1981 Japanese producers more than doubled their market share,
enjoying 22% of the American market in the early 1980s. During this period
competition from West German imports had diminished, as had the German
share of the market. By 1982 Japanese producers were able to revise their policy
on transfer pricing, shifting toward upward transfer pricing in the American
market. This was possible because of Japan's more entrenched market position
and because of substantial inflation in the United States which gave Japanese
producers greater pricing flexibility in the American market.

Since 1982 Japanese producers have employed the strategy of developing an American production base via FDI inflows. In addition, Japanese producers have been able to continue to transfer prices up in the U.S. market as a result of a contrived scarcity related to the voluntary import quota imposed on Japanese auto producers. It is now estimated that by 1988 Japanese producers will be manufacturing well over 800,000 motor vehicles per year in the United States.[13] The strategy of developing U.S. production facilities by direct investment is partly a reaction to proposals for legislation that would mandate a minimum percentage of domestic content for all motor vehicles sold in the United States.

In summary, the strategies of both the Volkswagen and Japanese automobile producers indicate that they have been able to employ FDI inflows to enhance their market positions in the United States at the expense of domestic firms. Over the past two decades foreign producers, especially Japanese firms, have increased market share from 5% to 38% of the U.S. domestic market. At the same time domestic producers have suffered from a decline in market share and, in the period since 1977–1978, a reduction in number of units produced.

State-Owned Enterprises

Another source of inequality between American and foreign industrial companies is state ownership. State or government ownership of industry has become fairly widespread in Western Europe and other parts of the world. It has a negative effect on American companies for private sector firms in the United States do not enjoy the low cost capital funds and other subsidies available to state enterprises. These advantages are of benefit to state enterprises both when they are selling their products at home and when they are seeking to gain or enlarge market position in the United States.

Foreign state enterprise has invested in American industry and generally operates from a relatively protected home base. European Airbus Industrie is an excellent example of a manufacturing consortium kept afloat by political will and taxpayer subsidies. Airbus, the European-based aircraft group owned and supported by the French and British governments, has reduced Boeing's dominance by winning orders for jet aircraft from America as well as from Europe and Third World nations. Outside the Communist bloc the aircraft business is dominated by Airbus, Boeing, and McDonnell Douglas. If the aerospace industry were governed only by commercial sales, the loser long ago would have been Airbus, which shipped only 57 aircraft in its first five years.[14] But Airbus is sponsored and supported by European governments, which indirectly own most of the consortium. These governments value aerospace for employment and technology spinoffs. Although the two American companies derive government subsidies in the form of research funding and military contracts, they are nowhere near the level achieved by Airbus.

Government maneuvering and creative financing have won Airbus orders for jet aircraft in the Middle East and Asia. Projections for the period 1984–2002 suggest that expenditures by the world's airlines for new jet aircraft will aggregate

$440 billion, of which the Airbus share could be $114 billion. It is clear that foreign state enterprises present a clear competitive challenge to America's position in world markets for sophisticated technology products.

In 1983 the U.S. Department of Commerce, International Trade Administration, published a report on direct investment in the United States by state enterprises covering their activities for the period 1974–1981.[15] This study identified 147 cases of direct investment in the United States by foreign companies wholly or partially controlled by a foreign government. These investments came from 29 countries. Financial details covering 70 of these completed investment transactions indicate that they had an aggregate value of $9.3 billion. Two very large transactions in 1981, the acquisition of Santa Fe International Corporation by Kuwait Petroleum Corporation, and the acquisition of Texasgulf Inc. by the French group Elf Acquitaine, accounted for an unusually large investment value. These two transactions together were worth more than $5 billion, or about 54% of all direct investment by foreign companies with government ownership recorded from 1974 through 1981.

The major industrial countries were the primary source of direct investment activity in the United States by foreign-owned firms for the period 1974–1981 (Table 1.7). Four of these countries—Canada, France, the United Kingdom, and West Germany—accounted for 65% of the completed transactions and almost three-quarters of the cases with known values. The United Kindgom ranked first in number of completed transactions and third in value of these transactions. France and the OPEC countries ranked first and second, respectively, in value of transactions. Companies wholly or partially owned by the government of Kuwait accounted for 90% of the OPEC share.

Table 1.7
Foreign Government Source Countries' Completed FDI Transactions, 1974–1981

Country	Total No. of Transactions	No. of Transactions Known Value	Total Value of Transactions (mil. dols.)
Canada	11	9	388.1
France	24	14	3,130.2
Japan	1	0	0
The Netherlands	1	0	0
United Kingdom	28	20	1,704.0
West Germany	17	7	582.5
OPEC[a]	17	10	2,833.2
Other Countries	25	10	630.0
Total	124	70	9,268.0

[a]The OPEC countries included here are Algeria, Iran, Kuwait, Libya, Nigeria, Saudi Arabia, and Venezuela.
Source: U.S. Department of Commerce, Office of Trade and Investment Analysis, March 1982.

Significant Issues

The fact that American industrial companies must compete at home against foreign state enterprises that invest in this country raises a number of significant policy issues:

1. *Influence on FDI Policy and National Security.* One concern is that large foreign investment holdings could hinder U.S. efforts in a national emergency. Alternately, foreign investors with significant U.S. holdings may attempt to influence or alter U.S. policy. Foreign government-controlled investments could be subject to foreign political pressures designed to support their respective governments' policy objectives.

2. *Domestic Competitive Behavior.* American suppliers could be placed at a disadvantage if foreign parent companies purchased their materials from abroad rather than from U.S. sources. State-owned corporations may be willing to sacrifice U.S. production to insure full employment in their respective home countries. Job redundancy has become a major issue in Western Europe.

3. *Global Monopoly.* Foreign corporations owned or controlled by a foreign government are in a position to create global cartels. By acquiring U.S. companies, these foreign firms could reduce effective domestic competition in U.S. markets. Any resulting global monopoly position would leave rival American firms at a serious competitive disadvantage.

4. *Tax Loss.* Some foreign investors enjoy tax advantages that result in lower U.S. tax liabilities than those of domestic investors. These advantages stem from tax treaties covering treatment of interest and dividends as well as capital gains. All business income is subject to U.S. tax, but certain investment income of foreign governments and their controlled entities may be exempt.

5. *Technology Transfer.* Critics assert that foreign investment could lead to the loss of U.S. technological superiority, a superiority which has accounted for the preeminence of U.S. companies in a number of industries and has also been a key factor in U.S. economic growth and military security. The acquisition of U.S. technology companies by foreign state-owned enterprises could give these enterprises an advantage that would threaten the remaining members of that industry sector. It could also create problems relating to the protection of national defense technology and other sensitive sectors closely linked to national interests.[16]

Reasons for U.S. Acquisitions by State Enterprises

In his analysis of the reasons why state enterprises make investments in the United States, Douglas F. Lamont underlines the threat which these enterprises pose for American business.[17] He points to four primary reasons for such investments: (1) to have a secure source of raw materials, (2) to sell valuable products to American consumers, (3) to have sufficient resources to supply the new market position, and (4) to oust American industries from market dominance.[18]

Table 1.8 describes the major direct investments by foreign state enterprises. These include smaller investments such as the VW $120 million acquisition of Pertec Computer Corporation and very large commitments such as British Petroleum's (BP's) acquisition of Kennecott Corporation worth $938 million. The industrial sectors include automobiles, steel, mining, computers, and pulp and paper. In each case there is a "new form of government-business union which we call the nexus: a merger that is stable, effective, and affords each partner what it wants."[19]

Foreign state enterprises present the United States with two challenges: an economic challenge, which involves an attack on America's market position abroad; and a political challenge, which is equally serious but difficult to see clearly. It is

the intent and methods of the political strategy employed in the United States and worldwide that give cause for concern. These nexus competitors are impairing our very ability to defend ourselves even when we finally choose to do so, not simply by building new economic power, but by assuring its strength and resilience through political means.[20]

What is the solution to this double challenge? Lamont suggests that we must enforce congressional policy of reciprocity, and even amplify it. The solution, he states, is not to pass a stringent foreign investment review code as the Canadians once did, which halts new investments, but rather to demand reciprocity as a quid pro quo.[21]

LIMITED FEDERAL REGULATION

Existing Federal Regulation

General Open Door Policy. With the exception of a few very specific areas of activity, the United States has followed a "let alone" policy with regard to FDI inflows. As C. Fred Bergsten notes:

The United States is almost alone among host countries, however, in eschewing any effort to control or at least direct the flow of incoming investments. No performance requirements are applied. No registration, let alone negotiation, is required of foreign firms. The United States is clearly the most open market in the world for foreign investors. I believe this policy has been strongly supportive of U.S. interests, but it does differ sharply from trends in the rest of the world at this time.[22]

The open door emphasis in U.S. policy applies to the application phase (foreign investors are not presently required to apply to federal authorities for permission to proceed with investment) and the activity phase (once investment is made, the government follows a hands-off policy).[23] However, since the early 1970s Washington has focused greater attention on FDI inflows as manifested by the Foreign Direct Investment Act in 1974, which authorized a thorough study of foreign investment in the United States. This study sought to determine whether such activity should be subject to greater federal regulation. Two years later the International Investment Survey Act was passed, which called for periodic anal-

Table 1.8
Major Direct Investment Transactions in the United States by Foreign Companies
Owned or Controlled by Foreign Governments, 1974–1981

Government	U.S. Company	State	SIC No./ U.S. Industry	Foreign Owner of Record/Pct. of Govt. Ownership	Value of Transaction ($ Millions)	Type of Transaction	Year of Investment
Austria	Bayou Steel Corp.	LA	33 Billets & Blooms	Voest-Alpine A.G. (et al.) (100%)	128.0	NP (100%)	1979
Canada	MacMillan Bloedel Inc.	AL	26 Pulp & Paper	MacMillan Bloedel Ltd. (1%)	274.0	PE (100%)	1981
France	American Motors Corp.	MI	37 Motor Vehicles	Regie Nationale des Usines Renault (92%)	167.5	EI (4.7% to 46.4%)	1980
	Texasgulf Inc.	CT	10 Mining	Societe Nationale Elf Aquitaine S.A. (67%)	2,500.0	Acq (63.1%)	1981
	Vickers Petroleum Corp.	KS	13 Oil/Gas Drilling	Cie Francaise des Petroles (CFP) (35%)	245.0	Acq (100%)	1980
Iran	Canal Place	LA	65 Real Estate	Bank Omran (100%)	250.0	JV (50%)	1976
Italy	Enoxy	KY	12 Cola Mining	Ente Nazionale Idrocarburi (ENI) (100%)	375.0	JV (50%)	1981

Country	Company	State	SIC / Industry	Foreign Parent	Value	Transaction Type/Status	Year
Kuwait	Santa Fe International Corp.	CA	13 Oil/Gas Field Services	Kuwait Petroleum Corp. (KPC) (100%)	2,500.8	Acq (100%)	1981
United Kingdom	Continental Illinois Properties	CA	65 Real Estate	National Coal Board (100%)	144.2	Acq (100%)	1979
	Crystal Block Mine	WV	12 Coal Mining	British Petroleum Co., Ltd. (39%)	318.0	Acq (100%)	1981
	Kennecott Corp.	CT	10 Copper Mining	British Petroleum Co., Ltd. (39%)	938.1	Acq (100%)	1981
West Germany	Ashland Coal Inc.	KY	12 Coal Mining	Saarbergwerke A.G. (98%)	102.5	Acq (25%)	1981
	Pertec Computer Corp.	CA	35 Computers	Volkswagenwerke A.G. (40%)	120.0	Acq (100%)	1979
	Volkswagen of America, Inc.	MI	37 Motor Vehicles	Volkswagenwerke A.G. (40%)	300.0	NP (100%)	1981

Key: *Transaction Type/Status*

Acq — Acquisition
EI — Equity Increase
JV — Joint Venture
NP — New Plant
PE — Plant Expansion

Source U.S. Department of Commerce, Office of Trade and Investment Analysis, March 1982.

yses of FDI activity and frequent gathering of data on such investment. In addition, the Ford Administration through Executive Order (in 1975) established a Committee on Foreign Investment in the United States. During the late 1970s regulatory legislative proposals appeared, one calling for a flat prohibition of any more than five % acquisition of voting stock of publicly traded American corporations by foreign investors.

Spheres of Restricted Activity. The federal government has applied regulation to six industrial or activity areas of FDI: antitrust, transportation, communications, natural resources, banking, and national defense.

Overseas investors have been particularly perplexed by U.S. antitrust laws and, as a result in some cases this has caused European company executives to alter or defer original investment plans. U.S. antitrust regulation has few parallels in other industrial countries. In addition, "U.S. authorities have tried at times in the past to give American antitrust provisions an extraterritorial dimension,"[24] causing foreign corporate investors concern that an investment in the United States could expose their non-U.S. activities to American antitrust provisions.

Transportation has long been considered an industrial activity sensitive, and therefore subject, to restrictions on foreign investor activity. Nonresident aliens are excluded from engaging in coastal or inland water shipping activities. The Merchant Marine Act (1920) holds that freight and passengers transported between points in the United States or its territories must use vessels built and registered in the United States, and owned by American citizens. To register a vessel for such activity the principal company officers must be Americans, and 75% of the company voting stock must be domestically controlled. Federal law requires approval by the Secretary of Commerce for foreign investment in the ship construction and repair industry. Federal and state law makes it extremely difficult for foreign firms to control the railway and airlines industries.

Federal legislation prohibits foreign-owned or -controlled business from operating instruments of communications, including radio stations.[25] Similarly, foreign ownership is strictly limited in the telegraph and communications satellite sectors.

FDI activity in natural resources development is limited by federal laws pertaining to the hydroelectric power and geothermal power sectors. In addition, the Mining Law of 1872 limits alien mining activity on federal lands. There are many loopholes in the law, however. The United States has reciprocal agreements in this area with other nations, which give foreign firms wide opportunity to exploit valuable coal, oil, gas, and other natural resource reserves. This sector has been a target of foreign investors, including a number of state enterprises.

In 1978 a federal law brought foreign banking activities in the United States into closer balance with what is permitted domestic banking institutions.[26] In general, this law equalized foreign bank activity in the interstate and investment banking areas of activity, where earlier they enjoyed competitive advantages over domestic banks.

National defense considerations prompted the federal government to tighten up on component sourcing with the Buy American Act of 1970. This law requires at least a 50% U.S. product content in defense procurement. Earlier legislation required that alien-owned firms be precluded from winning defense contracts unless they received necessary security clearances.[27] The Department of Defense scrutinizes all foreign-controlled or foreign-influenced firms that seek to do classified contract work for the U.S. government. If the foreign connection is considered to be potentially dangerous to U.S. interests, security clearance for the firm will be denied and the contract will be assigned to an alternate supplier.

Firms and industries essential to defense as part of the broad military-industrial complex are examined in Chapter 7. These firms and industries may not be directly associated with sensitive materials or products, but in a broad context the production capacity will be essential for military surge production capability.

State Activity

Whereas the federal government has maintained a hands-off, open door policy toward FDI inflows, the various state governments have actively solicited foreign investors. As mentioned earlier, Pennsylvania and its localities provided substantial financial benefits to win the battle for the Volkswagen plant. This is generally reflective of state efforts through the 1970s and continuing into the 1980s. By the end of the 1970s all 50 states had provided complete data to investors relating to plant location within their jurisdictions, and all but two states provided a broad range of financial assistance, loans, and incentives.[28] All now provide one or more tax incentives and most or all of the following special services to encourage industrial development: publicly owned industrial park sites, state funds for public works projects, state funds for city master plans, state programs to promote research and development, state programs to increase exports, funds for feasibility studies, and state recruiting of employees and training funds.

A federal government analysis of state programs published in 1977 noted that 24 states and 11 port authorities had already established information offices in Europe, 7 states had offices in Tokyo, and 2 in Hong Kong.[29] The same study pointed to a predictable relationship between foreign investment and job creation, with $30,000 to $40,000 of industrial plant investment needed to create one additional job. The report suggested a close relationship between the amount invested by a state and the amount of direct foreign investment attracted ($1 of state funds attracts $667 of FDI). A state expenditure of $60 could attract $40,000 of investment, adding one new job.[30]

NOTES

1. Sara L. Gordon and Francis A. Lees, "Multinational Capital Budgeting: Foreign Investment Under Subsidy," *California Management Review* 15, no. 1 (Fall 1982), 22–32.

2. The term "creeping expropriation" is doubly appropriate. First, foreign producers have taken over American markets and market share. Second, a large number of these

foreign producers are government-owned enterprises, so that their takeovers are akin to their respective governments expropriating American industry in the United States.

3. The term "relative decline" refers to the greater growth in production of industrial products in other parts of the world. This includes production of aerospace (in Europe by Airbus Industrie), motor vehicles (in Japan, Korea, and Mexico), and steel (Brazil and Korea), to mention a few specific illustrations. We are not in disagreement with Robert Z. Lawrence, who states that America is not deindustrializing and that any perceived slump in manufacturing observed since 1973 is a worldwide phenomenon. See Robert Z. Lawrence, *Can America Compete?* (Washington D.C.: Brookings Institute, 1984), pp. 5–6.

4. Robert Reich has argued that American industries have lost their competitiveness and that a combination of industrial policy and structural shift toward service activities is inevitable. See Robert B. Reich, *The Next American Frontier* (New York: New York Times Books, 1983), pp. 124–131.

5. This is analogous to the concept of income shifting effects from imports, discussed later in this work. For example, large increases in auto imports have shifted income from the United States to the exporting countries.

6. See Reich, *The Next American Frontier*, pp. 122–132. See also Felix Rohatyn, "Reconstructing America," *New York Review of Books* (March 5, 1981), p. 16.

7. Douglas Lamont, *Foreign State Enterprises* (New York: Basic Books, 1979), pp. 4–7.

8. U.S. Congress, Senate, Hearings Before the Subcommittee on International Economic Policy of the Committee on Foreign Relations, *U.S. Policy Toward International Investment*, 97th Cong., July 30, September 28, and October 28, 1982 (Washington, D.C.: Government Printing Office, 1982), 49–83.

9. Ibid., p. 54.

10. Ibid., p. 70.

11. Gordon and Lees, "Multinational Capital Budgeting," pp. 25–26, 30.

12. Ibid., p. 28.

13. Susan Chira, "For Mazda, a U.S. Car Plant," *New York Times*, December 1, 1984.

14. "Pan-European World Airways," *The Economist* (September 22, 1984): 79.

15. U.S. Department of Commerce, International Trade Administration, *Direct Investment in the United States by Foreign Government-Owned Companies 1974–1981* (Washington, D.C.: March 1983), pp. 9–11.

16. Ibid., pp. 6–8.

17. Lamont, *Foreign State Enterprises*, pp. 155–158.

18. Lamont uses the following illustrations in these four cases. In the first case, three European state enterprises—Veba, CDF (Charbonnages de France), and BP—use their control over American minerals to improve their world position. In the second case state enterprises have valuable products, such as DSM (Dutch State Mines) which can produce raw material for nylon with caprolactum without infringing on DuPont's patents. In the third case, CFP (Cie Françoise des Petroles) lacked adequate supplies of American crude until it made important acquisitions. In the fourth case, Polysar's rubber tubing investment should reduce the access of American firms to Canadian markets. Lamont, *Foreign State Enterprises*, pp. 155–158.

19. Ibid., p. 6.

20. Ibid., p. 12.

21. Ibid., p. 13.

22. C. Fred Bergsten, testimony in *U.S. Policy Toward International Investment*, p. 15.

23. Earl H. Fry, *Financial Invasion of the U.S.A.* (New York: McGraw-Hill, 1980), p. 47.

24. Ibid., p. 49.

25. The Radio Act of 1927 and the Federal Communications Act of 1934 are the basic federal laws covering these areas. Foreigners may own up to 25% of U.S. chartered corporations in most spheres of communications, and the Federal Communications Commission plays a watchdog role over these matters.

26. See Fry, *Financial Invasion of the U.S.A.*, ch. 5, for a detailed discussion of this legislation.

27. This legislation includes the Armed Services Procurement Act of 1947 and the Federal Property Administrative Act of 1949. Foreign investors are not barred from buying into companies that are already performing defense work, but they do run the risk of having these contracts canceled as a result of the foreign takeover. See Fry, *Financial Invasion of the U.S.A.*, p. 52.

28. Raymond J. Waldman, *Direct Investment and Development in the U.S.* (Washington D.C.: Transnational Investments Ltd., 1980).

29. U.S. Department of Commerce, Domestic and International Business Administration, *State Government Conducted International Trade and Business Development Programs* (Washington, D.C.: June 1977).

30. Fry, *The Financial Invasion of the U.S.A.*, p. 80.

2

Foreign Investment in the United States: Trends and Economic Performance ____

With the expansion in foreign business investment flowing into the United States, many questions come to mind with respect to the enormous changes that have taken place in the global economy. Only a few years ago the United States was the major provider of investment capital to Europe, Canada, and other parts of the world. The U.S. multinational company was almost unchallenged in its competitive position, backed up by relatively low cost capital funds, a vast technological leadership, and organizational talents beyond compare. World markets were growing and beckoning to U.S. companies.

Today all of this has changed. The U.S. multinational is at bay, and non-U.S. multinationals have attained a new independence and sovereignty over world markets. Much of the U.S. technological lead has been narrowed; some of it has been absorbed by foreign competitors or even stolen by Communist countries.[1] Interest rates in the United States are no longer among the lowest in the world, and multinationals in Japan, West Germany, and Switzerland enjoy far lower local borrowing costs.[2] World markets are not growing rapidly, and this slow growth may be viewed as a warning to multinational companies that belt-tightening is in order.

With these new world market and global competitive conditions, foreign business investment is flowing into the United States each year by the billions of dollars. Whereas in the past the United States was a major contributor of business investment, in recent years this country has become a major recipient of such flows. In the previous chapter we saw that by 1979 the United States was receiving as much as 40% of the global flow of FDI (Table 1.1). This chapter outlines the major trends and patterns in global FDI flows, and subsequent chapters consider the structure and rationale of foreign direct investment coming into the United States. In later chapters specific attention is given to investment and trade patterns in the steel and motor vehicle industries. Finally, the implications of the new pattern of FDI for government policy, as well as for the future viability of an integrated world economic system, are considered.

CHANGING TRENDS AND PATTERNS

The following discussion focuses on the changing fortunes of FDI from the point of view of the U.S. economy from 1946, after World War II, to the present. To provide a statistical backdrop, the average annual FDI flows from and to the United States are summarized, and, based on this analysis, six distinct subperiods are identified.

In the immediate post-war years U.S. dominance in global investment flows was reflected in the nearly $1 billion a year FDI outflow. By contrast, FDI inflows averaged somewhat in excess of $100 million a year. In this period (1946–1958) there was a worldwide dollar shortage, the U.S. export position was very strong, and Western Europe was slowly recovering its pre-war production and investment levels.

By 1959 the Common Market has been established, creating a regional preferential trading system. Between 1959 and 1968 the six members of the bloc removed all tariff restrictions on intratrade in industrial products. In 1958 American companies enjoyed a substantial export position in the Common Market, but, as the preferential trading zone developed an increasingly more discriminatory approach against outside producers, the United States faced the prospect of losing its advantage. The direction was clear: invest in the Common Market to produce and sell inside the tariff wall. The substantial increase in annual FDI outflows (to $3,135 million) is largely explained by this factor. At the same time inward FDI grew to $343 million per annum.

The balance-of-payments impact of expanding foreign direct investment outflows from the United States was one of several issues that confronted U.S. policymakers in the early 1960s. Other balance-of-payments flows that produced a deficit in U.S. payments included bank lending, U.S. tourism, and an increased volume of foreign dollar bond placements in New York. In 1965 the U.S. government imposed a comprehensive system of capital controls which were intended to close the door to foreign investment outflows. These controls applied to U.S. FDI outflows, bank lending overseas, and portfolio investment outflows. The effect on FDI is shown in Table 2.1, where in the period 1965–1969 annual FDI outflows stabilized at $5,166 million. In this period foreign business investment inflows to the United States averaged $703 million per annum. This reflects the substantial recovery that was taking place in Western Europe and the ability of European-based companies to venture into business investments in the United States.

In the fourth or transition phase (1970–1972) the United States experienced a breakdown of confidence in the dollar-oriented Bretton Woods system. The 1971 international financial crisis led to a major revision in international financial arrangements. Nevertheless, U.S. FDI outflows increased further to $7,651 million per year, while annual FDI inflows also advanced to $927 million.

Table 2.1
Direct Foreign Investment to and from the United States, 1946–1983[a]
(million U.S. dollars, annual average)

Period	U.S. Outflows		Foreign Inflows to United States		Net Flow
	New Equity and Debt Funds	*Reinvested Earnings*	*New Equity and Debt Funds*	*Reinvested Earnings*	
U.S. Dominance (1946–1958)	$ 999		$ 126		−873
European Regionalism (1959–1964)	3,135		343		−2,792
Early Capital Controls (1965–1969)	5,166		703		−4,463
Transition (1970–1972)	4,023	3,628	412	515	−6,724
	7,651		927		
Friendly Invasion of United States (1973–1977)	4,083	7,615	2,365	1,282	−8,051
	11,698		3,647		
Accelerated Flight to United States (1978–1983)	(796)	12,907	9,512	3,089	490
	12,111		12,601		

[a]U.S. outflows reflect foreign direct investments of U.S. investors; foreign inflows reflect foreign direct investments of non-U.S. investors in the Uinted States. FDI has two components: new equity and debt funds provided by parent company investors to foreign affiliates; and reinvested earnings. These components are indicated for the period beginning in 1970.

Source: U.S. Department of Commerce, *Survey of Current Business*, various issues.

In 1973–1974 the capital controls were removed, reflecting the need to open up the U.S. capital markets for the international financial intermediation of petrodollars. In the short span of three years OPEC earnings from oil exports flooded the world's financial markets with liquidity and opened up the possibility of massive international funds flows. This period provided opportunities for a massive escalation of foreign FDI into the United States. In part this was financed by a surge in global liquidity. If we examine the FDI outflows and inflows we find that inflows surged ahead, averaging four times what they were in the transition phase ($3,647 million per annum).

The past several years have brought further shifts in the balance between direct business investment flows from and to the United States. The accelerated flight of FDI into the United States in the period 1978–1983 was 3 1/2 times as large as during the previous period ($12,601 million per annum). As a result, the net outflows were reversed and became net inflows of $490 million per year.

The flow of business investment into and from the United States has been undergoing an important compositional change since 1970. FDI flows consist of (1) new equity and debt funds and (2) reinvested earnings. The first is a more active ingredient and reflects new commitments to foreign investment. The second involves a more passive financing of growth of existing operations with internally generated funds.

The massive buildup of U.S.-owned foreign investment in other countries now generates substantial earnings, part of which is reinvested each year. In 1970–1972 the amount of reinvestment was still somewhat below new equity and debt investment. In the period 1973–1977 reinvestment was nearly double new investment. In the most recent period analyzed, reinvestment accounted for all of the FDI from the United States. We should remember that there is a cyclical aspect to this trend and that the final period in Table 2.1 coincides with a worldwide recession, during which new equity and debt investment by many corporations would be at a low ebb. Nevertheless, there appears to be an unmistakable shift toward reinvestment accounting for a larger share of FDI flows from the United States.

The buildup of foreign-owned investment in the United States is also increasing the relative importance of reinvestment in the total amount of FDI taking place in the United States. Nevertheless, new equity and debt investment remain several times larger than reinvestment. Moreover, new equity and debt investment coming into the United States continues to exhibit a vigorous growth pattern. This indicates the heavy emphasis given to the United States as a safe place for private capital. For a large part of the period 1978–1982 the depressed U.S. stock market provided favorable takeover opportunities for non-U.S. investors.

FDI, AN EVOLVING ACTIVITY

FDI has undergone a complete metamorphosis over the past 35 years. The early 1970s (1972) may be considered a watershed in this respect. Since 1972

FDI has become a different type of activity in its orientation and goals; in its direction of flow; with respect to the impact of government policy; and with respect to the role played by principal participating countries.

Table 2.2 summarizes some of these changes in FDI. From the standpoint of government policy, items 3, 4, and 5 are very important. They reflect the growing role of government policy in international investment and trade. Wide sectors of industry in developed nations are influenced by government policy and/or government subsidies. British steel, French computers, German electronics, Japanese chemicals, and American aerospace manufacturers rely on government subsidies, government protection, or government R & D and investment support to maintain their competitive position in national and global markets. In some cases government ownership is involved. FDI flows in these and other industry sectors are similarly influenced by government subsidies and protection.

Private sector profit goals have, at least in part, given way to public sector objectives, as is manifested by host country demands that various performance requirements be met (employment, domestic content, and exports). The direction of FDI flow has changed, as have the important participating countries. Japan has become a more important investor, and the United States has become a more important host country. Several of the newly industrializing countries (NICs) have initiated their own FDI outflows.

These changes are important enough to warrant a closer examination of the role and importance of FDI for host and home countries alike. Because the United States now plays a dual role as host and home country for FDI, it becomes doubly important that this activity be evaluated in connection with its performance and overall contributions to the economy.

Table 2.2
FDI Flows before and after 1972

Pre–1972	Post–1972
1. FDI outflows from U.S. much larger than inflows.	1. FDI inflows into U.S. increase, nearly equal to outflows.
2. U.S. dominant source of FDI investment funds.	2. Globally diffused sources of FDI.
3. Private sector companies dominate FDI totals.	3. Government-owned corporations and government-subsidized corporations account for increasingly larger share of FDI flows.
4. Government policy plays moderate role in influencing FDI flows.	4. Government policy plays important role in shaping and influencing FDI.
5. Product cycle important—trade precedes investment.	5. Trade and investment are closer alternatives. Therefore, trade and investment issues are more closely intertwined.

CONTRIBUTIONS OF FOREIGN DIRECT INVESTMENT TO THE U.S. ECONOMY

General Contributions

Have direct foreign investments in the United States made favorable contributions to the domestic economy? To answer this question let us compare the performance of FDI affiliates of foreign companies operating in the United States with that of domestic companies in the same industry sector. Information made available by the U.S. Department of Commerce is used as the data base.

The actual contributions of FDI to the domestic economy in the United States are detailed in connection with employment, investment, income-generating, export, and other effects. This analysis considers these contributions based on the industry sector of the companies with activities in the United States. On the basis of this comparison industries are identified according to the following criteria:

1. Industries where foreign-owned affiliates have made contributions that are decidedly superior compared to domestic counterparts.
2. Industries where foreign-owned affiliates enjoy a small margin of advantage over comparable domestic industry sectors.
3. Industries where foreign-owned affiliates have performed on a par with domestic industry sectors.
4. Industries where foreign-owned affiliates have performed on a moderately less satisfactory basis when compared with domestic industries.
5. Industries where domestic firms have performed on a decidedly superior basis when compared with foreign-owned affiliates in that sector.
6. Industries where foreign companies have served U.S. markets primarily via exports to the United States, as contrasted with producing in the United States.

Data provided by the U.S. Department of Commerce permit a detailed comparative evaluation of the economic performance of foreign-owned and U.S. domestic companies. Table 2.3 presents data concerning business (plant and equipment) investment per worker and as a percentage of sales, sales revenues per worker, export data, profit margins, and compensation per employee for a number of industry sectors. For example, in the paper and allied products industry investment per worker was $14,560 or 12.2% of sales revenues. Sales per worker exceeded $118,000. Exports were 11.0% of sales, or $13,096 per worker. The profit margin was 4.1%, and annual employee compensation averaged $30,896. In all of these respects foreign-owned affiliates in this industrial sector performed better than the U.S. domestic industry.

Data for the U.S. domestic industry are presented in Table 2.4. For example, investment expenditures per worker for the U.S. domestic paper industry were $9,790, barely two-thirds of the amount spent by foreign-owned affiliates. Foreign-owned affiliates in the paper and allied products industry were able to exceed the contributions to the U.S. economy of U.S. domestic firms in all five categories of comparison (investment, sales, exports, profit margin, and employee compensation). For this reason, in this industrial sector foreign investor performance is considered to be decidedly superior to U.S. domestic companies.

Comparisons of the performance of foreign-owned affiliates and U.S. companies are tabulated and summarized in Table 2.5. Fourteen industrial sector categories and subcategories are compared. In five cases foreign-owned affiliates were classified as decidedly superior in their contributions to the United States (petroleum, primary metals, fabricated metals, textiles, and paper and allied products). In four cases foreign-owned affiliates were classified as enjoying a small margin of advantage in their contributions to the United States (mining, electrical machinery, rubber and plastics, and stone, clay, and glass). In only one case did domestic firms perform on a par with foreign-owned affiliates (transportation equipment). In this case this results from the opposite tendencies of the motor vehicle and commercial jet aircraft manufacturing sectors with respect to profitability, exports, and other performance areas. In four cases U.S. domestic firms performed in a decidedly superior manner compared with foreign-owned affiliates (manufacturing, food and kindred, chemicals, and machinery except electrical).

Finally, we reviewed the performance of foreign-owned affiliates in connection with their supplying U.S. markets with imports versus U.S. domestic production. A summary of these findings is presented in Table 2.6. Overall, foreign-owned affiliates relied on imports to provide slightly more than 16% of U.S. sales (Table 2.6). In manufacturing there was considerably less reliance on imports (imports were 9.4% of sales). In wholesale trade foreign-owned affiliates were considerably more dependent on imports (26% of sales).

The highest dependence of foreign-owned affiliates on imports to supply the U.S. domestic market is found in the motor vehicles and equipment sector, where over $20 billion of imports was shipped to U.S. affiliates of foreign manufacturers. This represents nearly one-fourth of all imports shipped to U.S. affiliates in 1981, and over 51% of motor vehicle and equipment sales in the United States by foreign-owned wholesalers.

Balance-of-Payments Effects

The information used for the following analysis of the balance-of-payments effects from FDI inflows to the United States consists of data found in Tables 2.3 through 2.6, as well as materials published by the U.S. Department of Commerce concerning U.S. balance-of-payments totals and foreign direct investment activity in the United States.

The balance-of-payments effects may be broken down into three basic components: (1) initial capital inflow to the United States, (2) continuing trade flows, and (3) continuing foreign investment and other remittances to foreign parent

Table 2.3
Performance Characteristics of Foreign-Owned Affiliates in the United States, by Industrial Sector, 1981

Industrial Sector	Plant & Equip. Expend. per worker 1	P & E Expend. as Pct. of Sales 2	Sales per worker 3	Exports as Pct. of Sales 4	Exports per Worker 5	Profit per Sales Dollar 6	Employee Compensation 7	Exports of Foreign Investors In United States as Pct. Total Exports 8	Trade Balance 9
Mining	$21,200	—	$123,331	19.6	$24,168	11.6	$33,347	—	+887
Petroleum	53,164	9.8	544,306	2.8	15,088	6.5	29,914	50.3	−8,090
Manufacturing	7,197	6.7	106,771	9.9	10,531	3.0	24,593	—	+574
Food & Kindred	3,657	3.2	115,419	4.9	5,703	10.3	18,759	2.4	−732
Chemicals	10,263	7.8	132,014	9.3	12,216	3.4	28,094	28.1	−1,564
Primary Metals	11,873	7.9	148,830	8.8	13,073	1.7	27,005	28.8	−500
Fabricated Metals	3,686	4.9	78,448	8.5	6,688	2.7	21,284	2.3	−17

Machinery, Except Electrical	4,006	4.5	88,180	18.2	16,008	Loss	25,142	4.2	+589
Electrical Machinery	5,583	7.2	77,238	12.3	9,501	2.6	22,178	11.8	−235
Textile Products	6,650	11.7	56,670	3.6	2,048	0.1	15,107	2.2	−35
Paper & Allied Products	14,560	12.2	118,920	11.0	13,096	4.1	30,896	13.5	+89
Rubber & Plastics	4,378	5.7	75,509	3.8	2,858	Loss	18,814	—	−119
Stone, Clay & Glass	6,243	5.8	107,344	2.5	2,662	Loss	25,445	—	+6
Transportation Equipment	4,789	4.3	110,916	17.2	19,031	Loss	30,878	4.0	+146
All Industries	10,677	—	214,989	12.7	27,341	2.3	22,584	—	−17,539

Source: U. S. Department of Commerce, *Survey of Current Business, 1984.*

Table 2.4
Performance Characteristics of U.S. Domestic Industries, by Industrial Sector, 1981

Industrial Sector	Plant & Equip. Expend. per Worker 1	P & E Expend. as Pct. of Sales 2	Sales per Worker 3	Exports as Pct. of Sales 4	Exports per Worker 5	Profit per Sales Dollar 6	Employee Compensation 7	Trade Balance 8
Mining	$ 1,463	—	—	—	—	—	$30,424	—
Petroleum	125,876	11.9	$1,062,236	1.7	$17,862	9.0	42,867	−$73,338
Manufacturing	6,270	6.3	99,747	—	—	—	—	—
Food & Kindred	4,889	3.0	161,891	11.1	18,019	1.6	21,210	+12,177
Chemicals	12,230	7.5	162,281	9.9	16,153	2.6	29,531	+11,996
Primary Metals	7,198	5.7	125,835	2.4	3,005	2.4	31,961	−5,741
Fabricated Metals	1,855	2.4	77,533	8.0	6,219	3.0	23,603	−2,594

Machinery, Except Electrical	5,294	6.6	80,712	25.6	20,667	4.1	25,968	+28,425
Electrical Machinery	4,895	7.3	66,569	9.2	6,134	3.8	22,875	+3,468
Textile Products	753	3.1	24,257	7.5	1,817	3.7	13,413	+1,209
Paper & Allied Products	9,790	8.4	116,962	6.2	7,242	2.9	$25,718	-635
Rubber & Plastics	2,402	3.3	72,148	—	—	—	—	—
Stone, Clay, & Glass	4,883	6.5	74,651	—	—	—	—	—
Transportation Equipment	9,668	8.9	107,898	16.6	17,881	Loss	32,153	-796[a]

[a]Involves approximately $34 billion each of exports and imports.
Source: U.S. Department of Commerce, *Survey of Current Business*, 1984.

Table 2.5
Comparison of Performance of FDI in the United States with Domestic Industry, 1981

Industrial Sector	Foreign Affiliates Perform Better 1	U.S. Companies Perform Better 2	Total 3	FDI Decidedly Superior 4	FDI Small Margin of Advantage 5	U.S. Domestic Companies Decidedly Superior 6	Foreign Affiliates & U.S. Companies on a Par 7
Mining	2		2		X		
Petroleum	6	1	7	X			
Manufacturing		5	5			X	
Food & Kindred	2	5	7			X	
Chemicals	2	5	7	X		X	
Primary Metals	5	2	7	X			
Fabricated Metals	5	2	7	X			
Machinery, Except Electrical	1	6	7			X	

Electrical Machinery	4	3	7			X
Textile Products	5	2	7	X		
Paper & Allied Products	7	0	7	X		
Rubber & Plastics	3	2	5		X	
Stone, Clay & Glass	3	2	5		X	
Transportation Equipment	3	3	6			
Totals	48	38	86	5	4	X / 1
Wins	9	4			4	
Ties		1				

Source: Tables 2.3 and 2.4.

Table 2.6
Imports Shipped to U.S. Affiliates of Foreign Direct Investors, Sales in the United States, and Percentage of Imports to Sales, 1981ᵃ

Industrial Sector	Sales in United States 1	Imports Shipped To U.S. Affiliates 2	Imports as Percentage of Sales in United States 3
All Industries	$503,745	$81,599	16.2
Petroleum	68,360	9,985	14.6
Manufacturing	137,717	13,009	9.4
Food & Kindred	14,674	1,457	9.9
Chemicals	54,550	3,432	6.3
Primary Metals	11,123	1,477	13.3
Fabricated Metals	2,639	242	9.2
Machinery, Except Electrical	11,953	1,581	13.2
Electrical Equipment	12,381	1,758	14.2
Wholesale Trade	221,387	57,571	26.0
Motor Vehicles & Equipment	39,161	20,132	51.4
Metals & Minerals	62,774	14,644	23.3
Farm Product Raw Materials	41,835	5,482	13.1
Other Nondurable Goods	14,277	5,301	37.1

ᵃAmounts are in millions of dollars.
Source: U.S. Department of Commerce, *Survey of Current Business*, 1984.

companies.[3] These magnitudes can be traced on a nearly current basis to ascertain their overall impact on the balance of payments of the United States in recent years. We can speculate on the direction or trend in which the overall effects may be heading. In this connection we can examine the structural shifts in the U.S. balance of payments over the past several decades, note the pressures stemming from increasing FDI inflows, and discuss to what extent these structural shifts may be related to foreign investment inflows.

With FDI inflows accelerating during 1978–1983, by the end of 1983 the foreign direct investment position in the United States had grown to $135.3 billion.[4] In 1982–1983 capital inflows averaged $12.7 billion per annum. At the same time the earnings distributed averaged $3.4 billion per year, and net interest paid foreign parent companies averaged $2.3 billion per year. In the early 1980s foreign-owned affiliates were running trade deficits of $16 billion per year (mostly concentrated in petroleum and wholesale trade).[5] In short, the annual balance-of-payments effects from FDI activity in the United States could be summarized as shown in Table 2.7. These effects reflect what are essentially long-term cumulative effects, that is, they are generated from many years of accumulated FDI activity. Table 2.7 reveals that as of the early 1980s FDI activity in the United States had produced a deficit in the U.S. balance of payments of approximately $9 billion per year.

The remainder of the discussion in this section focuses on changes in the structure of the U.S. balance of payments. U.S. balance-of-payments data are summarized in Table 2.8, reflecting only those key relationships required. In slightly more than two decades, the U.S. balance of payments has gone through three stages. In 1960–1965 the United States enjoyed a healthy balance of payments with a strong trade surplus and substantial foreign investment income. Outward investment flows were large, although curbed in 1965 by the capital controls imposed by Kennedy-Johnson. At this point the United States was an immature creditor (trade surplus, with long-term private capital outflows). By 1972 the trade accounts had reversed, and the United States experienced an $8.3 billion trade deficit. Nevertheless, income on U.S. investment abroad more than offset the trade deficit (and also offset the deficit on foreign investment income received from the United States). At this stage the United States had become a mature creditor (having a trade deficit, still investing overseas, with substantial net foreign investment income).[6]

Table 2.7
Balance-of-Payments Effects from FDI Activity in the United States, Early 1980s

Effect	Annual average (billions)
Capital Inflows	$12.7
Remitted Earnings	3.4
Remitted Interest	2.3
Trade Balance	16.0
Overall Effect	9.0

By 1980–1982 the balance-of-payments picture changed again. Between 1972 and 1980 the United States and the world economy experienced a series of dislocations, including two sharp increases in petroleum prices (1973–1974, 1978–1979), global inflation (1978–1982), global recession (1980–1982), and a shift to a floating exchange rate regime. With these changes the U.S. payments position also moved. The trade deficit magnified to the $17–36 billion range. At the same time foreign investment income earned and paid by the United States increased several fold. Foreign investment income earned reached $84.1 billion in 1982, and income received by foreign investors in the United States grew to $56.8 billion. More importantly, net private capital flows reversed direction. By

1980 the net long-term private capital outflow had declined to $2.2 billion. In 1982 there were net inflows of $11.7 billion. In 1982 the United States was moving into still another balance-of-payments stage. This could be termed mature creditor borrowing. As of 1985 the United States was shifting to a debtor stage as inflows exceeded outflows and as the net creditor position melted away.

Two questions emerge. First, can the United States afford to become a net

Table 2.8
Three Stages in the Changing Structure of the U.S. Balance of Payments (billion dollars)

Item	Immature Creditor		Mature Creditor Lending	Mature Creditor Borrowing[a]	
	1960	*1965*	*1972*	*1980*	*1982*
Merchandise Exports	$ 19.6	$ 26.5	$ 47.4	$ 110.4	$ 211.2
Merchandise Imports	14.7	21.5	55.7	127.5	247.6
Trade Balance	+4.9	+5.0	−8.3	−17.1	−36.4
Income on U.S. Assets Abroad	4.6	7.4	14.7	72.4	84.1
Income on Foreign Assets in United States	1.2	2.1	6.6	42.9	56.8
U.S. Private Capital Flow Direct	−2.9	−5.0	−7.7	−9.3	+3.0
Portfolio	−0.7	−0.8	−0.6	−2.1	−7.9
Total	−3.6	−5.8	−8.3	−11.4	−4.9
Foreign Private Capital Flow Direct	0.3	0.4	0.9	3.8	10.5
Portfolio	0.3	−0.4	4.5	5.4	6.1
Total	0.6	—	5.4	9.2	16.6
Balance on Private Capital	−3.0	−5.8	−2.9	−2.2	11.7

[a]Alternately can be termed Immature Debtor.

Source: U.S. Department of Commerce, *Statistical Abstract of the United States*, various issues, 1965–1984.

debtor and be able to discharge its global obligations? Second, how much did the FDI inflows contribute to the change in balance-of-payments structure? The second question is discussed here, and the first is reserved for Chapter 7.

FDI inflows represent one of several causes of the transition to the present balance-of-payments structure. Other important causes include (1) poor economic (macro) management, leading to budget deficits and high interest rates, strong inward capital flows, and an overvalued dollar; and (2) failure to adopt appropriate policies (macro and micro). Appropriate policies might include management of commodity trade flows to insure full reciprocity by trading partners, and management of the overall trade balance so as to give the United States greater flexibility in overall international economic policies.

FDI inflows have contributed in a major way to the evolution of the U.S. balance of payments—from immature creditor, to mature creditor, to immature debtor. Foreign direct investment in the United States has been one of the fastest growing categories on the liabilities side of the international investment position, accounting for approximately one-sixth of the total. Moreover, FDI activities have added to the trade deficit tendencies in the overall payments position, thereby providing relatively cheap dollars to the rest of the world for investment in the United States. The accumulation of foreign investment in the United States has swollen the income earned by foreign companies on their assets held in this country. The rapid growth of FDI investment, and reinvestment of earnings, has brought the U.S. balance of payments to a position of net capital inflows, reversing the cumulative creditor position enjoyed for so many decades.

In summary, FDI inflows have exerted significant additional pressures on the U.S. balance of payments. These have accelerated the evolution in the structure of international payments. Consequently, in a relatively short period of time the United States has shifted from immature creditor, to mature creditor, and finally to immature debtor.

This chapter reviews the trends in inflows and outflows to and from the United States. Inflows have accelerated, and there is virtually no net outflow of FDI in the most recent period of years covered in this study. FDI is an evolving activity, with the role of government policy changing over time.

A brief statistical comparison of the performance of FDI foreign-owned affiliates with U.S. domestic firms, by industry sector, permits us to evaluate FDI inflows to the United States. Certain foreign-owned industry sectors, on the basis of the performance areas utilized as criteria, performed more or less satisfactorily than their U.S. domestic counterparts.

Finally, the performance of foreign-owned affiliates is reviewed from the standpoint of their supplying U.S. markets with imports from parent companies versus U.S. domestic production. One sector in particular was found to be heavily dependent on imports in supplying U.S. markets, the motor vehicle sector. For this reason and others considerable attention is given to this industry sector in Chapters 5, 6, and 7.

NOTES

1. Communist countries obtain technology or high-tech products through illicit trading channels. For example, North Korea illegally obtained a number of U.S.-made Hughes helicopters. The helicopters apparently were diverted to North Korea via a West German distributor. "North Korea Illegally Got Hughes Copters," *Wall Street Journal*, January 4, 1985, p. 28.

2. Partly for this reason Robert Z. Lawrence argues that a combination of tight fiscal policy and easy monetary policy is needed in the United States. See Lawrence, *Can America Compete?*, (Washington D.C.: Brookings Institute, 1984), pp. 87–88.

3. N. Bruck and F. A. Lees, *Foreign Investment, Capital Controls, and the Balance of Payments* (New York: New York University, Institute of Finance, 1968).

4. R. David Belli, "Foreign Direct Investment in the United States in 1983," *Survey of Current Business*, October 1984, p. 26. Approximately three-fourths of this investment was in the form of parent equity; the remainder was intercompany debt.

5. U.S. Department of Commerce, *Survey of Current Business*, November 1983, p. 25.

6. Francis A. Lees, "Mature Creditorship and the Balance of Payments," *Economic and Business Bulletin* 22 (Spring-Summer 1970): 31–35.

3

The Theory of Foreign Direct Investment and the Inflow of Foreign Direct Investment into the United States

For much of the post-war period the United States has been the principal overseas investor. But during the past decade, the inward flow of FDI into the United States has accelerated rapidly. In this chapter we explore the characteristics of this inflow and seek to understand what motivated foreign-owned multinationals of other industrial countries to invest in the United States.

SOME ASPECTS OF THE THEORY OF FOREIGN DIRECT INVESTMENT

This section summarizes some of the theoretical literature regarding the rationale for FDI. Several distinct strands of thought are identified, notably (1) the industrial organization approach; (2) the MNC and the product cycle hypothesis; (3) internalization and the MNC; and (4) location theory and international trade.

By the early 1970s the leading theoretical explanation of foreign direct investment was the industrial organization or imperfect competition theory espoused by Stephen Hymer, Charles Kindleberger, and Richard Caves. According to this framework, large oligopolistic firms that produce differentiated products undertake FDI. Even though production abroad involves a number of disadvantages including additional costs and risks, firms engage in production abroad because they possess certain advantages, allowing them to obtain larger profits than domestic firms. These advantages enhance the profitability of producing abroad as opposed to producing at home and exporting. These advantages stem from the imperfections in the goods market, economics of scale internal and external to the firm, and government-imposed market imperfections.[1]

Hymer hypothesized that foreign direct investment belonged to the theory of imperfect competition because multinationals are usually large firms operating in imperfectly competitive markets. For firms to operate in imperfect markets abroad they must have certain net advantages over firms in the host country. Hymer found that the motives for investing abroad were similar to Joseph Bain's list of barriers to entry.[2] Bain classified barriers as those due to economies of scale, absolute cost advantage, and product differentiation advantages.

While stressing the idea that FDI belongs to the theory of industrial organization, Richard Caves also investigated the impact of MNCs on the host country in terms of promoting allocative efficiency. Because MNCs can overcome high entry barriers and upset local, entrenched oligopolistic firms, they produce more active rivalry and improve market performance, thus enhancing allocative efficiency. But the entry of MNCs also has a negative aspect, for it may raise seller concentration in the market of the host country, especially if the presence of the new rival induces mergers among domestic firms. In such cases, the entry of foreign firms may even raise domestic prices.

Charles Kindleberger also stresses the idea that foreign direct investment belongs to the theory of industrial organization. The investing firm earns more abroad than at home and can earn a higher return in the market where it is investing than existing or potentially competitive firms in that country because of the possession of monopolistic advantages. Kindleberger has classified these advantages under four headings: departures from competition in goods markets (product differentiation, marketing skills, administered prices, and so on) and factor markets (proprietary knowledge, discrimination in access to capital, and managerial skills); external and internal economies of scale; and government-imposed intervention to facilitate import substitution, which contributes to "defensive investment" undertaken to defend existing market shares.[3]

The idea of defensive investment was introduced by Alexander Lamfalussy. Firms undertake defensive investments which may offer a less than average rate of return in order to avoid losses on existing investments. Tariffs or exchange controls imposed to encourage the development of industries may encourage FDI.

In his theory of oligopolistic reaction, Fredrick Knickerbocker argued that firms in concentrated industries may engage in FDI to match the investment patterns of rivals.[4] Oligopolistic reaction is applicable after a leading oligopolistic competitor makes the first FDI in an industry. This FDI induces a clustering of investment by other leading oligopolistic competitors. Firms in a given industry perceive their mutual interdependence and follow the behavior of rival firms that undertake FDI. Using the Harvard School of Business Administration data for manufacturing FDI by 187 American MNCs, he constructed an entry concentration index (ECI). This index showed that entries of American firms into foreign markets are bunched in time. He also found a significant positive correlation between the ECI and U.S. industrial concentration ratio, which indicated that, except at very high concentration levels, a high level of industrial concentration produced reactions by rivals in the field of FDI.

Edward B. Flowers investigated the increase in FDI in the United States by European and Canadian firms during the period 1945–1975. His approach is a variation of the hypothesis of oligopolistic reaction developed by Knickerbocker to explain the timing of U.S. FDI in Europe. The study showed that in relatively concentrated industries, competitive interaction by the leading firms was involved in their undertaking FDI at roughly the same time. For each investing country the study regressed a measure of FDI entry concentration on a measure of industrial concentration. The ECI was computed to measure the strength of the FDI entry. The research indicated that in highly concentrated European and Canadian industries, the FDI of the leading firms in each country had a tendency to come into the United States in clusters of subsidiaries in response to the activities of the first investing firm in the industry, with the clustering of oligopolistically reactive FDI occurring within three years of the first investment by a leading firm. Industrial concentration of the investing industries was able to explain almost one-half of the European and Canadian FDI coming into the United States during the three decades.[5]

Raymond Vernon's description of the product cycle theory explains why innovative and oligopolistic firms undertake FDI. The innovating firm initially produces the technologically sophisticated product for its home market because of the availability of a demand for the product and the need to effectively coordinate R & D with production units. Production expands by taking advantage of economies of scale for the product, and it becomes cheaper to produce it as demand increases. A market for the product appears in other advanced economies, and the firm begins to export the product to other industrial countries. As foreign demand grows and the technology of producing the product stabilizes, production takes place outside the United States, often by U.S. subsidiaries who invest abroad as part of "defensive investment" in other advanced economies. The shift to production outside the United States coincides with an erosion in America's initial technological advantage. Finally, as technology in producing this product line becomes standardized, it is sold on the basis of price competitiveness, and the United States becomes a net importer. That is, in the final stage, the product line matures, and the rest of the world becomes a net exporter while the United States becomes a net importer. The MNC may undertake production in less developed countries because with standardization of technology low wages give LDCs a comparative advantage.[6] The product cycle theory was originally useful in explaining U.S. FDI in other advanced countries as well as the eventual production by MNCs in low labor cost economies. But the theory has become outdated. First, the United States is no longer the only dominant foreign investor. European and Japanese investors are contributing an increasing share to global FDI. Second, the MNCs are now able to develop, mature, and standardize products almost simultaneously and can differentiate their products without incurring significant time lags.[7] The product cycle theory was developed to explain U.S. FDI in Europe during the 1950s and 1960s and cannot explain all types of FDI. Some of the recent changes include the deterioration of U.S.

technological leadership and the leveling of the income differentials that once existed between the United States and other developed economies.

Vernon himself has indicated that the power of the product cycle to explain trade and investment is considerably weakened. The first reason is that large multinationals have spread their networks of subsidiaries around the world, and these producing units generally produce more than half the global output of their respective product lines. In the 25 years between 1950 and 1975 there was a dramatic increase in the overseas networks and geographic dispersion of U.S. and European MNCs. In addition, after examining the spread of new product lines by U.S. MNCs to their foreign subsidiaries, it appears that the time interval between the introduction of a new product in the United States and its initial production overseas has continuously deteriorated.

The second reason is that during the past two decades other advanced countries experienced rising incomes and the higher relative labor costs that had previously prevailed only in the United States, and demand for products that had previously been introduced in response to U.S. needs increased in Europe and Japan. These phenomena weakened the critical assumption of the product cycle theory that large MNCs encountered conditions abroad that differed markedly from conditions in their home markets.[8]

Market imperfections in capital markets have also been used to explain FDI. Robert Z. Aliber emphasizes imperfections in foreign exchange and capital markets.[9] Others have focused on other financial aspects of MNCs as explanations of FDI. For instance, T. B. Agmon and D. F. Lessard used portfolio theory to explain the relation of FDI to the needs of MNCs to diversity and stabilize earnings. They observed that at the corporate level, FDI rather than portfolio capital movements offered the multinational corporation an opportunity to diversify that was not otherwise available. Another approach is to explain FDI in terms of changes in the levels of exchange rates, associating overvaluation of a currency with the outflow of FDI and undervaluation with the inflow.[10]

According to Aliber, FDI is an outcome of the existence of different currency areas. FDI takes place because source country firms capitalize the same stream of earnings at a higher rate than host country firms because the market is able to give different capitalization rates to future streams of income that are denominated in different currencies. Different capitalization rates are attached because, according to the market mechanism, a premium must be paid for bearing uncertainty about exchange risk. This also means that the difference in the yields on equities from two different countries may reflect the expectation of depreciation of the weaker currency and a premium for bearing the uncertainty about the future price of the weaker currency in terms of the stronger currency.[11]

Accordingly, firms from countries with currencies that command a premium have an advantage in investing abroad because the market capitalizes the host country stream of earnings at a higher rate if it is earned by a source country instead of a host country. Aliber suggests that this "exchange risk" theory of FDI explains the geographic and industrial patterns of FDI. The geographic pattern of FDI is a reflection of different capitalization rates for different equities denominated in different currencies. According to this theory, FDI will be larger in the more capital-intensive industries because the larger the contribution of capital to production, the larger the advantage of the source country. Aliber also explains that the difference in capitalization ratios can cause FDI through takeovers.

Other researchers have attempted to explain FDI in terms of misalignments in the level of exchange rates, an overvaluation of a currency being associated with an outflow of FDI and an undervaluation with an inflow. According to J. Makin, an overvalued currency is a tax on exports and a subsidy to imports. Therefore, overvaluation of the currency reduces the size of both the firm's domestic and foreign markets and makes some of the firm's capacity redundant. In such a situation, unit costs of production might be reduced if some of the redundant capital is used to undertake FDI abroad.[12]

Stephen Kohlhagen has examined the effect of devaluations in the United Kingdom, France, and West Germany during the 1960s on FDI inflows. He develops a model of relative profitability in alternative production locations— the source country and the host country. The net result depends on the effect of a devaluation on costs and prices in the two locations, but the devaluation will probably increase relative profitability in a country with a devaluing currency. However, if the devaluing country has a very open economy and the domestic demand and supply for tradeable goods are relatively inelastic, production in the devaluing economy becomes relatively less profitable. The major devaluations in the United Kingdom, West Germany, and France during the 1960s increased the profitability of investment in the devaluing countries and induced inflows of FDI into these countries.[13]

Dennis Logue and Thomas Willet have analyzed the impact of exchange rate changes for the United States from 1967 to 1973 and found that exchange rate changes encouraged inflows of FDI.[14]

Exchange rate risk and discrete changes in exchange rates can offer some explanation for FDI. But, because changes in exchange rates may influence the timing of a particular FDI, Aliber's hypothesis that portfolio investors ignore exchange risk in earnings of foreign subsidiaries would apply only to holders of small portfolios and not to large institutional investors.[15] Several other criticisms have been levied against Aliber's hypothesis.[16] First, it has been argued that, in the long term, investor myopia does not explain FDI because speculators should be able to eliminate the bias causing the currency premium. Second, the theory explains neither the industrial distribution of FDI nor the phenomenon of simultaneous cross-investment between different currency areas but in one industry. It may also be noted that, although the theory can explain the post-war expansion of U.S. FDI to weaker currency areas, followed later by an extensive outflow of European and Japanese investment and the recent influx of such investment into the United States, it fails to explain the continuation of the inflow of FDI into the United States since 1981 when the dollar appreciated against other currencies.

As can be observed from the above sampling of FDI theories that have focused on market imperfections, during the past quarter of a century considerable research efforts have been devoted to explaining the growth and composition of foreign investment. Important contributions have been made by those who focused on market imperfections and the ownership advantages of foreign firms. Drawing on these contributions, several researchers have elaborated hypotheses that revolve around a particular aspect of ownership advantage. For instance, Harry G. Johnson points to the availability of superior technology as an ownership advantage,[17] and Caves emphasizes the idea that the ability to engage in product differentiation is responsible for FDI. Knickerbocker and Flowers, on the other hand, explain FDI in terms of defensive oligopolistic reaction strategies between different MNCs in the same industry and country.

More Recent Theories of FDI

None of these hypotheses offers a complete explanation for the determinants of FDI. In 1977 John P. Dunning proposed a general theory that integrated the existing body of knowledge surrounding the determinants of FDI. He brought together the different strands of FDI theories into one approach.[18] Earlier, in a paper written in 1973, he had concluded that trade and foreign production were alternative forms of international involvement that could be explained in terms of ownership and locational advantages. In the 1977 article subtitled "A Search for an Eclectic Theory," Dunning offered a theory that combined the different strands of thought with respect to FDI theory.[19] His theory drew on three areas of economics: industrial organization, theory of the firm, and international trade theory—and he explained the willingness and ability of firms to exploit markets as well as the reason they seek to exploit markets through foreign production. If ownership, internalization, and locational advantages exist, then the firms can engage in international production.

To serve particular markets, the investing firm, in contrast to firms of other nationalities, must possess net ownership-specific advantages in the form of intangible assets, which are exclusive or specific to the investing firm. Most of these advantages can be explained by industrial organization theory. These advantages consist mainly of firm size, established position, access to raw materials, and exclusive possession of intangible assets such as patents, trademarks, management and organizational skills, and marketing channels. Other advantages arise from the multinationality of the firm, such as accrued knowledge and more favorable access to foreign markets.

It is more beneficial for the firm itself to use these advantages rather than to sell or lease them to other firms. By extending its activities through foreign direct investment, the firm can internalize its ownership advantages. Such internalization results from market failure or may represent a shield against market failure. Public intervention in the allocation of resources may also encourage the internalization of activities. When multinationals serve foreign markets, they can allocate resources according to their own control procedures and can choose to replace or augment the market mechanism.[20] In imperfect markets, the firm may gain by improving the coordination of interdependent activities. The formation of the firm reduces the substantial coordination costs that would accrue with the operation of markets.

The idea that firms can bypass the market and internalize their ownership advantages draws upon developments in the theory of the firm that can be attributed to Ronald Coase, Kenneth J. Arrow, and A. Alchian and H. Demsetz. Erik Furubotn and Svetozar Pejovich present a good survey of the literature on property rights and economic theory.[21] Peter Buckley and Mark Casson, John McManus, G. Bauman, and Stephen P. Magee have expanded these concepts in the direct investment literature.[22]

Several writers have studied the role of multinational firms in reducing these coordinating costs. McManus theorizes that MNCs will emerge in industries characterized by a substantial amount of interdependence among producers in different countries and substantial costs of coordinating their activities through liscensing or the market mechanism.

Magee's appropriability theory of direct investment is parallel to Dunning's explanation that multinational firms internalize ownership-specific advantages. According to Magee, the need to appropriate the private returns from investment in information becomes an explanation of FDI. Multinationals, he states, specialize in producing information that is less efficient to transmit through markets than within firms. Because the appropriability of the social value of new ideas is higher for sophisticated technologies than for simple technologies, multinationals produce sophisticated rather than simple technologies and the appropriability of the returns from and complementarities among five types of information (information for product creation, product development, development of production functions, market creation, and knowledge of the degree to which creators of information can appropriate for themselves returns of the new information) dictate large optimum plant size. Firms invest abroad to increase the appropriability of information by reducing the rate of diffusion. Firms expand abroad to internalize the public goods aspect of new information.

In addition to market imperfections, Dunning points out that enterprises may internalize activities as a result of government intervention in the allocation of resources. One example of such intervention is the government's encouragement of the internalization of production and/or sale of technology. Governments have facilitated internalization by subsidizing R & D activities, continuing the patent system, and permitting a milieu in which firms internalize their knowledge-producing and knowledge-consuming activities. The second example of public intervention arises because the government's different economic policies lead to distortions in the allocation of economic resources. For instance, a firm may manipulate transfer prices to reduce the global tax burden.[23] Other reasons to internalize operations across borders are to minimize exposure from fluctuating exchange rates, take advantage of interest rate differentials, and cushion the adverse effects of government legislation.

Ownership and internalization advantages are firm-specific. Some research has shown that location-specific advantages are important determinants of FDI. During the 1950s and 1960s a number of researchers employed theories of location and international trade to explain why MNCs chose to produce in one country rather than in another. Among the location-specific advantages are prices, quality, and productivity of inputs; government intervention involving tariff and non-tariff barriers, tax rates, foreign investment incentives, and political stability; the available infrastructure; transport and communications costs; foreign exchange effects from locating in one country as opposed to another; the large size of markets in the host country; and the psychic closeness of cultures in the home and the host countries.

The eclectic theory explains FDI by combining the firm-specific ownership and internalization advantages with the location-specific advantages. Assuming that the firm can utilize ownership and internalization advantages, for FDI to occur it must be profitable to combine these advantages with certain location-specific advantages in the host country. Rather than introduce a completely new body of theoretical literature, the eclectic theory draws on a large body of knowledge. According to the eclectic theory a wide range of motivations could determine a FDI decision.

CHARACTERISTICS OF FDI INFLOW INTO THE UNITED STATES

The pattern of investment inflows into the United States since 1973 differs markedly from the pattern of the preceding period. Whereas previously the outward flow of U.S. FDI was greatly in excess of the inward flow, by the early 1980s this pattern was reversed. During the 1970s FDI represented an increasing, though still minor, share of Gross Domestic Fixed Capital Formation and total employment, thereby indicating that FDI was becoming relatively more important to the U.S. economy. Changes were also taking place in the sectoral allocation, with the service sector accounting for a relatively larger share of FDI infows compared to the extractive sector and manufacturing.

To a large extent, investment inflows mirror the changing nature of the international economy. First, many of the Japanese and European firms reached maturity during the 1960s and 1970s, and foreign investment flows became larger as these firms matured and were forced to compete with older, more established firms. Second, the percentage of global FDI going into the developed market economies has tended to expand in relation to the shares being invested in the developing nations.

FDI patterns also reflect the changing composition of economic activity in industrial countries. As the standard of living has increased in these countries, services account for an increasing proportion of national output. Thus, FDI inflows in all advanced economies including the United States show an increasing share going into the service sector relative to the extractive sector and manufacturing. In addition, the expanding foreign activities of multinationals require an increase in support services.[24]

Since 1976 when data first became available, mergers and acquisitions have comprised a major, though declining, share of FDI. In this chapter we seek to explain why acquisitions have played such an important role and demonstrate that industrial organization theory can help explain this phenomenon. We also examine the changes in the value of assets of enterprises acquired and established by foreigners, and the rates of return of the investment flows.

Foreign Direct Investment Flows

Since 1981 the United States has become a net importer of foreign direct investment (Table 3.1, Col. 3). In contrast, during the earlier postwar period the United States was the major exporter of direct investment capital. By 1981 the stock of U.S. direct investment capital abroad was $226 billion, almost four times the amount of the United Kingdom's total investment in overseas FDI. The United Kingdom is the second largest investor country. But the growth of U.S. foreign direct investment abroad had slowed down considerably, and FDI outflows by the six EEC countries, Canada, and Japan continued to grow. In contrast to 1965–1969 when the United States contributed 65% to this outflow, by 1980–1981 this share had declined to 28%.[25] By way of contrast, the six EEC added 48.6% to world FDI flows, Canada 9.7%, and Japan 7.6%.[26]

The growth of inward FDI to the United States has characterized the years since 1973. This flow became particularly large after 1977. By 1984 the stock of FDI in the United States was twelve times its size in 1970. The data for the 1980s indicate that these inflows continued to undergo growth even during a period of severe world recession.

Although foreign direct investment into the United States grew continuously during the two decades under review, this growth was particularly pronounced between 1977 and 1984, when the absolute amount of FDI in the United States more than quadrupled, rising from $34.6 billion to $159.6 billion. The rate of growth between 1977 and 1982 was sustained at an average level of 24% per annum.[27] From 1980 to 1983, a recession period, it grew by 18%, a slower growth rate reflecting the recession that lasted until the first half of 1983. In 1984 the low rate of inflation and strength of the U.S. recovery led to a new surge in FDI. In conjunction with this growth since 1977 was a large increase in the number of large investments. The U.S. Department of Commerce notes that not only was the increase in number of affiliates large after 1977, but also there was a vast increase in the number of new investments valued at $100 million or more, and many were much larger than $100 million. Between 1977 and 1981 the number of investments over $100 million increased from 3 to 51, and then fell to 34 in 1982.[28] Table 3.2 lists all transactions of over $300 million during the years 1977–1982. Most of the largest transactions involved acquisitions by petroleum companies and banking establishments.

Since 1950 the industrial mix of foreign direct investment in the United States has shifted (Table 3.3). The share in manufacturing rose from one-third to 42% in 1966, but declined to about one-third by 1982. Over the same period the

Table 3.1
The U.S. International Foreign Direct Investment Position, 1950–1983

Year	Additions to U.S. Direct Investment Position Abroad (1)	Additions to FDI Position in United States (2)	Net International Investment Position (3)	U.S. Company FDI Position Abroad (4)	Foreign Company FDI Position in United States (5)
1950	1,088	325	−763	11,788	3,391
1955	1,766	443	−1,323	19,396	5,076
1960	2,039	306	−1,733	31,866	6,910
1965	4,994	434	−4,560	49,475	8,797
1970	7,387	1,452	−5,935	75,480	13,270
1971	7,280	5,688	−1,592	82,760	13,914
1972	7,118	4,588	−2,530	89,878	14,868
1973	11,435	2,518	−8,917	101,313	20,556
1974	8,765	3,108	−5,657	110,078	25,144
1975	13,971	3,825	−10,146	124,050	27,662
1976	12,759	7,854	−4,905	138,809	30,770
1977	9,181	11,991	−2,810	145,990	34,595
1978	16,737	7,874	−8,863	162,727	42,471
1979	25,131	11,991	−13,140	187,858	54,462
1980	25,517	16,918	−8,599	215,375	83,046
1981	12,973	24,401	11,428	228,348	107,590
1982	−6,836	16,000	22,836	221,512	123,590
1983	5,119	12,384	7,118	226,962	137,061
1984	6,450	22,510	16,060	233,412	159,571

Sources: Columns (1) and (2): U.S. Department of Commerce, *International Direct Investment: Global Trends and the U.S. Role, 1984,* 1984, pp. 54 and 65 and U.S. Department of Commerce, *Survey of Current Business,* October 1984.

Column (3): Column (1) minus Column (2).

Columns (4) and (5): U.S. Department of Commerce, *International Direct Investment,* pp. 54, 55, 61, and 65 and U.S. Department of Commerce, *Survey of Current Business,* August 1984, p. 40, August 1985, pp. 30, 47.

Average Annual rates of growth:

A. Change in U.S. FDI position abroad: 1. 1950–1966, 9.7%; 2. 1966–1982, 9.5%; 3. 1977–1982, 8.7%.

B. Changes in Foreign FDI position in United States: 1. 1950–1966, 6.3%; 2. 1966–1982, 16.3%; 3. 1973–1977, 13.9%; 4. 1977–1982, 24.1%; 5. 1980–1983, 18.0%.

Table 3.2
Foreign Direct Investment Transactions in the United States over $300 Million, 1977–1982

Country	Reported Total Cost (mil. dol.)	Foreign Investor	U.S. Company
		1977	
Canada	350.0	Olympia and York Ltd.	Real Estate
		1978	
Netherlands	485.0	Unilever Group	Natl. Starch and Chem. Corp.
		1979	
Canada	310.0	Genstar Ltd.	Flintkote Co.
France	363.0	Schlumberger Family	Fairchild Camera & Instrument Co.
Netherlands	3,650.0	Royal Dutch Shell Group	Belridge Oil Co.
	349.2	Nationale-Nederlanden N.V.	Life Ins. Co. of Georgia
United Kingdom	429.0	Natl. Westminister Bank Ltd.	Natl. Bank of N. America
	375.0	ICI Ltd.	Corpus Christi Petro-Chemicals Inc.
	372.0	Standard Chartered Bank Ltd.	Union Bancorp
	300.0	Swire, John & Sons Ltd.	Real Estate
		1980	
Canada	1,000.0	Olympia and York Ltd.	Real Estate
	500.0	N.B. Cook Corp.	Real Estate
	500.0	Olympia and York Ltd.	Real Estate
Hong Kong	314.0	Hong Kong & Shanghai Banking Corp.	Marine Midland Banks Ltd.
Netherlands	680.0	Royal Dutch Shell Group	A. T. Massey Coal Co.
United Kingdom	630.0	Imperial Group Ltd.	Howard Johnson
	415.0	Grand Metropolitan Ltd.	Ligget Group, Inc.
		1981	
Australia	591.2	CSR Ltd.	Delhi Int'l, Oil Corp
Canada	2,580.0	Bronfman Family	E. I. Dupont de Nemours
	630.0	Hiram Walker Consumer Home Ltd.	Davis Oil Properties
	400.0	Campean Corp.	Real Estate

Table 3.2 (*continued*)

Country	Reported Total Cost (mil. dol.)	Foreign Investor	U.S. Company
	370.0	Alsten Holding Ltd.	Real Estate
	360.0	Reichman Family	Real Estate
	300.0	Cadillac-Fairview Ltd.	Real Estate
	300.0	Campean Corp.	Real Estate
France	2,500.0	Societe Nationale Elf-Acquitaine	Texasgulf, Inc.
	305.3	Lafarge Copper SA	General Portland
Italy	375.0	Ente Nationale Idrocarbur	Enoxy
Japan	500.0	Nissan Motor Co., Ltd.	Nissan Lfg. USA
Kuwait	2,500.8	Kuwait Petroleum Corp.	Santa Fe Int'l Corp.
South Africa	309.0	Oppenheimer, Harry & Family	Newmont Mining Corp.
United Kingdom	938.1	British Petroleum Co., Ltd.	Kennecott Corp.
	820.0	Midland Bank Ltd.	Crocker National Bank
	500.0	Grand Metropolitan Ltd.	Intercontinental Hotels
	318.0	British Petroleum Co., Ltd.	Crystal Block Mine
West Germany	300.0	VW	VW of America Inc.
		1982	
Bahrain	454.0	Arab Banking Corp.	Arab Banking Corp.
Belgium	581.6	Petrofina SA Oil Leases	Texas Oil and Gas Corp's.
Canada	500.0	Bramalea Ltd.	Dallas Main Ctr.
	400.0	Cadillac-Fairview Ltd.	California Plaza
	400.0	Markborough Properties Ltd./Costain	Scottsdale Ranch
	310.0	Canadian Pacific Ltd.	Giddings and Lewis Inc.
	300.0	Bramelea Ltd.	Corporate Park Complex
Japan	330.0	DAIEI Ltd.	Hawaii Properties
United Kingdom	539.0	British Petroleum Co. Ltd.	Oil/Gas Leases
	455.0	Goldsmith, Sir James	Diamond Int'l. Corp.
	365.0	BAT Industries PLC	Marshall Field & Co.
	300.0	European Ferries Ltd.	Andrau Airpark

Source: U.S. Department of Commerce, *International Direct Investment: Global Trends and the U.S. Role*, Appendix B, 1984, pp. 77–80.

Table 3.3
Foreign Direct Investment Position in the United States by Industry, 1950–1982 (millions of dollars)

Industry	1950	1959	1966	1974	1982[b]
Petroleum	405	1,184	1,740	5,614	20,488
Manufacturing	1,138	2,471	3,789	10,387	32,186
Trade	[a]	614	739	4,387	20,630
Finance and Insurance	1,065	1,734	2,072	2,723	14,844
Other Industries	784	601	714	2,032	13,696
Total	3,391	6,604	9,054	25,144	101,844
Percentage Distribution					
Petroleum	11.9	17.9	19.2	22.3	20.1
Manufacturing	33.6	37.4	41.8	41.3	31.6
Trade	[a]	9.3	8.2	17.4	20.3
Finance and Insurance	31.4	26.3	22.9	10.8	14.6
Other Industries	23.1	9.1	7.9	8.1	13.4

Note: Figures may not add up to totals exactly due to rounding.
[a]Included in "Other Industries."
[b]Figures for 1982 do not correspond to those in Table 3.1, which uses data revised in 1984.
Sources: U.S. Department of Commerce, *International Direct Investment: Global Trends and the U.S. Role*, 1984, p. 63; and U.S. Department of Commerce, *Survey of Current Business*, October 1984, p. 26

share in petroleum almost doubled, rising to 20% of the total, while finance and insurance combined dropped from over one-third to 15%. Several large investments of over $1 billion contributed to the large rise in petroleum. Trade rose from 9.3% in 1959 to 20.3% in 1982. The large expansion in trade can be explained by the growth of wholesale distributorships of imported cars and trucks and large commodity price increases.[29]

The importance of FDI to the U.S. economy can be illustrated by comparing the magnitudes of such investment to a number of different economic variables. Tables 3.4–3.7 reflect (1) the percentage of total U.S. assets held by foreign-owned or -controlled U.S. affiliates; (2) the percentage of total U.S. equity held by foreign-owned or -controlled U.S. affiliates; (3) the percentage of total U.S. employment accounted for by foreign-owned or -controlled enterprises; and (4) the flow of FDI as a percentage of Gross Domestic Capital Formation. Since 1977 the percentage of assets in mining, manufacturing, wholesale trade, and retail trade held by foreigners has increased substantially, and in 1981 foreigners owned or controlled 13% of total assets in these four industries. Total U.S. equity in these four industries held by foreign-owned or -controlled enterprises increased to 6% by 1980. In manufacturing the percentage of equity owned or controlled by foreigners rose to 11%. Total U.S. employment by foreign-owned or -controlled U.S. affiliates rose from 1.6% in 1977 to 3.1% in 1981.

Another indication of the growing role of FDI in the U.S. economy is the flow of direct investment as a percentage of Gross Fixed Capital Formation. In the United States this percentage increased substantially in the two decades between 1960 and 1979, rising from 0.4% in 1960 to 1.9% in 1979.[30] During the 1980s this share continued to grow.

As other industrial economies prospered, their corporations became larger and more mature, and engaged increasingly in FDI abroad. The number of source countries that invested heavily in the United States increased. As a consequence, the relative importance of countries that initially were major source countries declined. Over the period 1950–1983 Europe continued to contribute about two-thirds of the investment flow. The United Kingdom and the Netherlands remained the major source countries, but the share of the United Kingdom declined from 33% in 1950 to 24% in 1983, while the Netherlands' share rose from 9.8% to 21.3%. The shares of Germany and France increased in relative importance. The roles of Japan and Latin America (particularly the Netherlands Antilles) increased in relative importance, and Canada's role was sharply reduced.

Table 3.4
Percentage of Total U.S. Assets Held by Foreign-Owned or -Controlled U.S. Affiliates, Selected Industries, 1977–1981

Industry	1977	1978	1979	1980	1981
Mining	9	9	8	10	15
Manufacturing	6	6	7	8	12
Wholesale Trade	17	17	17	18	28
Retail Trade	2	2	3	4	4
Average	7	7	8	9	13

Source: U.S. Department of Commerce, *International Direct Investment: Global Trends and the U.S. Role* (Washington, D.C.: 1984), p. 21.

Table 3.5
Percentage of Total U.S. Equity Held by Foreign-Owned or -Controlled U.S. Affiliates, Selected Industries, 1974 and 1980

Industry	1974	1980
Mining	6	6
Manufacturing	4	6
Wholesale Trade	7	11
Retail Trade	2	3
Average	4	6

Source: U.S. Department of Commerce, *International Direct Investment: Global Trends and the U.S. Role*, p. 21.

Table 3.6
Percentage of Total Employment by Foreign-Owned or -Controlled U.S. Affiliates, 1977–1981

Industry	1977	1978	1979	1980	1981
Mining	2.1	2.3	2.4	2.6	3.6
Manufacturing	3.6	3.9	4.7	5.8	6.8
Wholesale Trade	3.0	3.3	4.7	4.2	4.6
Retail Trade	0.9	1.1	1.5	2.0	2.2
Other Industries	0.5	0.4	0.7	0.9	1.0
(excl. banking)					
Average	1.6	1.8	2.2	2.7	3.1

Source: U.S. Department of Commerce, *International Direct Investment*, p. 22.

Table 3.7
Flow of Direct Investment as a Percentage of Gross Fixed Capital Formation, 1960–1979

Year	Percentage	Year	Percentage
1960	0.4	1973	1.2
1965	0.3	1976	1.6
1967	0.5	1978	2.1
1970	0.9	1979	1.9

Source: United Nations, Centre on Transnational Corporations, *Salient Features and Trends in Foreign Direct Investment* (New York: 1983), p. 42.

Acquisitions and Assets of Acquired and Established Enterprises

Data for acquisitions by foreign investors are available only since 1976. After that year acquisitions accounted for between 61 and 86% of foreign direct investment outlays in the United States, with only a minor share spent on new establishments (Table 3.8). It also appears that the share going into new establishments has increased in recent years. Of the amount spent for new establishments, the major share went into real estate. Between 1979 and 1983, between 55 and 74% of FDI went into real estate each year. The share dropped to 54% in 1984, reflecting a slowdown in appreciation of real estate values. Only a minor part of all FDI that was directed into the establishment of new business was involved in productive activities. Even though most FDI in directly productive activities took the form of acquisitions, investments still had an impact on productivity and employment. An example is the takeover by Sanyo Electric Company Ltd. of Warwick Electronics in 1976, a plant that was owned by Whirlpool and produced color television sets. Because of continuing problems

Table 3.8
Investment Outlays and Assets of Acquired and Established Enterprises, 1976–1984 (mil. dol.)

Year	Investment Outlays			Assets Acquired and Established	Assets Acquired	
	Total	Acquisitions				
		Value	Percent of Value		Value	Percent of Value
1976	$ 3,108	$ 2,100	67	—	—	—
1977	3,825	3,300	86	—	—	—
1978	7,874	6,100	77	35,581	—	—
1979	15,317	13,179	86	36,627	32,351	88
1980	12,127	8,974	74	49,694	42,591	86
1981	25,219	18,151	72	87,757	76,254	87
1982	10,817	6,563	61	31,852	24,603	84
1983	8,091	4,848	60	22,311	14,510	65
1984[a]	13,018	10,599	81	34,538	28,749	83

[a]Preliminary data.

Sources: 1976–1978: Investment outlays-acquisitions; Sarkis, Khoury, *Transnational Mergers and Acquisitions in the United States* (Lexington, Mass.: D.C. Heath and Co., 1980), pp. 21–23. Other data: U.S. Department of Commerce, *Survey of Current Business,* various issues.

caused by poor product quality, Warwick was facing a severe financial crisis. Sears, its largest buyer of color televisions, had given up on its products and had approached Sanyo, its largest supplier of television sets, concerning the prospect of U.S. production. The new management immediately took steps to improve quality at the plant, cleaning and rearranging the production floor and making changes in lighting and assembly line conditions. The new management also improved communications with employees and won the cooperation of the union. Japanese technicians with many years of television manufacturing experience were brought in to work alongside Americans on the assembly line, so that the employees might learn to work together to produce a top quality product.[31]

As noted above, one interesting trend that is becoming evident is the rise in the share of FDI investment outlays that is being spent on new establishments. The dollar appreciation and increase in stock market prices during the early 1980s may have contributed to this phenomenon. Furthermore, Japanese investors, who have increased their inflow of FDI into the United States, prefer to establish new ventures rather than engage in acquisitions.

Because the total assets of U.S. business enterprises acquired and established each year greatly exceed investment outlays, figures for investment outlays in any given year do not indicate the full extent of foreign control over U.S. resources. According to the Department of Commerce methodology, investment outlays relate only to equity interests obtained, whereas total assets relate to the total operations of the acquired or established enterprises. For example, between 1977 and 1984 total investment outlays ranged from $3,825 million to $25,219 million, whereas assets of established and acquired enterprises ranged from $19,866 million to $87,657 million (Table 3.9). In terms of total FDI position, between 1977 and 1983 gross fixed assets of U.S. affiliates rose from $61,696 million to $231,723 million, compared to a direct investment position of $34,595 million in 1977 and $135,313 million in 1983.[32]

If we examine the breakdown of assets acquired and established by industrial sector, two industries (banking and manufacturing) accounted for over one-half of all assets acquired and established during most years in the period 1979–1983.

Acquisitions comprised most of the investment outlays and assets. For acquisitions, the relationship between total assets and investment outlays depends on several factors. To acquire 100% of an enterprise, the cost is usually less than the value of total assets because the buyer is purchasing equity (the difference between total assets and total liabilities). If ownership is less than 100%, the difference between investment outlays and assets is even larger. The difference can be large for banks because the assets and liabilities constitute a dominant portion of balance sheets.[33] Furthermore, for both acquisitions and newly established enterprises, the market value of the enterprise may differ from the value carried on the books.

Because banking assets include loans outstanding, a few bank acquisitions can have a profound effect on total assets of enterprises acquired and established in that year. For instance, in 1980 about $16 billion of the $20 billion of assets acquired in banking (32% of assets of enterprises acquired and established that year) resulted from the acquisition of Marine Midland Bank by a Hong Kong bank. In 1981 assets acquired in banking were high because a British bank acquired Crocker National Bank, the twelfth largest bank in the United States. In 1982 most of the banking assets acquired by foreign investors were concentrated in three banks.[34]

Manufacturing contributed the second largest share to assets of enterprises acquired or established. Again, most of these assets were accounted for by enterprises that had been acquired by foreign investors.

Income and the Rate of Return on Investment

Wide variations are evident in both earnings and rate of return on FDI in the United States (Table 3.10). From 1977 to 1980 investment income increased by 400% to $9,470 million, and the average rate of return on investment rose from 8.7% to 15.4%. Increasing income and rates of return were evident in all economic sectors. However, the growth in petroleum was particularly pronounced, with the rate of return rising to 31.1% in 1980 as a consequence of greatly increased petroleum prices over the period.

These high levels of earnings and rates of return were followed by substantial reductions in 1981–1983 as a result of the worldwide recession and an excess market supply situation for petroleum. Income from FDI and rates of return declined in all industrial sectors as the U.S. economy reached the trough of the worst recession since the Great Depression. Between 1980 and 1982 income from FDI in the United States fell from $9,470 to $3,050 million. This collapse

Table 3.9
Assets of Acquired and Established Enterprises, by Industrial Sector, 1979–1983 (mil. dol.)

Industry	1979	1980	1981	1982	1983	1984[a]
Agriculture & Forestry	176	354	457	442	218	124
Mining	387	b	3,876	1,387	75	2,556
Petroleum	4,239	741	2,942	1,650	977	4,222
Manufacturing	7,231	6,942	29,754	5,318	3,951	5,457
Wholesale Trade	756	967	891	1,227	426	1,065
Retail Trade	2,064	1,179	1,703	1,626	324	1,286
Banking	13,141	20,418	24,667	7,238	6,732	11,385
Other Finance	1,414	8,613	14,696	4,524	5,045	3,514
Insurance	2,096	1,587	728	1,541	331	646
Real Estate	4,250	5,540	5,417	4,122	3,491	1,680
Other	873	b	2,527	2,777	730	2,403
All Industries	$36,627	$49,694	$87,657[c]	$31,852	$22,311[c]	$34,538[c]

[a]Preliminary data.
[b]Suppressed to avoid disclosure of individual companies.
[c]Totals may not add up due to rounding.
Source: U.S. Department of Commerce, *Survey of Current Business*, various issues.

Table 3.10
Income and Rates of Return on FDI in the United States, 1977–1984 (mil. dol. and percent)

Industry	1977		1978		1979		1980	
	Income	ROR	Income	ROR	Income	ROR	Income	ROR
Petroleum	836	13.4	1,239	17.9	2,037	13.1	3,476	31.1
Manufacturing	900	6.8	1,149	6.4	1,699	8.9	2,390	10.3
Trade	655	9.8	805	8.6	1,066	10.3	1,410	10.9
Insurance	96	4.3	445	8.5	599	17.3	828	17.4
Other	347	8.2	573	11.0	956	14.1	1,375	14.3
All Areas[d]	2,834	8.7	4,211	10.5	6,357	13.1	9,470	15.4

Industry	1981		1982		1983		1984[c]	
	Income	ROR	Income	ROR	Income	ROR	Income	ROR
Petroleum	3,392	22.3	2,256	13.0	1,657	9.2	2,659	12.3
Manufacturing	934	3.4	2	—	819	1.8	2,678	5.4
Trade	1,508	9.4	14[a]	.1[a]	1,138[a]	5.8[a]	2,632[a]	11.7[a]
Insurance	185	3.3	[b]	[b]	[b]	[b]	[b]	[b]
Other	1,435	9.5	778	1.9	778	4.2	2,219	4.0
All Areas[d]	7,454	9.4	3,050	2.6	5,598	4.3	10,187	6.9

[a] For 1982, 1983, and 1984, retail trade is included in "Other." Trade data show only whole-sale trade.
[b] For 1982, 1983, and 1984, insurance is included in "Other."
[c] Preliminary data.
[d] Totals do not add due to rounding.
Source: U.S. Department of Commerce, *Survey of Current Business*, various issues.

in FDI income took place during the trough of the recession. In 1983, with the revival of economic activity, FDI income rose to $5,598 million. In addition, the rate of return dropped precipitously, from 15.4% in 1980 to 2.6% in 1982. With the recovery in the pace of economic activity, the rate of return rose to 5% in 1983 and 6.9% in 1984. Although rates of return in petroleum declined throughout the 1981–1983 period, they rebounded in 1984.

Earnings and rates of return in manufacturing were more volatile. By 1982 earnings had declined to almost zero, and the only industry to show a sizable improvement was food products where the earnings of affiliates increased. In 1983, when the recovery was underway, the most pronounced gains were in manufacturing. Although the improvement in earnings was widespread throughout manufacturing, only in chemicals and food products were earnings substantial. The income of manufacturing affiliates increased sharply in 1984,[35] and the rate of return rose from 1.8% in 1983 to 5.4% in 1984.

By comparing corporate profits for the U.S. economy with income from FDI, one finds that for the years 1977–1983 corporate profits exhibited substantial volatility. The variations for gross profits averaged 14.4% over the period and 9.3% for net profits. Earnings in FDI exhibited much greater volatility, with variations averaging 61.1% over the same period. In part, this can be explained by the large growth in FDI over the period which produced a substantial rise in earnings. Because of revised reporting techniques, data for income before 1980 are not comparable to data in later years. However, the data still show that the earnings of affiliates fluctuated much more than earnings in the economy as a whole.

Because some of the variability in FDI income may be caused by statistical discrepancies, an effort was made to achieve greater comparability between data for FDI earnings and corporate profits. When corporate profits after taxes were compared to FDI corporate earnings, the results still showed FDI earnings to have been much more highly volatile than for overall U.S. corporate profits.

FACTORS EXPLAINING THE INFLOW OF FDI INTO THE UNITED STATES

The factors motivating the surge in FDI inflows are discussed in this section in terms of the eclectic theory which incorporates trade and location theory, industrial organization theory, and theory of the firm.

The U.S. Department of Commerce explanation of FDI into the United States typifies recent location theories for this phenomenon. Among the locational factors it cites are: (1) the growing recognition among foreign multinationals of the large size of the U.S. market, (2) the political stability and economic strength of the United States, (3) the depreciation of the dollar until late 1980, which reduced the dollar cost of acquiring U.S. companies, building new facilities, and expanding existing affiliates (and increased the cost of exporting to the United States), (4) the narrowing of the spread between production costs in the United States and other industrial countries, (5) the pursuit of foreign investors by individual states with the offer of subsidies and other incentives, and (6) a growing concern over U.S. protectionism which encouraged the acquisition or new establishment of U.S. facilities.[36] Another locational factor that is frequently mentioned is the increase in the cost of fuels and other resources during the 1970s which encouraged foreign investment in resource-based industries.[37]

The only other major factor noted in the Commerce Department study has to do with size of the firm—namely, the emergence of large foreign MNCs who, because they had been able to compete with U.S. firms in their home market and other countries, become convinced that they could compete with U.S. firms on their own home territory.[38] Underlying this explanation is the idea that firms desire to grow and to increase sales volume, and to do that they choose to invest abroad. This point of view fits in with the theory of the firm. As is shown later in this chapter, factors having to do with the theory of the firm and industrial organization theory can help to explain the recent surge of FDI into the United States, as well as the wider geographic dispersion of source countries accounting for this inflow.

General Explanation for the Phenomenon

The industrial organization theory of foreign direct investment offers reasons for such investment in terms of the advantages possessed by large multinational enterprises. When writing about the eclectic theory, Dunning explains FDI in terms of the ownership advantages of the firm, the ability of the firm to internalize its advantages, and the locational advantages of the host country. Ownership advantages can be a legally protected right or a commercial monopoly. Such advantages may also be caused by the technical characteristics or size diversity of the firm.[39] These advantages include size of firm, management and organizational expertise, technological advantages, marketing economies, access to domestic markets, knowledge about natural resources, and capital availability and financial expertise.

A number of studies have attempted to explain why foreign firms choose to invest in the United States. The U.S. Department of Commerce, for example, published a nine-volume benchmark study in 1976[40] which found that the growth in size and capabilities of foreign firms motivated FDI. European and Japanese firms had developed ownership advantages, including experience in operating in international markets through FDI, and had developed export markets in the United States prior to undertaking their initial manufacturing investments. They had also made progress in producing a competitive or superior product, and had achieved equality in marketing ability and technology. All of these factors figured strongly in their investment decisions.

According to the study, the locational advantages which the United States offered as a host country also served as causal factors. During the early 1970s the weaker dollar and the depressed stock market helped to trigger the surge in FDI inflow that to a large extent was motivated by ownership advantages. For some investors, security of raw material and energy supplies, and growing concerns over political risk in other parts of the world were important considerations.

In their 1979 *Directory of Foreign Manufacturing in the U.S.*, David A. Ricks and Jeffrey F. Arpan provided an explanation for FDI in the United States.[41] In their survey, they found that the most frequently cited reasons for FDI were the size and rate of growth of the U.S. economy. Factors related to the growth of foreign firms were also important. Because firms in countries that are smaller than the United States require a larger market than their domestic market if they are to continue growing, they are more dependent on international business. In order to develop a position that is competitive, firms must achieve a certain scale or size of operations. To achieve this size, foreign firms must develop a multinational posture by undertaking FDI, and with the growing number of foreign-based multinationals, the necessity of investing in the United States is enhanced. This suggests that FDI in the United States is a natural oligopolistic reaction of foreign MNCs.

Although Arpan and Ricks found that the primary motivation was the massive size of the U.S. market, another important influence would be the small size of foreign countries and the dependence of their firms on international business as an initiator of growth. Other factors would include the dollar devaluations of the 1970s, which increased the cost of exporting to the United States and decreased the cost of foreign investment into the United States. The depressed condition of the U.S. stock market also reduced the cost of foreign acquisition investment in the United States. In addition, the reduction in the gap in relative labor costs between the United States and other developed countries made it less advantageous to export to the United States. Other motivations for FDI into the United States included a better supply and price situation for natural resources, including energy; increased tax burdens in Europe resulting from the proliferation of government-funded social programs; and improved access to suppliers. One motivation peculiar to Japan was the increasingly protectionist position of industrial countries against Japanese goods; this provided a powerful incentive for Japanese investment in the United States and Europe.

Arpan and Ricks conducted a survey in the early 1970s which showed that local incentives affected the decision to come to a particular state or locality. Proximity to a particular market was the major reason given for coming to a particular state (cited by 34% of the respondents), transportation facilities ranked second (24% of respondents), labor market factors third (15%), and tax considerations fourth (9%). With respect to community selection, the major factors were closeness to markets (cited by 25%), labor considerations (23%), and tax considerations (25%).

In 1981 Riad A. Ajami and David Ricks identified the most important reasons for FDI in the United States, based on responses from 39 firms with recent investments in the United States. The large U.S. market was the single most important reason cited by respondents. Other important reasons were the desire to enter a new market, the need for preserving markets established by exports (defensive investment), the attractive political climate in the United States, and a favorable attitude toward FDI inflows in the United States. Interestingly, factor analysis revealed that the group of variables most useful in explaining the behavior of investing firms centered on the desire to acquire U.S. technology and know-how.[42]

Lawrence Franko stresses the role of the advantages acquired by European and Japanese firms which enable them to engage in FDI.[43] By the early 1970s continental European and Japanese firms had become skilled at managing large MNCs. The capabilities of these firms in product and process innovation grew relative to the U.S. and U.K. firms, and productivity rates of growth in manufacturing were greater than in the United States. But an even more important advantage was the European and Japanese firms' becoming more skillful at developing and producing energy-saving processes and products, whereas innovations in the United States had historically been biased toward labor-saving products and processes which by their nature were energy- and material-intensive. As the price of energy rose during the 1970s, the demand for energy-saving products and processes increased, giving European MNCs advantages in overseas competition. Demand for energy-efficient products undoubtedly provided an impetus for Michelin to produce radial tires and for Bosch of Germany to manufacture fuel injection equipment in the United States. It also explains why Volkswagen, Honda, Nissan Motors, and Toyota began to undertake production in the United States.

David McLain suggests a new perspective for examining FDI and understanding the direct investment process.[44] This approach involves using Tobin's q, the ratio of the market value of an asset to its replacement cost.[45] The use of q integrates portfolio decisions concerning the allocation of wealth among existing stocks of assets with decisions to accumulate new capital. If the asset is perfectly durable, costs p to produce, and yields a perpetual real return of R, an investor who pays qp for the asset receives a return of $r = R/q$. McLain adopted E. B. Lindenberg and S. A. Ross's notion that Tobin's q could be used as a bound for or measure of monopoly rents.[46] Monopoly rents are attributable to factors that act as barriers to entry. The possession of special factors that lower a firm's production costs relative to those of marginally competitive firms allows the firms to earn "Ricardian rents." According to Lindenberg and Ross, in the absence of taxes, $q - 1$ becomes the capitalized value of the Ricardian and monopoly rents which are scaled by the replacement cost of the firm's capital stock.

Using individual firm data, Lindenberg and Ross constructed an 18-year time series for the period 1960–1977 for measures of q for 246 firms. Large q values can be associated with "monopoly rents," or with rent resulting from special factors possessed by the firm. Industries possessing high values of q have unique products or factors of production (e.g., the average q for Avon Products was 8.53; for Polaroid Corporation 6.43; Xerox, 5.52; and Searle, 5.27). Low q values can be associated with firms that are in a competitive market environment, a highly regulated market structure, or a dying industry (firms that are not replacing their capital stock). Some companies with low q ratios are National Steel Corporation, with 0.52, B. F. Goodrich with 0.89, Kaiser Aluminum and

Chemical Corporation at 0.80, and Dan River Company at 0.67.[47]

Average q values for different industries for the period 1960–1977 are illustrated in Table 3.11, with values ranging from 3.08 for measurement and photographic equipment, to 0.85 for metal products.

Table 3.11
Average Industry Values of q, 1960–1977

Industry	q
Measurement and Photographic Equipment (SIC 38)	3.08
Oil and Gas Extractions (SIC 13)	2.94
Chemicals (SIC 28)	2.42
Electric Machinery (SIC 36)	1.79
Food Products (SIC 36)	1.72
Machinery (nonelectric) (SIC 35)	1.67
Printing Industries (SIC 27)	1.66
Leather Products (SIC 31)	1.66
Building Materials (SIC 52)	1.60
Lumber and Wood Products (SIC 24)	1.59
Bituminous Coal Mining (SIC 12)	1.54
General Merchandise Stores (SIC 53)	1.42
Miscellaneous Retail (SIC 59)	1.41
Tobacco Manufacture (SIC 21)	1.39
Petroleum Refining (SIC 29)	1.39
Nondurable Wholesale (SIC 51)	1.35
Miscellaneous Manufacture (SIC 39)	1.33
Stone, Clay, and Glass (SIC 32)	1.29
Metal Mining (SIC 10)	1.24
Rubber and Plastics (SIC 30)	1.23
Food Stores (SIC 54)	1.23
Unclassified (SIC 99)	1.20
Transport Equipment (SIC 37)	1.17
Construction (other) (SIC 16)	1.15
Apparel Products (SIC 23)	1.13
Paper and Allied Products (SIC 26)	1.09
Communication (SIC 48)	1.08
Fabricated Metals (SIC 34)	1.04
Electric, Gas, and Sanitation Services (SIC 49)	0.94
Furniture and Fixtures (SIC 25)	0.93
Textile Products (SIC 22)	0.92
Primary Metal Products (SIC 33)	0.85

Source: Eric B. Lindenberg and Stephen A. Ross, "Tobin's q Ratio and Industrial Organization," *Journal of Business* 54, no. 1, p. 26. See that article for adjustments and other details in the calculation of these ratios. Table reproduced from David McLain, "Foreign Direct Investment in the United States: Old Currents, 'New Waves,' and the Theory of Direct Investment," in Charles P. Kindleberger and David B. Audretsch, eds., *The Multinational Corporation in the 1980's* (Cambridge, Mass.: M.I.T. Press, 1983), p. 303.

The industrial organization approach to the theory of FDI predicts that foreign firms that have the Ricardian and monopoly advantages will compete in the U.S. market and will engage in FDI. With this in mind, McLain explores the relationships of these q ratios and the distribution by industry of U.S. FDI. If it is assumed that q provides an upper bound on monopoly rents and the industrial organization theory is correct, a greater concentration of FDI would be observed in industries possessing a high value for q. When the industrial distribution of gross product of U.S. affiliates of firms in Table 3.12 is compared with the results in Table 3.11, there is the suggestion of a greater concentration of FDI in industries having a higher value of q. For instance, U.S. affiliates are heavily concentrated in chemicals and food products industries which have high values

Table 3.12
Gross Product of All U.S. Businesses and U.S. Affiliates of Foreign-Owned Businesses, 1974 (bil. dol.)

Industry	All U.S. Business Gross Product (1)	Affiliate Gross Product (2)	(2) as pct. of (1)	Distribution All	Distribution Affiliate
Mining	12.1	0.7	2	1	3
Petroleum	32.2	5.9	5	3	24
Manufacturing	323.1	11.2	3	29	45
Food	31.0	2.2	7	3	9
Printing	16.5	0.5	3	1	2
Chemicals	24.5	2.8	12	2	11
Primary Metals	30.7	1.4	4	3	1
Instruments	8.2	0.3	3	1	a
Other	212.2	4.0	2	19	16
Transport, Communications, Utilities	121.5	0.7	1	11	5
Wholesale Trade	110.6	3.0	3	10	12
Retail Trade	132.8	1.2	1	12	5
Finance, Insurance, Real Estate	116.7	1.5	1	10	6
Other Industries	274.6	0.7	a	24	3
Total	1,123.6	24.7	2	100	100

aLess than $50 million.
Source: U.S. Department of Commerce, *Survey of Current Business*, January 1979. Table reproduced from David McLain, "Foreign Direct Investment in the United States," in Kindleberger and Audretsch, eds., *The Multinational Corporation in the 1980's*, p. 284.

for q and are not concentrated in primary metals which have low values for q.

To test the relationship between q and gross product, McLain correlated q and gross product of U.S. affiliates of foreign firms, and q and the share of gross products of U.S. affiliates in total U.S. gross product.[48] The mining and petroleum sectors were excluded from the analysis. The correlation for q and gross product of U.S. affiliates was 0.33, and the correlation for q and the share of gross product of U.S. affiliates in total gross product was 0.45. A correlation for the industry values of q and the number of U.S. affiliates in each industry was 0.58. At even the 5% levels of significance, the correlations were significantly different from zero. McLain concluded that, at least in the manufacturing sector, the results gave some confirmation to the industrial organization approach to the theory of FDI.

McLain also tested the roles of real exchange rate changes and changes in stock market valuations in the timing of FDI during the floating rate period, 1974–1980.[49] Whereas he acknowledged that exchange rate theories for FDI could only be adequately examined in a simultaneous setting in which all influences on FDI were given a proper weighting, he performed several primitive tests for the influence of exchange rate changes. For eight countries (the United Kingdom, the Netherlands, Sweden, Canada, Switzerland, Germany, Japan, and France) he calculated time series correlations of the annual real flow of FDI into the United States with changes (absolute and percentage) in the real exchange rate (current and lagged) for 1974–1980. Using data for these eight countries, he also calculated correlations of the ratio of the flow of FDI in the United States to the flow of Gross Fixed Capital Formation in the home country with the absolute change in the real exchange rate for these countries. For four countries (the United Kingdom, France, Germany, and Switzerland), the data suggested a significant (and negative) correlation at the 10% level of significance, for either absolute or percentage changes in real exchange rates and real FDI flows. In the United Kingdom and France, the factor producing a change in the real exchange rate was changes in relative price levels and not changes in nominal exchange rates. Similar results were obtained for the correlations when the FDI flow was scaled by the flow of Gross Fixed Capital Formation in the home country.

McLain tested the frequently expressed view that changes in the nominal exchange rates in conjunction with changes in the relative stock market values of American and foreign countries contributed to the growth of FDI in the United States. First, he correlated real FDI flows with current and lagged changes in the ratio of the stock market index in the home country to the U.S. stock market index. For this exercise, both indices were expressed in a common currency and adjusted for price level changes. He also correlated FDI flows scaled by home country investment with changes in the stock market index ratio. The results of these two exercises suggest that in the late 1970s, for Canadian, British, Japanese, and French investors, low-priced U.S. stocks may have been associated with FDI flows into the United States.

McLain cautions that, while the results of his correlations are not conclusive, they do provide mixed evidence concerning the role of both nominal exchange rate changes and changes in stock market valuations in the timing of FDI under the floating exchange rate regime of the 1970s. It is interesting to note that for the period covered, when FDI inflows increased, the price of the dollar was relatively low and stock market prices were simultaneously depressed.

Jane S. Little focuses on the locational choices of foreign manufacturers during the surge of investment in 1978–1979.[50] Using foreign-owned plants per thousand manufacturing employees as a guide, she showed that New England and the Southeast ranked first and second, respectively, as the two most attractive regions in the country for foreign investors. Although locational decisions are both subjective and complex, the primary motivation is proximity to relevant markets. The second most important factor is the availability of labor. Little suggests that foreign investors give relatively greater importance to wage differentials between states than U.S. investors, in part because since 1967 in most industrial countries hourly compensation and unit labor costs have risen more rapidly than in the United States. The quality and attitude of labor are also important, because foreign investors want to maintain their product quality. Another important factor is transportation, especially port facilities, because many foreign investors may begin their U.S. operations by importing parts to be assembled in the United States. Quality of life for managerial employees was also considered important.

It is indeed interesting that tax incentives and financial aid were considered of lesser importance. Such incentives did not alter the fundamental decision to undertake the investment, but, given similar situations, they would make one location more favorable than the other.

Country-Specific Explanations for FDI

The studies cited above do not distinguish foreign investors by nationality. In the studies cited below, we examine the motivating factors for British, German, and Japanese multinationals.

In his study of German foreign direct investment in the United States, J. M. Stopford stresses the role of the Germans' traditional strength in science and technology.[51] Three-fourths of German FDI was in manufacturing, with a heavy emphasis in chemicals and engineering industries; these investments are concentrated in oligopolistic industries in which firms have acquired ownership advantages. Like Franko, Stopford emphasizes that European firms have responded to the scarcity of raw materials and fuels by innovating in materials-saving and energy-saving processes. Examples of such expertise are Bosch's fuel injection equipment and Solvay process techniques for soda ash.[52]

Until the later 1960s, German firms preferred exporting to FDI, partly because of their fear of the confiscation of assets such as had occurred during both world wars (when they lost valuable brand names such as Bayer) and the need to use excess industrial capacity. More recently, union resistance to the established patterns of investment and fears about integrating U.S. affiliates into their world-wide network have also made German firms hesitant to invest in the United

States. Only during the late 1960s did German firms begin to invest in the United States on a large scale.

According to Stopford, four factors contributed to these changes. The first was the relative depreciation of the dollar and the increase in relative production costs in Europe which made the United States a relatively inexpensive manufacturing site. The second factor was the decline during the 1970s in the U.S. stock market where many listed firms were selling below book value, which along with the dollar depreciation of the 1970s enhanced the attractiveness of acquiring U.S. companies. The two remaining factors were the increasing social costs of doing business in Germany (which in conjunction with a declining real rate of economic expansion have reduced prospects for future economic growth and profitability) and concerns regarding energy supplies.

Stephen Young and Neil Hood's study of British investors in the United States during the 1970s shows that, unlike their European and Japanese counterparts, most British firms did not have monopolistic advantages.[53] They did not have the technology or marketing expertise that provided many corporations with ownership-specific advantages essential for success in the unfamiliar U.S. markets. Instead, cash-rich firms engaged in acquisitions and mergers in the United States in areas in which they could profitably utilize their experience in managing large enterprises. It appeared that they were using the acquisition route to purchase technology or to be close to new technical and marketing developments.

In terms of number of transactions completed for foreign direct investors as a group, completed acquisitions were of decreasing importance from 1976 to 1978. Only the British and the Swiss continued to channel much of their FDI into acquisitions. For the British, almost all of the large transactions involved acquisitions and equity increases, and most of the acquired firms were in manufacturing.

The Hood and Young study of British FDI in the United States suggests that firms lacking ownership-specific advantages but possessing plentiful supplies of cash to invest will attempt to acquire ownership advantages. Thus, the authors conclude that key explanations for continued long-term growth of British acquisitions in the United States are access to managerial and technological expertise for manufacturing concerns as well as access to marketing and service networks. Even though some of the acquisitions were made for short-term reasons during the late 1970s—that is, reasons associated with a strong pound and depressed U.S. stock market—the long-term strategies explain the sustained high level of British acquisitions in the United States.

In recent years Japanese manufacturing companies have expanded production in the United States and Europe. As a percentage of the total stock of FDI in the United States, the Japanese share rose from 0.5% in 1974 to 8.2% in 1983. Trade restrictions imposed on television set imports in the early 1970s and on autos in the early 1980s have helped to exacerbate this inflow. Seven Japanese television producers now produce (assemble) television sets in the United States, holding a total of one-third of the U.S. market. The year after voluntary export restraints were imposed, Honda began producing cars in the United States. Nissan Motors is assembling small pickup trucks, Toyota and GM have a joint venture to produce small cars in the United States,[54] and Mazda also has planned to produce here.[55] Mitsubishi and Chrysler are planning a joint venture. In the electronics market, NEC (Nippon Electric Company), a major communications machinery manufacturer, and Fujitsu are two companies that produce in the United States. Nippon Kokan K.K. has acquired a one-half interest in National Steel Corporation, and Komatsu, the world's second largest construction equipment manufacturer, has announced plans to construct a $35 million plant in the United States, aiming for 15% of the U.S. market in 1990.[56]

The Japanese Institute for Social and Economic Affairs attributes the recent surge in Japanese FDI to three factors: a growing number of Japanese businesses have become internationally competitive through their growth in technical, management, and financial capabilities; the gap between labor costs in Japan and other industrial countries has narrowed; and particularly acute are the problems encountered by increasing trade protectionism in the United States and Europe.[57] Because Japan's growth has been export-led, the rising protectionist sentiment in the industrial countries threatens the very core of Japanese economic expansion.

Lawrence Franko's study of Japanese multinationals analyzes the motivation for FDI in the United States. Unlike American and European multinationals, very little Japanese FDI was motivated by the need to defend a product lead in international markets because, until recently, the Japanese did not have very much in the way of product lead over their foreign competitors.[58] Rather, the Japanese had developed manufacturing processes and economies of scale that were tied in with Japanese human resources and the large homogeneous Japanese market.

Franko lists three motives for Japanese investment in Europe (as well as for investment in the United States): real or threatened protection, the learning of Western technology (by taking advantage of the skills of employees and their connections in scientific institutions), and the promotion of Japanese exports of components and intermediate products to be used in vertically integrated operations.[59] Two additional motivations that apply to investments in North America include the need to procure foodstuffs and raw materials, and the desire to shift production of certain processed foods, chemicals, and metals to countries with lower land, water, minerals, and chemical feedstock costs.[60]

Tetrutomo Ozawa has described some of the characteristics that distinguish Japanese from U.S. multinationals.[61] One characteristic is the immaturity of the majority of Japanese investing firms, especially in manufacturing. They are immature in terms of scale of operations, technological sophistication, and financial strength. Whereas U.S. multinationals are oligopolistic firms selling differentiated products, one-half of Japan's overseas investments were made by small and medium-sized enterprises. Japan's multinationalism is clustered in competitive industries that produce standardized or traditional goods.

For the most part Japanese firms have used Western technologies and have not introduced significant technologies that could be imitated abroad on a large scale. Therefore, Japanese FDI does not fit the product cycle model described earlier.

Ozawa identified two types of Japanese FDI. One type of Japanese investment was undertaken in order to take advantage of lower production costs; such investment is characteristic of Japanese investment in Asia. The second type of Japanese investment occurs when followers who have improved new products by innovation invest in the original market in which the product was developed. The followers originally attained technological maturity by exporting to overseas markets which were more advanced than their own home markets. When they are threatened by protection, they invest overseas. Once they have invested in the advanced market, they can capitalize on conditions such as an innovation-conducive atmosphere and the technological resources of the advanced markets.

Thus, although Japanese firms originally played the role of followers, they eventually turned into innovators and invested in the original innovator's home markets. They invested in the advanced market at an earlier phase than that in which U.S. firms invested overseas. By doing so, the Japanese can take advantage of the technological resources of the advanced Western nations and can also capture promising markets for their own innovations. By investing in the U.S. market, they have moved into the world's most attractive market, so that they can improve their technological capabilities.[62] Thus, Ozawa characterizes Japanese firms as being in a "post product cycle stage of industrial adaptation."[63]

Examples of Japanese investment in the United States include Japanese-owned steel mini-mills which need a cheap source of scrap and electric power, soy sauce plants using soybeans as a raw material, and textile firms that depend on U.S. cotton. During the mid–1970s the Japanese made a greenfield investment in Auburn Steel located in Auburn, New York, to produce construction bars. Kikkoman soy sauce invested in Wisconsin. In addition, a number of Japanese textile ventures are concentrated in the Southeastern United States.[64]

Sony's investment in San Diego is one example of a response to a fear of protectionism and the desire to adapt U.S. technology. The anti-dumping case which the U.S. government brought against Sony in 1970 was one reason why Sony commenced assembly of television sets in the United States. During its early days, Sony had made extensive use of U.S. technologies. By using both the technologies it adapted and its original R&D, Sony was able to develop its own differentiated product. The United States has served as a technological laboratory from which Sony has acquired the latest ideas and technical knowledge, and has been able to test and introduce new products.[64] Several years after Sony's initial venture into the United States, as a consequence of the voluntary export restraints imposed in 1977 (which limited the importation of color television sets to 1.75 million units), Sanyo and Matsushita took over existing television producing companies. Sharp and Toshiba have also begun assembly in the United States.[65]

The Japanese challenge in the color television industry has been instrumental in eliminating domestic producers from a substantial part of the U.S. market. Through exports and, more recently, investment in production facilities the Japanese are also making substantial inroads into the domestic auto industry, as well as steel. Moreover, the newest Japanese challenge is in the area of high technology, and the Japanese have begun to make very significant inroads into the U.S. technological lead.

CONCLUSION

Foreign direct investment in the United States surged upward during the 1970s, especially after the advent of floating exchange rates. Whereas, until 1980, the outward flow of FDI from the United States exceeded the inward flow, beginning with 1981 the situation was reversed with the inward flow exceeding the outward flow. The increasing importance of FDI to the United States becomes evident when one examines a number of different economic variables. The percentage of U.S. assets owned or controlled by foreign affiliates continued to grow over the period. Foreign-owned and -controlled affiliates accounted for an increasing percentage of total U.S. employment, and the flow of FDI as a share of Gross Domestic Fixed Capital Formation also continued to grow.

In conjunction with the increasing maturity of firms in other industrialized countries, there has been a widening geographic dispersion of source countries. As a consequence, the share of FDI owned by firms that initially invested heavily in the United States has declined, as other countries, such as Japan, have begun to contribute an increasing proportion of investment inflows.

Motivation for FDI in the United States includes both the desire to take advantage of ownership-specific advantages and the locational factors offered by the United States.

Among the ownership-specific advantages are (1) experience in operating in international markets through exports and FDI, (2) the ability to produce a competitive or superior product, (3) the achievement of technological capabilities, (4) the development by foreign firms of skills required to manage large multinational firms, (5) the ability to produce energy-saving products and processes, and (6) the ability to earn monopoly and Ricardian rents.

Studies show that a wide range of locational advantages offered by the United States as a host country have motivated FDI. The size and rate of growth of the United States as a market is probably the most frequently cited reason for investing in the United States, but other important reasons have been the dollar devaluation by the United States and the depressed state of the U.S. stock market during the 1970s, the reduction in the gap in relative labor costs between the United States and other developed countries, the supply and price situation for natural resources, the desire to preserve markets established by exports (defensive investment), the attractive U.S. political climate, and the desire to acquire U.S. technological know-how.

The locational advantages offered by different regions of the country have also affected the choice of where to invest in the United States. The most important reasons are proximity to the relevant markets, labor and wage differentials, and transportation, especially port facilities. Tax incentives and financial incentives did not alter the initial incentive to undertake the investment, but did make one situation more favorable than another.

Motivations also differed according to the nationality of the source country. The Germans invested in chemicals and engineering industries, sectors in which German firms have ownership advantages. The relative depreciation of the U.S. dollar and the decline of the U.S. stock market during the 1970s, the increased social costs of doing business in Germany, and concerns regarding the availability of labor supplies motivated the investments.

Most investing British firms did not have monopolistic advantages. Instead, cash-rich firms undertook mergers and acquisitions. Such firms were using this route either to purchase technology or to be proximate to marketing and technical developments. Access to managerial expertise and marketing and service networks also were important considerations.

The growth in Japanese investment in the United States was stimulated by Japan's need to defend market share in the face of real or threatened protection, and the desire to learn U.S. technology and improve technical capabilities. Other reasons include the promotion of export of components to vertically integrated industries, the desire to be closer to the sources of foodstuffs and raw materials, the need to shift production of certain products to countries in which land, water, mineral, and chemical feedstock costs are lower, and the attempt to capture new markets for their own innovations.

NOTES

1. Stephen A. Hymer, *The International Operations of National Firms: A Study of Foreign Direct Investment* (Cambridge: M.I.T. Press, 1976); Charles P. Kindleberger, *American Business Abroad: Six Essays on Direct Investment* (New Haven: Yale University Press, 1969); Richard E. Caves, "International Corporations: The Industrial Economics of Foreign Direct Investment," *Economica* 38 (February 1971): 1–27.

2. Hymer, *The International Operations of National Firms*; Joe S. Bain, *Barriers to New Competition* (Cambridge: Harvard University Press, 1956).

3. Kindleberger, *American Business Abroad.* See also Charles P. Kindleberger, ed., *The International Corporation: A Symposium* (Cambridge: M.I.T. Press, 1970).

4. Fredrick Knickerbocker, *Oligopolistic Reaction and Multinational Enterprises* (Cambridge: Harvard Business School, Division of Research, 1973).

5. Edward B. Flowers, "Oligopolistic Reactions in European and Canadian Direct Investment in the U.S.," *Journal of International Business Studies* 7 (Fall/Winter 1976): 43–55.

6. Raymond Vernon, "International Investment and International Trade in the Product Cycle," *Quarterly Journal of Economics*, 80 (May 1966): 190–207.

7. Peter Buckley, "A Critical Review of Theories of the Multinational Enterprise," *Assenwirtschaft* 36, Heft I (1981): 70–87.

8. Raymond Vernon, "The Product Cycle Hypotheses in a New International Environment," *Oxford Bulletin of Economics and Statistics* 40 (1979): 255–267.

9. Robert Z. Aliber, "A Theory of Foreign Direct Investment," in Kindleberger, ed., *The International Corporation.*

10. T. B. Agmon and D. F. Lessard, "Investor Recognition of Corporate International Diversification," *Journal of Finance* 33, no. 4 (1977): 1049–1055; J. H. Makin, "Capital Flows and Exchange Rate Flexibility in the Post-Bretton Woods Era," *Essays in International Finance* 103 (Princeton, N.J.: Princeton University Press, 1977), pp. 43–52.

11. Aliber, "A Theory of Foreign Direct Investment," pp. 28–29.

12. Makin, "Capital Flows," pp. 7–10.

13. Stephen Kohlhagen, "Exchange Rate Changes, Profitability, and Direct Foreign Investment," *Southern Economic Journal* 44 (1977): 43–52.

14. Dennis Logue and Thomas Willet, "The Effects of Exchange Rate Adjustment on International Investment," in Peter B. Clark, Dennis E. Logue, and Richard Sweeney, eds., *The Effects of Exchange Rate Adjustments* (Washington, D.C.: U.S. Department of the Treasury, 1977).

15. J. Agarwal, "Determinants of Foreign Direct Investment: A Survey," *Weltwirtschaftliches Archiv* 116, no. 4 (1980): 257.

16. Buckley, "A Critical Review," p. 74.

17. Harry G. Johnson, "The Efficiency and Welfare Implications of the International Corporation," in Kindleberger, ed., *The International Corporation*, pp. 35–57.

18. John P. Dunning, "Trade, Location of Economic Activity and Multinational Enterprises: A Search for an Eclectic Approach," in John H. Dunning, ed., *International Production and the Multinational Enterprise* (London: George Allen and Unwin, 1981), pp. 21–45.

19. Dunning, "The Determinants of International Production, " *Oxford Economic Papers* 25 (January 1973): 289–336.

20. Dunning, "Trade, Location of Economic Activity and Multinational Enterprises," pp. 28–32.

21. Kenneth J. Arrow, "Economic Welfare and the Allocation of Resources for Invention," National Bureau of Economic Research, *The Rate and Direction of Inventive Activity: Economic and Social Factors* (Princeton: Princeton University Press, 1962), pp. 609–625; Ronald Coase, "The Nature of the Firm," *Economica* 4 (November 1937): 1–40; A. Alchian and H. Demsetz, "Production, Information Costs, and Economic Organization," *American Economic Review* 62 (December 1972): 777–795; Erik Furubotn and Svetozar Pejovich, "Property Rights and Economic Theory: A Survey of Recent Theory," *Journal of Economic Literature* 10 (December 1972): 1137–1162.

22. Peter Buckley and Mark Casson, *The Future of the Multinational Enterprise* (London: Macmillan, 1976), pp. 32–65; G. Bauman, "Merger Theory, Property Rights and the Pattern of U.S. Direct Investment in Canada," *Weltwirtschaftliches Archiv* 7 (1975): 676–698; John McManus, "The Theory of the International Firm," in Gilles Paquet, ed., *The Multinational Firm and the Nation State* (Toronto: Collier-Macmillan, 1975), pp. 66–93; Stephen P. Magee, "Information and the International Corporation: An Appropriability Theory of Foreign Direct Investment," in Jagdish Bhagwati, ed., *The New International Economic Order* (Cambridge: M.I.T. Press, 1977), pp. 317–340.

23. Dunning, "Trade, Location of Economic Activity and Multinational Enterprise," pp. 30–31.

24. United Nations, Centre on Transnational Corporations, *Salient Features and Trends in Foreign Direct Investment* (New York: 1983).

25. U.S. Department of Commerce, International Trade Administration, *International Direct Investment: Global Trends and the U.S. Role* (Washington D.C.: 1984), p. 7.

26. Ibid., pp. 4, 46.

27. Due to revisions resulting from the 1980 Benchmark Survey conducted by the U.S. Department of Commerce, data are not strictly comparable, and the rate of growth in the foreign direct position is higher than if the data depended on the results of the 1974 Benchmark Survey.

28. U.S. Department of Commerce, *International Direct Investment*, Appendix B.

29. Ibid., p. 20.

30. United Nations, *Salient Features and Trends*, p. 44.

31. Marilyn Wilson, "How the Japanese Run U.S. Subsidiaries," *Dun's Business Month* 121 (October 1983): 34–35.

32. U.S. Department of Commerce, *International Direct Investment*, p. 71. U.S. Department of Commerce, *Survey of Current Business*, October 1984.

33. U.S. Department of Commerce, *Survey of Current Business*, August 1980, p. 66.

34. Ibid., June, 1983, p. 31.

35. Ibid., October 1984, p. 30.

36. U.S. Department of Commerce, *International Direct Investment*, p. 20.

37. U.S. Department of Commerce, *Survey of Current Business*, August 1981, p. 32.

38. U.S. Department of Commerce, *International Trade Administration*, p. 20.

39. John H. Dunning, *International Production and the Multinational Enterprises* (London: George Allen and Unwin, 1981), p. 47.

40. U.S. Department of Commerce, *Foreign Direct Investment in the United States*, Vol. 1, April 1976, pp. 97–113, and Vol. 5, Appendix G, pp. G–1 to G–339.

41. Jeffrey F. Arpan and David A. Ricks, *Directory of Foreign Manufacturing in the United States*, 2d ed. (Atlanta: College of Business Administration, Georgia State University, 1979), Introduction, pp. ix–xiv.

42. Riad A. Ajami and David A. Ricks, "Motives of Non-American Firms Investing in the U.S.," *Journal of International Business* 12, no. 3 (Winter 1981): 25–34.

43. Lawrence G. Franko, "Multinationals: The End of U.S. Dominance," *Harvard Business Review* 56, No. 6 (1978): 93–101.

44. David McLain, "Foreign Direct Investment in the United States: Old Currents, 'New Waves' and the Theory of Direct Investment," in Charles P. Kindleberger and David B. Audretsch, eds., *The Multinational Corporation in the 1980's* (Cambridge: M.I.T. Press, 1984), pp. 278–333.

45. W. Brainard and J. Tobin, "Pitfalls in Financial Model Building," *American Economic Review* 58 (May 1968): pp. 99–122. J. Tobin, "A General Equilibrium Approach to Monetary Theory," *Journal of Money, Credit and Banking* (February 1969): 15–29.

46. E. B. Lindenberg and S. A. Ross, "Tobin's q Ratio and Industrial Organization," *Journal of Business* 54, No. 1 (1981): 1–32.

47. Ibid., pp. 19–20.

48. McLain, "Foreign Direct Investment in the United States," pp. 321–326.

49. Ibid., pp. 321–326.

50. Jane S. Little, "Locational Decisions of Foreign Direct Investors in the U.S." *New England Economic Review* (July/August, 1978): 42–63. Jane S. Little, "Foreign Direct Investment in the U.S.: Recent Locational Choices of Foreign Manufacturers," *New England Economic Review* (November/December 1980): 5–22.

51. J. M. Stopford, "German Multinationals and Foreign Direct Investment in the United States," *Management International Review*, 20, No. 1 (1980): 7–15.

52. Ibid., p. 9.

53. Stephen Young and Neil Hood, "Recent Patterns of Foreign Direct Investment by British Multinational Enterprises in the United States," *National Westminster Bank Quarterly Review*, (May 1980): 20–32.

54. Thomas M. Hout, "Trade Barriers Won't Keep Out Japan," *New York Times*, April 29, 1984, p. D1.

55. Susan Chira, "For Mazda, a U.S. Car Plant," *New York Times*, December 1, 1984, p. D1.

56. Steven Greenhouse, "Komatsu Plans to Make Equipment in U.S. Plant," *New York Times*, February 11, 1985, pp. D1 and D14.

57. Keizai Koho Center (Japan Institute for Social and Economic Affairs), KKC BRIEF, "Japanese Investment in U.S. and Europe Aids Mutual Development," No. 15, February 1984.

58. Recently, the Japanese have been undertaking increasing R&D efforts and have started to develop product leads in products such as video recorders. Lawrence Franko, *The Threat of Japanese Multinationals: How the West Can Respond* (New York: John Wiley and Sons, 1983), pp. 73–74.

59. Ibid., p. 71.

60. Ibid.

61. Tetrutomo Ozawa, *Multinationals, Japanese Style* (Princeton, N.J.: Princeton University Press, 1979), pp. 25–29.

62. Ibid., pp. 50–54.

63. Ibid., p. 54.

64. Ibid., pp. 119–120.

65. Ibid., pp. 117–118.

4

Foreign Direct Investment in the U.S. Steel Industry

In the spring of 1984, National Steel Integrated Inc. announced plans to sell 50% of its National Steel Corporation, the seventh largest U.S. steel producer, to Nippon Kokan K.K. for $292 million. Nippon Kokan is Japan's second largest steel producer.[1] Even though the Japanese have made several smaller investments in the U.S. steel industry, the proposed merger represents the first investment activity of such a magnitude. Nippon Kokan and other Japanese competitors moved into the U.S. market because they feared rising protectionism, because lower cost steel from developing nations was taking a growing share of the Japanese market in the United States, and because Japan had an excess steel-producing capacity.

Japanese investment in the United States has largely been prompted by fear of protectionism. In the late 1960s anti-dumping procedures against Sony Corporation encouraged Japanese investment in consumer electronics in the United States. It was charged that Sony had been dumping (selling below cost) in the U.S. market. In the 1980s Japanese producers of motor vehicles made investments in the United States to protect themselves against impending protectionism. Similarly the U.S. steel industry has recently obtained import relief in the form of voluntary restraint agreements (VRAs). Investment in the United States to protect newly acquired market shares has become increasingly important to the Japanese.

The developing countries, as low cost steel producers, have become competitive with the Japanese and have made major encroachments on the U.S. market. For instance, between 1979 and 1983 Japan's share of total steel mill products imported into the United States fell from 36.2% to 24.8%. During the same period developing country imports rose from 13% to 29%.

As a result of a decline in the growth in demand at home, the Japanese steel industry is faced with excess domestic supply. In early 1984 Nippon Kokan, which owns Japan's largest steel mill, was operating at less than 50% domestic capacity and the company as a whole was using about 65% of its capacity.[2]

National Steel Corporation may be expected to receive substantial benefits from the merger. First, the steel industry has been experiencing a shortage of capital funds. National Steel Corporation is undertaking a five-year capital spending program of $800 million, and the partnership is expected to accelerate the program's completion to two years. National can also benefit from the transfer of research and technology. The Japanese have improved on steelmaking technology, and access to this technology as well as the ability to engage in scientific collaboration with Nippon Kokan could improve National's technological base. However, gains from the transfer of technology would depend on whether Nippon Kokan chose to make its technology and scientific facilities and personnel available to National Steel Corporation. The Japanese company believes that further changes in technological improvements and management style can add $45 million to National's annual profitability.[3]

Another benefit is the avoidance of adverse effects from antitrust legislation. In late 1983 Jones and Laughlin (LTV) and Republic Steel proposed a merger, but the Justice Department would not grant approval until the firms sold off two of their plants. At the same time, a merger of a giant foreign steel producer with a domestic integrated steel producer was more readily given approval because the merger activity was less likely to violate antitrust legislation. The existing antitrust climate in the United States favors mergers of a giant foreign producer with a domestic producer over mergers of two domestic producers.

This chapter examines foreign direct investment in the U.S. steel industry, an industry that has recently encountered very serious economic and financial difficulties. In order to comprehend these difficulties, we first outline the problems of the U.S. industry, including the technologically obsolete state of some of the integrated plants and their inability to be cost competitive with foreign suppliers. This inability to be competitive is also shown to be a result of high raw material prices, reduced international shipping rates, failure to adopt the latest technology, high wage rates in U.S. steel companies, and a shortage of capital funds. Issues for public policy, including the role of foreign direct investment, antitrust legislation, subsidization of capital for the steel industry, and macroeconomic issues affecting industrial performance and U.S. exports and imports, are considered.

THE PROBLEMS OF THE U.S. STEEL INDUSTRY

Since the late 1950s, the U.S. steel industry has undergone substantial changes, and the nation has become much more dependent on imported steel.

From 1960 to 1983 major changes occurred in the pattern and growth of world steel production. The U.S share of world steel output declined from 26.4% to

11.6%, and the share of the European Economic Community (EEC) declined from 28.2% to 16.5%. At the same time the shares of output in Japan, the developing countries, and the Communist countries increased (Table 4.1). Total world output of raw steel rose by 91.7% to 731.6 million tons. Western output rose by 68.6% to 448.5 million tons, and the output of the Communist countries rose by 144.3% to 283.1 million tons. During this period growth of output in the industrialized world was in sharp contrast with that of the developing countries. The output of the industrial countries as a group increased by 47.6% to 378.1 million tons. Whereas output in Japan rose by 338.1% from 24.4 to 107.1 million tons, output in the ten EEC countries rose by only 11.7% to 120.6 million tons and output in the United States declined by 15% to 84.6 million tons (Table 4.2). The developing countries as a group emerged as significant producers of steel with production rising from 9.6 to 70.4 million tons over the period.

Among the reasons given for the shifts in relative positions are the slowdown of growth in industrial countries, the reduction in the use of steel per dollar of gross national product (GNP) generated, management decision-making with respect to long-term planning, product and process innovations, and the general and social environment in which the steel industry operates in different countries.[4] These factors have affected relative production costs and the international competitiveness of national steel industries. Management decision-making has an important role in the achievements of the Japanese steel industry. Furthermore, in a number of countries, government policies affect trade, savings and interest rates, industrial infrastructure and the ability of steel producers to set prices and lay off workers.

Table 4.1
Percentage Shares of Major Producers in World Steel Output, 1960 and 1983

Area	1960	1983
Western World	69.6	61.3
Industrialized Countries	67.1	51.7
EEC (10)	28.2	16.5
United States	26.4	11.6
Japan	6.4	14.6
Developing Countries	2.5	9.6
Communist Countries	30.4	38.7
USSR	18.9	22.9
Eastern Europe	6.0	8.9
China and North Korea	5.5	6.9
World	100.0	100.0

Sources: International Iron and Steel Institute, *Statistical Yearbook, Steel, 1982*, pp. 27–34. American Iron and Steel Institute, *1983 Annual Statistical Report*.

Table 4.2
Major Producers of World Steel Output, 1960 and 1983

Area	1960	1983	Growth Rate
	(Mil. Net Tons)		(Percent)
Western World	265.7	448.5	68.6
Industrialized Countries	256.2	378.1	47.6
EEC (10)	108.0	120.6	11.7
United States	99.3	84.6	− 14.8
Japan	24.4	107.1	338.9
Developing Countries	9.6	70.4	633.3
Communist Countries	115.9	283.1	144.3
USSR	72.0	167.6	132.8
Eastern Europe	22.8	65.1	185.6
China and North Korea	21.0	50.4	140.5
World	381.6	731.6	91.7

Sources: International Iron and Steel Institute, *Statistical Yearbook, Steel, 1982*, pp. 27–34.
American Iron and Steel Institute, *1983 Annual Statistical Report*, pp. 114–115.

Government Policies and Steel

The policy measures of foreign governments can affect the relative cost competitiveness of overseas steel producers. A critical issue involves subsidies to steel producers in other industrialized countries. Exports are subsidized through the provision of loans, loan guarantees, interest subsidies, and other assistance to exporters. A study by the Office of Technology Assessment (OTA) of the U.S. Congress describes different types of government policies affecting steel production and/or exports.[5] For example, the Commission of the EEC has developed policies to minimize problems related to overcapacity, has helped finance programs for capital investment by lending European producers capital at below-market interest rates, and engages in long-term planning for the iron and steel industry. In addition, European steelmakers receive favorable financing and are given attractive fiscal incentives to meet the cost of regulatory compliance. They also benefit from accelerated depreciation for pollution abatement equipment. European steelmaking is largely government owned and receives generous subsidies and low interest rate loans. European steelmakers also receive export incentives in the form of export credit insurance and below-market financing, as well as rebates on the value-added tax on imported merchandise.[6]

The OTA study also enumerates a number of areas in which the industrial policies of the Japanese government have affected the steel industry. Because steel is considered a priority sector, Japanese steel producers have easily obtained loans from the private lending institutions. Given the high savings rate in Japan, the banks have a large supply of capital to lend to industries, and most of the capital assets of Japanese steel companies have been debt financed. (Stock ownership accounts for only about five % of capital assets.) During crucial time periods, the Japanese steel industry has been assured of the capital it needs to expand and modernize its plants.

The Ministry of International Trade and Industry (MITI) and other government agencies carry out various planning functions for the steel industry. MITI prepares long-term forecasts of demand, establishes target production goals, and helps in economic stockpiling to assure a source of ferrous scrap and raw materials. MITI also funds and directs R&D steelmaking through the Agency of Industrial Science and Technology. The Japanese government actively engages in the export promotion of steel products to overseas markets and promotes the sale of steelmaking technology, especially to developing countries.

Developing countries such as Mexico, Brazil, and South Korea have become more important exporters of steel during recent years, and it is necessary to take note of the policy measures pursued by some of these countries. In general, the governments of developing countries have been heavily involved in promoting the production and exportation of steel. In most cases, the steel mills are state-owned enterprises.[7]

The Brazilian government is heavily involved in the steel industry. The Conselho Nacional de Nav Ferrosos e de Siderurgia supervises and coordinates the national steel plan, and the government has expanded its ownership stake. Brazil had planned to increase raw steel production capacity to 20.2 million tons by 1980, and three government-owned mills were to be involved in the expansion. The projects received financing from the International Bank for Reconstruction and Development, the Inter-American Development Bank, and the Agencia Especial do Financiamento Industrial (a Brazilian government agency), and credits from foreign governments. The Brazilian government guaranteed the loan.[8]

Mexico has aided the steel industry through long-range planning and the offer of direct financial assistance. The Steel Coordinating Commission organizes and advises public and private companies producing coal, coke, iron, and steel. As in Brazil, government financing has been used. International and national financing organizations have invested in the steel industry. For instance, a Mexican public sector enterprise, Siderugica Lazaro Cardenas-Las Truches SA (SICRSTA), recently completed a steel mill with production capacity of 1.2 million tons. A World Bank loan and a long-term loan from a group of industrialized countries that was guaranteed by the Mexican government paid for infrastructure facilities including a railroad spur, workers' housing, and expanded port facilities. Similar financing paid for Mexinox SA, a joint French-Mexican venture for producing stainless steel.[9]

It therefore becomes obvious that foreign governments have been directly involved in the planning, coordinating, and financing of steel. When national and international entities make capital available at below-market interest rates, a subsidy element is involved, and the existence of this subsidy makes the foreign producer more competitive vis-à-vis domestic U.S. steel producers.

In addition to subsidizing capital financing, it is often contended that many other forms of government intervention by foreign governments affect the unit costs of major steel producers. The U.S. government has attempted to identify and determine the effects of these policies.[10] Because U.S. producers have been filing countervailing duty cases against foreign steel producers, it is necessary for the U.S. Department of Commerce to investigate the issues involving countervailable actions by foreign governments.[11]

The participation of foreign governments in steel production has produced a large outcry from representatives of the U.S. industry who claim that some governments provide their own steel producers with a variety of subsidies, and, as a consequence, steel enters the United States at prices that are less than the cost of production. It is also said that steel producers in many countries are willing to continue to produce steel at prices that are below average costs of production over much of the business cycle. The argument is made that imports of subsidized steel have made the United States more dependent on imports at the same time that the U.S. steel industry continues to operate with low capacity utilization.

A serious problem is the strong value of the U.S. dollar which has severely reduced the competitiveness of manufacturers, including steel producers. Table 4.3 shows the impact of the dollar on relative costs of steel in the United States, Japan, and West Germany during the fourth quarter of 1978 and February 1985. In 1978 the dollar traded for 191 yen and 1.87 Deutsche Mark and by February 1985 it traded for 263 yen and 3.4 deutsche mark. In 1978 pre-tax steelmaking costs in dollars were $401 per ton in the United States compared with $440 and $465 in Japan and West Germany, respectively. In terms of local currency, between 1978 and February 1985 steel costs increased by 36% in the United States compared with 26% in Japan and 46% in West Germany. However, with the appreciation of the U.S. dollar, in 1985 the U.S. pre-tax cost was $545 per ton as contrasted with $404 in Japan and $374 in West Germany. Even after allowing for freight charges of between $80 and $90 per ton, U.S. steel was unable to compete with foreign steel. But had the exchange rates for the yen and for the Deutsche Mark remained the same as in 1978, the U.S. pre-tax cost of $545 would have compared favorably with costs of $555 in Japan and $656 in West Germany.

Whereas it can be argued that in the very short run consumers gain from the purchases of cheap imported steel, in the longer term adverse effects will accrue to both U.S. consumers and producers. On the production side, continued excess capacity will be met by plant closures. Inability to finance investment in new facilities will result in a lag in productivity advance. Simultaneously, the United States would become increasingly dependent on imported steel. At the same time, if the world economic recovery continues, demand for steel in the United States as well as in the rest of the world will increase. If the world steel industry operates at close to full capacity, imported steel will not be discounted, and prices to U.S. consumers will soar.

Table 4.3
International Steelmaking Costs and the Dollar, 1978 and 1985

Steelmaking Costs	Fourth Quarter 1978					February 1985				
	U.S. $	Japan $	Yen	West Germany $	DM	U.S. $	Japan $	Yen	West Germany $	DM
Currency/Dollar	—	—	191		1.87	—	—	263		3.40
Operating Rate (Pct.)	89	66	66	53	53	75	70	70	70	70
Pre-tax Costs	401	440	83,900	465	870	545	404	106,000	374	1,272

Source: Peter F. Marcus and Karlis M. Kirsis (World Steel Dynamics of Payne-Webber), "Steel's Survival Challenge," paper presented to the Warren, Ohio, Area Chamber of Commerce, March 21, 1985, p. 8.

For instance, the U.S. Department of Commerce indicated that U.S. steel consumption would rise to 101 million tons in 1985, as contrasted with an average consumption of 90 million tons during 1980–1983, and 98.9 million tons in 1984. This is contrasted with an average of 108 million tons for the 1970s. Three permanent influences have reduced the consumption of steel in the United States: the reduction in the size of automobiles, other technological trends which have reduced the use of steel per unit of durable goods output, and the trend toward service industries and away from the goods-producing industries. All of these factors are reflected in declining steel intensity of GNP (the consumption of steel per unit of GNP in constant prices). It is expected that as the downsizing of cars is completed, the rate of decline of "steel intensity" will decrease at the same time that economic growth should increase demand for capital-intensive goods and reverse the decline in aggregate steel use. The expectations of accelerated economic growth and the reduction in the rate of decline of "steel intensity" form the basis for the assumption that steel consumption might rise to 105 million tons per annum by 1988.[12] If imports average 19 million tons (assuming that the voluntary restraint agreements do succeed in reducing imported steel to 18.5% of consumption), domestic shipments will rise to 86 million tons compared to an average of 76 million tons in the early 1980s.

As of this writing, the dollar has declined in value but is still overvalued. A continued reversal of the rising value of the dollar would be expected to increase the price of imports, including steel. This should exert a counterforce to the rise in steel imports. Although the dollar depreciated by about 17% between February 1985 and the beginning of December 1985, it will take many months before the impact on merchandise trade, including steel imports, will become evident.

Problems of the U.S. Steel Industry

The steel industry comprises three categories of firms: integrated companies, alloy/specialty companies, and nonintegrated companies. Integrated companies have facilities for primary raw materials, ironworking, steelmaking units, and finishing mills. Alloy/specialty companies produce alloys and specialty products and do not generally deal with raw materials. Nonintegrated companies have melting and casting units and fabrication mills, and produce a limited range of products. The operation of "mini-mills" is included in these activities. Mini-mills have a capacity of less than 544,200 tons per year, but there is a wide variation in the size of these plants. In 1978 the integrated plants were in the 0.9 million to 8.2 million tons per year range, in contrast to Japan which operated eight post-war plants with capacities of about 9.1 million tons per year. Figure 4.1 shows a flow line for steelmaking. The flow line indicates all the major material inputs and operations. Integrated steel mills would perform most of these operations, whereas nonintegrated plants would be involved in only a few of these operations. When an integrated plant produces steel, pelletized iron ore generally goes into a blast furnace to produce pig iron which then goes through a steelmaking furnace.

Figure 4.1

Schematic Flowchart for Integrated and Nonintegrated Steelmaking

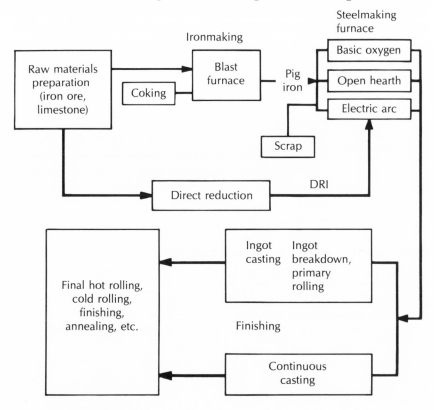

Possible major routes:

Integrated:	coking-blast furnace-basic oxygen-ingot casting-finishing.
Nonintegrated:	scrap-electric furnace-continuous casting-finishing.
Semi-integrated:	direct reduction + scrap-electric furnace-continuous casting-finishing.

Source: U.S. Congress, Office of Technology Assessment, *Technology and Steel Industry Competitiveness*, 1980, p. 188.

According to the OTA study, a non-integrated plant has a blast furnace for melting scrap, continuous casting units to produce slabs or billets, and rolling mills. A specialty steel plant might have only an electric furnace with some secondary steel refining equipment such as vacuum degassing units, electroslag rolling equipment, argon-oxygen decarbonization units (AOC), in addition to special forming and rolling facilities. Mini-mills would be included in the non-integrated plants.[13] Whereas most of the operations can be performed over a wide range of operating scales of production, blast furnaces and sheet rolling mills require large production units to achieve sufficient economies of scale.

Today, three-fourths of U.S. steel is produced in integrated steel mills where the iron ore is processed into molten products. The remaining one-fourth is produced in mini-mills in which scrap is placed in a steelmaking furnace and then either processed into steel ingots before being made into finished products or, alternatively, molten steel may be continuously cast into finished products. The integrated steel mill companies and the mini-mill companies may be regarded as realistically comprising two separate industries. Many of the problems facing the steel industry in recent years are the problems of the integrated steelmakers, and not the mini-mills which are considered to be the most efficient part of the industry. It is the integrated steelmakers that have been of declining importance in the United States. These companies have lagged behind their foreign competitors in adopting the latest steelmaking technologies and have lost a substantial portion of their domestic market share to foreign competitors as well as to domestic mini-mills. The mini-mills have been successful largely because of: (1) their use of abundant supplies of low cost ferrous scrap; (2) their introduction of new forms of efficient electric steelmaking furnaces and continuous casting machines; (3) their successful experimentation with new forms of labor management relations to raise productivity; and (4) their construction of low cost steel plants well adapted to the size and location of new markets. As a consequence, the mini-mills have steadily expanded and increased their share of output in relation to integrated steelmakers which have been slower to introduce advanced technology into the production process.[14]

At present some of the integrated plants are technologically obsolete. In addition, some of the large integrated plants are poorly located with respect to mass markets and raw materials sources.

Even though there is some merit to the industry's argument that foreign steel is unfairly traded, a major source of the industry's difficulties lies in its inability to be cost competitive in comparison with foreign suppliers. A Brookings Institute study states that "although there are many reasons for the decline in the U.S. position in the world steel market, three are predominant: raw materials prices, shipping costs, and new technology."[15] In addition to these three areas, the following are generally alleged to have contributed to the competitiveness problems faced by the U.S. integrated steel producers: high wage rates paid by U.S. steel producers, low productivity, and the lack of capital for investments in large-scale facilities.

Failure to Introduce New Technology

Three of the most significant technological developments in the steel industry have been the introduction of the basic oxygen furnace, the use of continuous casting, and, more recently, direct reduction. The basic oxygen furnace has replaced the open hearth furnace as the most important steelmaking device. It has been readily accepted, and it is estimated that by 1990 oxygen steelmaking will be producing about two-thirds of the world's steel.[16] In the United States, the basic oxygen furnace was introduced in 1955, and open hearth furnaces now produce only a little over ten % of total steel output. Initially, the United States was slow to adopt oxygen steelmaking because in the 1950s, when the industry was rapidly expanding, oxygen steelmaking was not fully developed. By contrast, because the Japanese and European steel industries were growing in the 1960s after the process was fully developed, they more readily adapted oxygen steelmaking.

Integrated steelmakers in the United States have been slower to adapt continuous casting into the productive process in part because the steel industry found it difficult to obtain a product with uniform quality by using continuous casting. In addition, steel consumers were not inclined to accept steel sheets that came from a slab that had been previously cast.[17] By 1978 Japan was using continuous casting to produce 50% of its steel, the EEC 29%, and the United States only 15%. Large-scale introduction of continuous casting would make the U.S. industry more competitive with other countries. The OTA study finds that, in order to become more technologically competitive at a minimum cost, the whole industry would need continuous casting by 1990. Yet, even though they estimate that the returns on investment from adoption of this technology would be at least 20%, capital availability is insufficient for the accomplishment of this goal.[18]

The direct reduction of iron ore outside of the blast furnace offers an excellent possibility for the industry to become more cost competitive. Direct reduction (DR) refers to several processes that are alternatives to the blast furnace in removing oxygen from iron ore and converting it to steelmaking iron. DR involves the use of gas or solid fuels, for example, low grade coal, which is readily available in the United States to remove the oxygen from the ore. The OTA report indicates that the capital costs of introducing DR would be relatively low and DR could help to revitalize integrated plants by the replacement of both blast furnaces and coke ovens.[19] The report suggests that the nation could benefit from increased use of DR in several ways: use of DR in conjunction with coal gasification plants to create new ironmaking capacity at competitive cost; use of directly reduced iron (DRI) as a substitute for scrap; and use of DRI to substitute for ore in blast furnaces, thereby improving the productivity of blast furnaces and reducing the amount of coke required for fuel.[20]

To date little investment has taken place in DR. The world's DR capacity at the end of 1980 was 15.5 million tons.[21] The United States has only 7% of this capacity and produced 9% of DRI. Future increases in U.S. DR will need to rely on the reducing agents derived from coal, but at present coal-based technologies are the least advanced both commercially and technologically. For future adaptation in the United States, the further development of coal-based technologies will be necessary.[22] However, the OTA believes that coal-based reduction of iron ore has the greatest advantages technologically and offers the best possibility of being adopted commercially within five to fifteen years.

The Small Amount of R and D in Integrated Steelmaking

Another problem involved in the development and commercial introduction of new steel technology in the United States is the small amount of R and D undertaken by integrated steelmakers. R and D expenditures as a percentage of sales have been declining and are lower than for all basic industries in the United States with the exception of textiles. For instance, in 1977 and 1979 steel industry R & D spending represented 0.5% of industry sales, whereas during 1963–1971 it represented 0.7%. These are very low figures compared with spending in other major industries and the amounts spent in foreign steel industries. For instance, Japan spends 1% of sales on R and D. In foreign countries generally, there is much more government support of R and D. Japan provides significant government support for university research, and in 1980 the EEC spent some $36 million on R and D, of which the government financed $20 million. In the United States federal funding for steel-related activities is very low, accounting for only 1.5% of R and D in 1977 compared with 9% for the chemical industry, 14% for the machinery industry, 47% for the electrical equipment industry, and 78% for the aircraft industry.[23] Academic spending on R and D is also low. By comparison with average employment levels of technical personnel in other U.S. manufacturing industries, the steel industry has a low use level. As a percentage of total employees, the number of scientists and engineers in the petroleum, refinery, and chemical industries is three times greater than in steel.[24]

It is important to ask why the emphasis on R and D in steel has been so low. Low profitability of the investment in R and D activities, especially for long-range activities, has been one reason for this small amount of spending. R and D spending that does occur is generally for short-range activities that have a quick payoff, and little spending goes for research.

Also accounting for the low level of R and D spending is management's cautious attitude toward research, preferring to deemphasize innovation and willing to be second, not first, to use a proven technology. The high costs of demonstration projects and a declining percentage of domestic production in domestic sales also play a role.[25] By not spending much on long-range research and innovation and by using borrowed technologies, the U.S. industry reduces its potential to resume its competitive role in world markets.

The Reduction of Raw Material Prices and Freight Charges

Large reductions in both raw material prices and shipping charges during the past 25 years have greatly enhanced the ability of foreign steel producers to become competitive in international markets. To a large extent, lower freight charges have contributed to the decline in raw material prices. And location of newer foreign steel plants near deep water ports has contributed to lower freight charges. For instance, lower freight charges have allowed Japan to enhance its competitiveness. Table 4.4 shows the movement in prices for coking coal and for iron ore for the United States and for Japan. Prices for iron ore for the United

Table 4.4
Iron Ore and Coking Coal Prices in the United States and Japan, 1956–1984 (in current dollars per ton)

Year	Coking Coal		Iron Ore	
	United States	Japan	United States	Japan
1956	9.85	22.14	9.63	16.69
1960	10.56	15.63	11.15	12.88
1964	9.25	14.65	12.00	12.85
1972	15.74	20.00	14.55	10.90
1980	52.50	65.00	36.00	25.00
1984[a]	61.00	73.00	43.00	29.00

[a]Estimated.
Sources: 1956 and 1960: Robert W. Crandall, *The U.S. Steel Industry in Recurrent Crisis* (Washington, D.C.: Brookings Institute, 1981), p. 21; 1964, 1972, 1980, and 1984: U.S. Congress, Congressional Budget Office, *The Effects of Import Quotas on the Steel Industry* (Washington D.C., July 1984), p. 25.

States rose continuously between 1956 and 1984, rising from $9.63 to $43 per ton. Simultaneously, prices for Japan declined from $16.69 to $10.90 in 1972, and then with worldwide inflation during the 1970s, rose to $25 by 1980 and $29 in 1984. Since the late 1960s the price of iron ore in Japan has remained considerably below the U.S. price.

After the war there were fears of iron ore shortages in the United States. The policies that ensued were to have disastrous consequences for the U.S. steel industry. Processes were sought for using the Mesabi taconite ores, and the industry developed new methods of beneficiating low grade ores. They sought new sources of iron ore in other countries, including Venezuela and Canada. To ship iron ore, they developed lower cost bulk ocean liners. During the 1960s these efforts led to a sharp rise in the available supply of foreign and U.S. ores. The price of iron ore remained fairly stable throughout the 1960s. The U.S. steel industry had lost its advantage of having low cost domestic ores, and imports of foreign ore began to increase, from less than 10 million tons a year during the Korean War period to 35 million tons in 1959–1960.[26]

In addition to a fall in the world price of iron ore, the decline in the price Japan paid for coking coal (Table 4.4) also contributed to the growth of the Japanese steel industry. It may be added that Japan is one of the countries that has been able to purchase raw materials at a cost lower than that paid by U.S. rivals,[27] partly because the Japanese have been actively involved in overcoming their earlier disadvantage in raw materials. By building ships able to carry large quantities of materials, the Japanese can ship high-quality ore and coal from long distances at a cost cheaper than the cost of shipping ore from Minnesota to Pennsylvania. Furthermore, they have invested in countries producing raw materials in order to assure sources of supply and have constructed plants at sites with access to deep water ports which enables them to use higher quality and lower cost sources of raw materials. Thus, the Japanese now have a cost advantage in raw materials.[28] Furthermore, lower shipping costs reduced not only the costs of raw materials, but also the price of exporting steel. The United States and Canada contributed to lowering shipping costs by building the St. Lawrence Seaway.[29]

High Wage Rates and Low Productivity

Labor costs in the United States represent a significant cost item in steelmaking. It is generally assumed that the very high wages paid in the U.S. steel industry are a principal cause of the loss of U.S. international competitiveness. The industry is fairly labor intensive, and between 1972 and 1976 labor received 64% of the industry's value added. In the past, the possibility of substituting capital for labor was fairly limited. Let us examine three aspects of wage costs in the steel industry: wage rates in steel compared with wages in other U.S. manufacturing; the relative rate of increase during the past decade; and the U.S. wage rate and productivity in foreign steel industries.

As in the automobile industry, wages in the steel industry have greatly exceeded the average for all manufacturing. Figures for average U.S. wage rates in steel show that for two decades the average U.S. wage rate for production workers in steel exceeded wage rates for all manufacturing. (Table 4.5). The difference in wage rates in automobiles and steel may be attributed to two factors—strong labor unions and the fact that workers tend to be older and to have achieved more seniority. In 1979 steel workers received an average of $10.77 per hour, which was over two-thirds the value for wages paid in all U.S. manufacturing.

Table 4.5
Average Wage Rates in Steel Compared with Motor Vehicles and All U.S. Manufacturing, 1960–1979

Year	Steel	Motor Vehicles	All U.S. Manufacturing
1960	$ 3.08	$2.91	$2.26
1965	3.46	3.45	2.61
1970	4.22	4.44	3.35
1975	7.11	6.82	4.83
1976	7.86	7.45	5.22
1977	8.67	8.22	5.68
1978	9.70	8.97	6.17
1979	10.77	9.74	6.69

Source: U.S. Congress, Office of Technology Assessment, *U.S. Industrial Competitiveness: A Comparison of Steel, Electronics, and Automobiles* (Washington, D.C., 1981), p. 59.

More relevant than comparisons of one industry to another is the trend in labor costs over time.[30] During most of the 1960s, the average wage rate in steel rose at about the same rate as in other U.S. manufacturing industries. For instance, in the 1960s and early 1970s average wages paid in steel were less than 50% above the national average for manufacturing, but by 1981 they were 74% above the national average. This trend may be reversed in the future, because, recently, management and labor have negotiated givebacks.

There are several reasons why, after succeeding in moderating wage increments during the 1960s, the steel industry allowed its wages to escalate in the 1970s. One important reason was the dollar devaluation of 1971–1973 which raised the relative price of steel imports and helped increase the profitability of the steel industry. In 1972–1973 production and exports increased and the steel industry acquiesced to labor demand to keep the domestic labor peace.

The voluntary quotas under the voluntary restraint agreements on steel imports also contributed to reduced imports and permitted rising profit margins. A third factor was the poor timing of labor negotiations in 1974 when the contract expired in the middle of a price explosion on world export markets. To avoid a strike at a time when the industry was so profitable, the steel industry was willing to pay a high price. A fourth reason was the expiration of the wage and price controls in 1974. Finally, in 1977 the industry chose to give support to the more moderate contender for the leadership of the United Steelworkers by reaffirming its support of the 1973 Experimental Negotiation Agreement (ENA) which provided for an annual increase in compensation at three % per annum if the rate of inflation continued at six % a year.[31] The ENA apparently had an important impact on hourly compensation rates. In 1973, before ENA, hourly labor costs in the steel industry were 40% greater than the average for all manufacturing. By 1981, the year before ENA was finally allowed to expire the difference was 74%.[32]

Compared with foreign wage rates, hourly wage rates in the United States are considered to be high. But the difference in average wage rates between countries understates the impact on competitiveness. If U.S. industries granted wage increments in excess of their expected productivity, inflation would contribute to an exchange rate adjustment and competitiveness would not be impaired. International competitiveness is affected because of the existing differences between wages in the U.S. steel industry and other manufacturing in the United States. Compared with foreign countries, the premium enjoyed by U.S. steelworkers is greatly in excess of the premium in other countries. For instance, whereas in the United States in 1978 the premium was 69%, on the average, wage costs for steelworkers abroad were about 25% above the average.[33]

In the steel industry, labor costs are an important cost component per unit of output. Estimates vary, but using World Steel Dynamics data it has been shown that in 1976 labor represented an estimated $115.84 out of a total cost per ton of $282.57.[34] By 1985 labor costs were $146 and cost per ton amounted to $538.[35] The cost of labor per unit of output rises as hourly wage rates increase and falls with rising productivity. Because the measure of productivity chosen can affect comparisons of competitiveness, the OTA study used two measures of competitiveness: value added per production worker and physical output per employee hour, the productivity index used by the U.S. Bureau of Labor Statistics (BLS).[36] Table 4.6 gives data for value-added per production hour in steel compared to manufacturing as a whole. Relative to other industries, steel productivity declined in the 1960s and remained low during the 1970s (with the exception of 1974). For the period as a whole, it remained above other manufacturing. However, according to the BLS index (in which all workers, and not only production workers, are counted in calculating output per person employed) for the period 1967 to 1979, with the exception of 1972–1974 productivity in steel remained below that of other manufacturing. Thus, the steel industry experienced competitive difficulties resulting from low productivity.

The OTA study on steel also compared productivity growth in physical output per ton unit for both Japan and the United States. Over the period 1970–1979, productivity in U.S. manufacturing grew by 23% compared to an almost similar rate of increase (22%) for steel. In Japan, productivity growth grew at an overall rate of 90% for all manufacturing compared with a rate of 82% for steel. What is important is the growth position of a particular sector relative to all manufacturing in the domestic industry.[37] It appears that U.S. steel, in contrast to productivity growth in all manufacturing, performed somewhat more optimally than in Japan. But because of the large growth in productivity, Japanese productivity in steel is now greater than that of the United States.

The Problem of Capital Funds

A major complaint of the steel industry is the lack of capital necessary to modernize plants and invest in new steel facilities and technology. Traditionally,

Table 4.6
Value Added per Production-Worker-Hour in Steel Compared with Motor Vehicles and All U.S. Manufacturing, 1960–1977

Year	Steel	Motor Vehicles	All U.S. Manufacturing
1960	$ 8.23	$ 9.57	$ 6.80
1965	10.27	12.08[a]	8.50
1970	11.37	15.42	11.30
1975	20.31	23.36	18.40
1976	21.67	28.30	20.20
1977	22.49	30.14	21.90

[a]Estimated.
Source: U.S. Congress, Office of Technology Assessment, *U.S. Industrial Competitiveness: A Comparison of Steel Electronics, and Automobiles* (Washington D.C.: 1981), p. 55.

internal corporate funds and equity financing have provided the major source of funds for the steel industry. In Japan borrowed funds have been the major source of finance for the industry. For the steel industry, during 1972 the debt-to-equity ratio was 6.3:1 in Japan compared to 0.83:1 in the United States.[38] In 1983 the ratio increased to 0.98:1 in the United States.[39] As indicated above, the Japanese steel industry has always been assured of debt capital at minimum cost.

At different time periods various estimates have been made of the amount of capital the steel industry would require to modernize and adapt new technology. In the late 1970s, the capital needs of the steel industry were analyzed by both the Office of Technology Assessment and the American Iron and Steel Institute (AISI).[40] Both studies agree that there is a need to improve profitability and to achieve the same increase in productive capacity. They assume that open hearth furnaces will be eliminated, a large increase in continuous casting will occur and one-half of existing coke ovens will be replaced. But there were differences between the studies. The OTA's renewal scenario assumed a greater expansion of nonintegrated steel companies at relatively low capital costs, and modernization and replacement of integrated plants at relatively low capital cost. AISI also emphasized the need to exand capacity in the integrated sector of the industry. In 1978 dollars, the OTA projected capital needs of $3 billion for the renewal scenario, whereas AISI projected $4.9 billion a year. The OTA projected a need for a 50% increase over the annual average for the past decade as contrasted with 150% increase for the AISI projections. The central issue that emerges is whether the integrated part of the industry would be able to sufficiently reduce its production costs to justify large capital expenditures in integrated plants or if steel expansion in the 1980s would occur by minimum cost modernization and replacement in the integrated sector and by expansion in the nonintegrated sector.

Because profitability of the steel sector was very low, especially during 1982 and 1983, capital spending programs were sharply curtailed. In 1983 the steel industry had planned to spend $3.2 billion, but it wound up spending $1.88 billion. In 1984, capital spending fell to $1.189 billion. Even if the industry downsizes and reduces capacity, capital is required to install equipment incorporating the newest technology in order to maintain competitiveness. Recent estimates of capital spending needs vary. It was recently estimated that $25 billion must be invested in the industry to maintain competitiveness.[41] In 1983 Donald H. Trautlein, chairman of Bethlehem Steel, had indicated that $5 billion a year must be devoted to modernization, much above the $1.88 billion spent in 1983 and the $1.189 billion spent in 1984 for the industry to remain competitive and to insure long-term survival.[42]

It has been pointed out that there are two ways to look at the discrepancy between outlays and estimated capital requirements. One is to say that the discrepancy between outlays and requirements is a spending shortfall that must be filled. Alternatively, one can ask why integrated firms have been unable to reach the investment levels they claim they require. It has been suggested that relatively poor investment choices in the past may be the "underlying reason for persistence of alleged capital shortage."[43]

A number of suggestions have been made to augment the resources available to the industry to enable it to modernize and remain competitive. This matter is discussed in the final section of this chapter.

SOME POLICY OPTIONS FOR U.S. STEEL INDUSTRY PROBLEMS

The steel industry is vital to the economic growth and national security of the United States. But since the 1960s the industry has been besieged by serious problems. Modernization involves the creation and adoption of new technology if the industry is to become competitive. As indicated above, hampering modernization are the problems of unfairly traded imports, low profitability, inadequate capital formation, and insufficient expenditures on R and D by both the private sector and government. Furthermore, the increasing participation of foreign governments in their national steel industries is reputed to have eroded the ability of the market mechanism to efficiently allocate economic resources. The existence of such an environment increases the desirability of the public sector adopting a policy position with respect to the steel industry. A policy position should include measures to adequately resolve the financial, technological, trade, and labor problems experienced by U.S. industry and to facilitate the achievement of a competitive international position.

Both sector-specific and macroeconomic policies at the federal level can aid the steel industry. First, the industry has frequently demanded protection, and whether trade policy is the appropriate means to revitalize the steel industry merits discussion. Second, there has already been some foreign investment in the U.S. steel industry, and appropriate policy measures at the federal level may be useful in monitoring foreign direct investment in the United States. A third area in which government intervention may be necessary is in the promotion of capital formation by helping to make capital funds more readily available to the industry. Because of low profitability in recent years, the industry is not in a position to undertake large amounts of investment activity. Another area in which policy changes may be necessary is in the area of antitrust legislation. Current antitrust policy makes it difficult for large domestic steel companies to merge. However, the government does not appear to be overly concerned about the effects on competitiveness when one company is owned by a foreign entity. It may be necessary to consider some revision of antitrust policy when a merger between two large producers may aid in the rationalization and modernization of production facilities to facilitate the lowering of per unit cost of production. Finally, recent fiscal policy has produced record budgetary deficits accompanied by high interest rates and an overvalued exchange rate. This affected U.S. international competitiveness adversely and necessitates a shift in economic policies. (This subject is discussed in Chapter 8.)

Trade Policy and Steel Imports

Since the late 1960s when imports were beginning to make sizeable inroads into domestic consumption, the steel industry has lobbied for protection from foreign competition. In the first four months of 1984, steel imports rose to 25% of the domestic market,[44] and by July of 1984 imports comprised one-third of the domestic market. The steel industry was actively seeking protection.

The General Agreement on Tariffs and Trade (GATT) restricts dumping and other unfair trade practices. The steel industry, as well as other domestic industries, has maintained it is not sufficiently protected from the unfair trading practices of foreign firms.[45] This situation has resulted in part from the U.S. attempt to maintain an open market and its avoidance of using anti-dumping laws against foreign steel producers, especially European. In addition to the desire to maintain good relations with its allies, the U.S. government fears retaliation against exports and foreign investment. In order to avoid having to engage in anti-dumping proceedings, the government implemented the voluntary restraint agreements on steel in 1968, and, later, the Trigger Price Mechanism in 1978.

In 1968, a year of record imports, the steel industry sought protection from foreign competition. The Johnson Administration was able to successfully negotiate agreements with Japan and most of the other steel-importing nations. These nations voluntarily agreed to limit their imports into the United States; their quotas were permitted to grow by five % a year. It was hoped that the VRAs would help the industry become more competitive again.[46] The agreements produced a decline in imported steel, with imports falling by 22% in 1969 and 5% in 1970. The agreements were extended in 1972 and expired in 1975. However, given the 1973–1974 boom on world export markets, extension of the VRAs was probably not necessary. Even though the VRAs permitted U.S. steel production to rise above its 1968 level and the industry became more profitable, capital expenditures remained well below the 1968 level.[47]

By 1977 the industry was in a slump, major mills were closing, and there were renewed requests for protection. In 1977 the Carter Administration requested that Under Secretary of the Treasury Anthony Solomon formulate a program for the steel industry. This action was taken largely to prevent the steelmakers from engaging in anti-dumping suits against European steelmakers.

The Administration implemented only a portion of the plan, the most significant part being the Trigger Price Mechanism which set reference prices for 32 categories of steel products (covering 90% of steel imports). The established prices were based on the cost of production in Japan, the lowest cost producer, and were to include transportation costs plus eight % for profits and another ten % for overhead. If imports were sold below the trigger price, a dumping investigation would ensue. Because the trigger price was based on prices in Japan, the most efficient producer, it did give the industry some import relief, but at the same time it allowed the Europeans to export to the United States at less than half their costs of production.[48]

Since 1982, a number of steel-producing nations have agreed to voluntarily limit exports to the United States. In an agreement with the Reagan Administration, European producers, many of whom are subsidized by their governments, agreed to limit their steel imports to the United States to 5.2% of domestic consumption. There is also an informal understanding with Japan to restrain its steel imports into the United States.[49] In the face of a number of unfair trade suits that have been filed by U.S. steel companies, a number of developing countries were involved in negotiating voluntary restraint agreements,[50] and Mexico, South Africa, and Brazil had agreed to limit exports.[51]

Domestic steelmakers have recently requested protection against foreign steel producers. On June 25, 1984, the U.S. International Trade Commission (ITC) issued the results of a study showing that 70% of U.S. imports were damaging to the domestic industry. The majority of the ITC determined that in nine product categories domestic industries had been seriously injured. These products include both semi-finished steel products and more advanced or finished products. These products comprise (1) ingots, blooms, slabs, and sheet bars; (2) plates; (3) sheets and strip; (4) wire rods; (5) wire and wire products; (6) railway-type products; (7) bars; (8) structural shapes and units; and (9) pipes and tubes. It was determined that all of these industries were faced with increasing imports and were either threatened with serious injury or had already faced serious injury. The ITC recommended a five-year program of tariffs and quotas. It was recommended that the President impose a tariff rate quota on imports of semi-finished steel and impose quotas on imports of plates; sheets and strip; structural wiring; and tariff increments on imports of wire products.[52]

Two of the three commissioners who voted in favor of the finding that serious injury existed recommended that a continuation of import relief be conditional on firms presenting plans describing how the five-year period of relief would be used to adjust in an orderly manner to import competition. It was also recommended that relief be granted for five years and reductions in the levels of relief granted in the fourth and fifth years were specified.[53] The years 1979–1980 were used as the representative years for imports of these products.[54] Since 1979–1980, however, steel exports by the developing countries increased substantially. Using the period 1979–1980 as representative years would seriously have restricted imports from countries such as Mexico, Brazil, and South Korea.

In September 1984 the Reagan Administration recommended that voluntary restraint agreements be negotiated with steel-importing nations in order to reduce steel imports to 18.5% of the U.S. market. By May 1985 VRAs had been negotiated with all major steel-exporting nations.

The VRAs are non-tariff barriers and can have an impact similar to that of a quota. Quotas, which are one of a whole series of non-tariff barriers, can have welfare effects that are similar to a tariff, with the exception that the importer receives the compensation that would have accrued to the government with a tariff.

The results of a recent study that assessed the impact of earlier restrictions on steel—the VRAs and the Trigger Price Mechanism (TPM)—give some idea about the impact of the current restraints.[55] Estimates were made of the effect of VRAs and the TPM on the producer price and the import prices of five categories of finished steel: hot rolled sheet, cold rolled sheet, bars, structurals and plate. The estimated effects of the VRAs on the import prices of these five categories in 1971 and 1972 ranged from $4.34 to $11.68 a ton, or on the average the costs to importers for the five steel mill products rose from a minimum of 6.3 to a maximum of 8.3%. As to U.S. producer prices, the average increase due to the VRA was estimated to be between 1.2 and 3.5%.

The study also estimated the impact of trigger prices for 1979. They were estimated as having had a maximum impact of 11.5% on import prices and 1.1% on domestic producer prices. Given that imports comprised 15% of U.S. shipments, the maximum impact of the TPM was calculated as 2.7%.[56]

In the study, the distributional effects as well as the deadweight losses (efficiency losses) from the TPM were estimated for 1979.[57] It was assumed that the elasticity of supply was 3.5. The rents transferred to domestic resource owners (suppliers of labor and capital) amounted to $371 million for the 85.9 million tons that would have been produced without the TPM and a share ($45 million) of $1,305 million for the additional resources attracted to the carbon steel industry. However, the TPM was estimated to have transferred total rents of $519 million to foreign resource owners. The deadweight loss in consumption was estimated at $9 million and the deadweight loss in production was estimated at $22 million. This made the total loss in consumer surplus equal to almost $1 billion.

The $31 million in deadweight losses represent a loss to the economy resulting from the misallocation of resources. The $371 million is the increase in producer's surplus. With a tariff, the $519 million would have accrued as government revenues, and the TPM benefitted foreign resource owners as much as the owners of domestic resources.

It has been shown that with both the VRAs and the TPM, the impact was much larger on import prices than on domestic prices. For domestic prices to have increased sufficiently to have provided producers with adequate funds for modernization, the impact on domestic prices would have had to have been much larger. But this would have required more severe import restraints. In addition, the TPM did involve a large transfer of resources from consumers to resources engaged in steel production. But unlike a tariff, the restraints involved a large transfer to foreign resource owners. There is little evidence that domestic steel producers could have been able to increase profitability sufficiently to engage in large-scale modernization efforts. It does not appear that a period of increased protectionism for steel would be able to make the industry more competitive in the long run. To enhance competitiveness, measures of protection must be accompanied by at least three additional policy measures. First, increased protection should be continued only if integrated producers demonstrate they are making efforts to modernize their facilities. Second, subsidies and loan guarantees will be necessary to provide funds for firms that do make the effort to modernize and reduce production costs. Finally, macroeconomic policies aimed at achieving exchange rate, and hence trade balance adjustments, must be implemented.

More recently, the Congressional Budget Office (CBO) had estimated the effects of a House of Representatives and Senate bill which, for a period of five years, would limit the share of imports to 15% of total U.S. steel consumption[58] (expressed in tonnage, rather than values). Effects were estimated for both the steel market and the economy. In response to a reduction in the available supply of steel, prices for imported and domestically produced steel would rise, resulting in a transfer of income from consumers to both domestic and foreign steel firms. In conjunction with higher prices, consumption would decline, with the extent of the reduction depending on the elasticities of demand and supply in response to a change in price. Although the quota would have positive effects on output and employment in the steel industry, higher prices and a misallocation of economic resources would occur in the rest of the economy.

It was projected that the average price of steel consumed in the United States would rise about 10% over the five-year period. In the first year of the quota, domestic steel prices would be 3% higher and in the fifth year of the quota about another 7% higher. (Because a quota reducing imports to 15% of domestic steel consumption represents a fairly substantial reduction in imports, and because the estimates cover adjustment over a five-year period, price effects would be substantially in excess of those for the TPM.) It was also estimated that a ten % average increase in the price of steel mill products would increase the producer price index for intermediate materials by 0.65%.

The distributional effects (income transfers) and deadweight losses (efficiency losses) were also estimated. The rents that would be transferred to domestic resource owners (domestic steel industry) would rise from $1.7 billion in 1985 to $4.5 billion in 1989 when measured in current dollars and from $1.5 billion in 1985 to $3.4 billion when measured in 1983 dollars. It was estimated that total rents transferred to foreign resource owners would range from $1.5 billion in 1985 to $2.1 billion in 1989 when measured in 1983 dollars. The transfer results because the foreign producers receive the gains generated by the higher prices prevailing with a quota.

Because it would be necessary to divert U.S. resources from other uses to production of steel, the quota would impose a deadweight loss of about $900 million for each year that the quota was in effect as a result of diverting U.S. resources from other uses to otherwise uneconomic steel production.

In summary, the loss in consumer surplus equals the sum of the distributional effects (economic rents transferred to domestic resources and foreign firms) plus the deadweight losses (efficiency losses). Because the discrepancy between domestic prices with and without the quota becomes larger during the later years of the quota, the total value of the distributional effects (rent transfers) and deadweight losses increases over the five-year period the quota is in effect. The loss in consumer surplus increases from $4.8 billion in 1985 to $7 billion in 1989 measured in current dollars, or from $4.3 billion to $5.9 billion in 1983 dollars.

FOREIGN DIRECT INVESTMENT IN THE STEEL INDUSTRY

The merger of National Steel Corporation and Nippon Kokan K.K. was motivated predominantly by a fear of protectionism, and to date it represents the largest single foreign direct investment in U.S. steel. Recently, it was announced that three other U.S. firms—California Steel Corporation which purchased the Kaiser steel works in Fontana, California, United States Steel Corporation, and Wheeling-Pittsburgh—had become recipients of foreign direct investment inflows. On September 23, 1984, subsequent to the Reagan Administration's announcement that it would seek to negotiate voluntary restraint agreements with some fifty steel-producing nations with an aim of keeping steel imports within 18.5% of domestic consumption, an article in the *New York Times* noted that the Administration's import proposal might make it more attractive to invest in American companies because investing in U.S. companies might be a way to offset the negative impact of import restraints.[59] To a certain extent, the recent investments in National Steel Corporation, United States Steel Corporation, Wheeling-Pittsburgh, and California Steel Corporation appear to signal the beginning of an inflow of foreign investment into the integrated companies. In past years, European, Japanese, and Canadian firms did make some investments in U.S. steelmaking facilities, predominantly mini-mill operations, but it is apparent that the recent movement toward protectionism has been accompanied by an increased flow of foreign investment into the large, integrated companies. There can be little doubt that investments of the magnitude of the recent merger of Nippon Kokan K.K. and National Steel Corporation would have substantial impact on the steel industry and on the economy of the United States. In this section, we investigate the nature of this impact as well as policy measures with respect to foreign direct investment in steelmaking.

Foreign Direct Investment in U.S. Steelmaking

To date, as already noted, the most significant foreign direct investment activity in U.S. steelmaking has been the merger of Nippon Kokan and National Steel Corporation in the first half of 1984 which cost the Japanese company $292 million. Over the same period, two other integrated steelmakers—Wheeling-Pittsburgh and California Steel Corporation—became recipients of foreign direct investment inflows.

On February 17, 1984, Japan's Nisshim Steel Company agreed to purchase ten % interest in Wheeling-Pittsburgh Steel Corporation for $17.5 million. At the same time Wheeling-Pittsburgh bought $5.3 million of Nisshim's stock. The motivation for the joint venture was the planned construction of a $50 million coating plant to make corrosion-resistant steel in West Virginia. The coating plant will produce galvanized or aluminized steel for automobile parts, appliances, and construction products. Both companies will share in the cost of the coating plant, but $8.38 million will come from an Urban Development Action Grant to the city of Follansbee. The city will lend the money at a 6.5% rate of interest to Wheeling-Pittsburgh. The joint venture with Nisshim Steel Company was part of an effort to modernize Wheeling-Pittsburgh which had been experiencing serious financial difficulties.[60] By May 1985 the situation deteriorated to the point where Wheeling-Pittsburgh was forced into undertaking a financial reorganization under Chapter 11 of the bankruptcy law.

Japanese capital was also involved when Kawasaki Steel Corporation agreed to become a 25% equity participant in California Steel Corporation, which had agreed to purchase Kaiser Steel Corporation's idle Fontana, California, plant constructed in 1943 to make steel to be used in shipbuilding. California Steel Corporation agreed to purchase Kaiser's steelmaking assets for $25 million cash and an $85 million five-year note. Another foreign stockholder of California Steel Corporation is Cia Vale de Rio Doce, a Brazilian government-controlled iron ore concern that also owns a 25% interest. Rio Doce Ltd. is a subsidiary of the world's largest iron ore producer, Companhia Vale de Rio Doce of Brazil. A California businessman holds a 50% interest. Initially, the venture will use only the plant's finishing mills and is expected to purchase 800,000 tons of raw or semi-finished steel annually. The imported steel is to be produced in a new plant, Companhia Siderurgica do Turbaraîa, located on Brazil's southern coast. Kawasaki Steel owns 24.5% of the plant, with the remainder being owned by Brazilian and Italian interests. The Fontana plant will be making coils, sheets, piping, and construction steel to be sold in the West Coast market. Because the Fontana plant was closed, imports supplied most of these goods to West Coast markets. Because of its location, the plant will be in a good position to supply steel sheet to the G.M.-Toyota venture which is producing small cars in Fremont, California. Kawasaki Steel Corporation already has an established relationship with Toyota in Japan.[61]

The three ventures announced in 1984 appear to have been occasioned largely by fears of impending protectionism in the United States. The foreign companies participating in these ventures will be in a better position to maintain market shares if they already have equity ownership in a U.S. company. Furthermore, the investment by the three Japanese companies—Nippon Kokan K.K., Nisshim, and Kawasaki—may represent part of a trend to export Japanese steelmaking technology. During recent years, the Japanese have been actively involved in exporting steelmaking technology to the developing countries. The joint venture and merger activities in the United States will probably be accompanied by the export of Japanese steelmaking technology to the United States.

On December 17, 1985, the U.S. Steel Corporation announced a joint venture with South Korea's Pohang Iron and Steel Corporation. U.S. Steel and Pohang

Iron and Steel will invest $300 million on a 50–50 basis to modernize U.S. Steel's finishing plant located at Pittsburgh, California. The two companies plan to become equal equity participants in the joint venture, and each will also contribute $90 million to purchase the plant. Beginning in 1986, Pohang will supply 40,000 tons of hot-rolled steel a year to the Pittsburgh plant, and after President Reagan's program to curb imports ends in 1989, Pohang will supply the Pittsburgh plant with 1 million tons a year. Previously, the plant was supplied by U.S. Steel's Geneva plant located near Provo, Utah. It is expected that the new venture will cause a significant reduction in steelmaking operations at the Utah plant, since the plant is considered obsolete because of its open-hearth furnaces that cannot be attached to continuous casting machines.

Pohang is among the world's lowest-cost steel producers and has achieved a reputation for supplying quality steel at low prices. Because ocean transport costs are low, it will be cheaper to ship the steel to the California plant from Korea than from Utah.[62] The joint venture which will supply U.S. Steel with a low-cost source of semi-finished steel, was obviously designed to enhance the competitive position of U.S. Steel.

Other foreign investments in the U.S. steel industry include:

1. Raritan River and Chapparal Steel Companies, which are owned by Co-Steel International of Canada. (Chapparal is owned jointly by Co-Steel and Texas Industries.)

2. Atlantic Steel, which is owned by Ivaco, a Canadian firm.

3. Copperweld, which is a subsidiary of a French firm.

4. Bayou, which is controlled by Voest Alpine, an Austrian firm.

5. Auburn Steel, which is Japanese owned.

In 1980 Chapparal Steel Company undertook a $200 million expansion of its steel-producing plant at Midlothian, Texas. The plant produces over 1 million tons of raw steel each year and uses the latest production machines and methods. One ton of steel can be produced with only 1.8 man hours of labor, a record even for mini-mills.[63] Co-Steel holds 100% ownership in Raritan River Steel Company. Construction of the $130 million plant commenced in 1980. The plant uses the latest technology, including the electric-arc furnace as well as high powered and high-speed equipment guided by computer controls. Ivaco, a Canadian firm, holds 51% ownership in Laclede Steel and 100% ownership in Atlantic Steel. Ivaco acquired Atlantic Steel for $50 million in 1979. In 1978 Voest Alpine formed a joint venture with Bayou Steel Company to build a $120 million steel mill in Louisiana. The annual output of the mill is about 600,000 tons of steel billet.

The first Japanese steel mill in the United States began operation in Auburn, New York, during the late 1970s. The mill produces construction-related bars. The investment was motivated by the desire of the Japanese to be near a stable source of scrap and supplies of land and electric power that are relatively cheap by Japanese standards.

As indicated above, a number of foreign investments have taken place, but 1984 marked a new phase, largely as an outcry for protectionism by the U.S. steel industry. In particular, the Japanese had decided that they risked losing a large part of their U.S. market and decided to invest in the United States. Because the VRAs negotiated by the Reagan Administration appear to be less restrictive than some of the legislation originally requested by the industry, foreign-owned steelmakers may find less of an incentive to invest in the United States.

An additional incentive for investment by the Japanese is to be able to supply Nissan, Toyota, and Honda, which are producing in the United States. The possibility of the passage of a domestic content bill would enhance the attractiveness of investment in the U.S. steel industry.

The Impact of Foreign Direct Investment on the U.S. Economy

The recent foreign investments in the U.S. steel industry have been largely in the form of mergers and joint ventures. Thus, it may not have the same impact as would the establishment of new facilities designed to expand steel output. Some of the areas in which such investment might have significant effect on the U.S. economy include balance-of-payments impacts; the externalities that might result from technology transfer and the training of labor; linkage and employment effects when there is expansion of capacity or when unutilized capacity is refurbished and placed back into operation; and the impact on allocative efficiency.

In the short run, balance-of-payment effects would be positive. The inflow of foreign capital and the reduction of steel imports should have positive effects on the balance of payments. However, because the United States has lagged behind in the development of steelmaking technology, it will be necessary to import modern technology and equipment from abroad. For instance, in 1979 Nippon Steel, Japan's largest steelmaker, extended technological cooperation to the Wheeling-Pittsburgh Steel Corporation to help construct and operate a rail production plant. This represents the first export of rail technology to the United States from Japan. Under the agreement, Nippon Steel was to license Wheeling-Pittsburgh to use its railmaking technology, provide engineering advice, and train engineers at its steel mill in Tokyo.[64]

Furthermore, if the foreign investor invests in a steel finishing operation, raw steel might be imported from abroad. Even if the investment were in an integrated steel mill such as the recent merger of Nippon Kokan K.K. and National Steel Corporation, it is possible that raw steel would be imported to be used in finishing operations if they ran short of materials to be finished at the U.S. facility. Because of the need to import steel technology from the foreign parent, the possibility of importing raw steel to be used in finishing mills, and the repatriation in the long run of dividends, interest, and royalties, any positive impact on the balance of payments might be minimal, especially in the long term.

The U.S. steel industry has to import foreign technology because it has not been involved in the development of steel technology. Most of the recent foreign investment in the steel industry has been accompanied by a transfer of technology. Thus, Nippon Kokan K.K., one of the world's leaders in steel technology, and National Steel Corporation have shared technical know-how for 20 years, and National already uses Japanese technology. The merger gives National Steel Corporation further access to Japanese technological expertise. The Raritan River Steel Company plant, a Canadian-owned firm, makes use of an electric arc furnace which is a technological advance in steelmaking pioneered by Co-Steel in Canada in 1954. As indicated above, Nippon Steel Corporation made the first export of rail-producing technology from Japan when it assisted Wheeling-Pittsburgh. These cases highlight the role now being played by foreign investors in transferring technology to the United States. The foreign investor can create positive externalities when it transfers technology to the host country. The externalities are created when other steelmaking firms adopt the technology which the foreign investors introduce. Presumably the existence of more firms in the United States using modern technology would speed-up the introduction of these technological advances in other large firms. However, until the problem of low profitability in the industry improves, it would be difficult for many of the integrated firms to introduce these new technologies.

The training of labor is another potential externality from the foreign investment. In several of the cases of investment in the U.S. steel industry, labor training was part of the investment package. In 1979, when Nippon Steel Corporation extended technological cooperation to Wheeling-Pittsburgh to construct and operate a rail production plant, Nippon also agreed to teach engineers from Wheeling-Pittsburgh at the Tokyo steel mill to operate the rolling equipment.[65] Nippon Kokan also intends to make changes in technology and management style at National Steel Corporation.

The creation of investment linkages also holds out a possibility of benefits to the host country. Even in the case of mergers and joint ventures, substantial investment linkages can be created if the investment involves sufficient refurbishing of existing plants or construction of new facilities. Most of the foreign investment activity involves considerable amounts of investment that should lead to a reduction in cost per ton and/or expand existing capacity. For instance, new construction was involved in the Chapparal and Raritan River plants. In addition, the joint venture between Nisshim Steel and Wheeling-Pittsburgh was for the purpose of constructing a $50 million coating plant in West Virginia with both companies splitting the cost of the plant. The Nippon Kokan partnership arrangement is expected to accelerate National Steel's $600 million capital spending program from five to two years.

The impact of an increase in basic steel output on total output and employment has been shown by the Congressional Research Service.[66] Using 1972 dollars, it is calculated that a $1 increment in basic steel output would result in a $2.20 growth in total output. More than 52,000 new jobs would result from a $1 billion rise in basic steel output.

The Data Resources Incorporated (DRI) interindustry model was used to estimate increases in output and employment of all sectors resulting from a change in the output and employment of any one sector. The model estimated both direct and indirect output effects. The direct effects are the effects on output and employment of the sector benefiting from the stimulus, and the indirect effects are the effects on all other sectors supplying the sector experiencing the stimulus.

Table 4.7 shows that of the $2.20 gain in total output, $1.189 would occur in basic steel and steel mill products and 85% of the remainder would occur in 13 other sectors. Each sector listed in the table contributed a minimum of one % of the total gain in gross output in all sectors combined. These include the backward linkages on services, mining, utilities, construction, and manufacturing. Forward linkages should result from the investment activity if low cost steel is produced as a result of the foreign investment. Because steel is used in so many other economic activities, the production of more low cost domestic steel should have an impact on economic activities, such as motor vehicle production, which are heavy users of steel.

The effects on employment in selected sectors due to a $1 billion real increase in basic steel production are shown in Table 4.8. The 14 sectors shown in the

Table 4.7
Effects of a $1 Increase in Output of Basic Steel on the Output of Selected Economic Sectors

Economic Sector	Increase in Output
All Sectors	$2.200
Basic Steel and Steel Mill Products[a]	1.189
Transportation and Warehousing	0.108
Business Services	0.089
Iron Ore Mining	0.079
Wholesale and Retail Trade	0.077
Utilities	0.072
Other Ferrous Metals Industries	0.044
Chemicals and Chemical Products	0.043
Real Estate and Rental	0.042
Maintenance and Repair Construction	0.036
Coal Mining	0.034
Other Fabricated Metal Products	0.026
General Industry Machinery	0.024
Crude Petroleum and Natural Gas	0.023

[a]The increase in Basic Steel and Steel Mill Products includes the initial $1 increase in output of this sector and its effects on production in this sector.

Source: U.S. Congress, House, Committee on Banking, Finance, and Urban Affairs, *Establishment of a National Development Bank and Other Matters*, Hearings before a Subcommittee on General Oversight and Renegotiation, on H.R. 638, 98 Cong., 1st Sess., 1983, p. 367. Calculated by Congressional Research Service based on Data Resources Incorporated (DRI) simulations.

Table 4.8
Effects of a $1 Billion Increase in Basic Steel Production[a] **on Employment in Selected Economic Sectors**

Economic Sector	Increase in Employment (persons)
All Sectors	52,180
Basic Steel and Steel Mill Products	15,560
Transportation and Warehousing	3,670
Business Services	2,940
Iron Ore Mining	1,860
Wholesale and Retail Trade	4,500
Utilities	820
Other Ferrous Metals Industries	8,780
Chemicals and Chemical Products	560
Real Estate and Rental	130
Maintenance and Repair Construction	1,170
Coal Mining	1,130
Other Fabricated Metal Products	820
General Industry Machinery	740
Crude Petroleum and Natural Gas	170

[a] The increase in output in constant 1972 dollars.
Source: U.S. Congress, House, Committee on Banking, Finance, and Urban Affairs, *Establishment of a National Development Bank and Other Matters*, Hearings, 1983, p. 368. Calculated by the Congressional Research Service based on Data Resources Incorporated (DRI) simulations.

table contribute more than 80% of the projected increase in output and employment caused by the growth in the steel industry. Basic steel and steel mill products contribute over 30% to the total gain in employment, and other ferrous metal industries contribute 17%.

From the above it can be assumed that foreign investment in the U.S. steel industry that contributes to low-cost production could raise the level of output and that this growth in output would have substantial direct and indirect effects on the overall level of output in a number of sectors, including basic steel, and on employment.

Another effect of foreign direct investment would be the impact on the allocative efficiency that occurs when the presence of the additional firms that have invested in the host country enhances the degree of competition. The steel industry is composed of about 15 large, integrated firms as well as a substantial number of mini-mills. In the past, foreign firms invested in a number of mini-mill operations. More recently, they invested in Wheeling-Pittsburgh and National Steel Corporation which are large, integrated firms. It has been pointed out above that the mini-mill sector is the most efficient, least cost part of the industry. In 1980 there were 45 such firms operating 58 plants throughout the United States.[67] As indicated earlier, the main advantage of these firms is that they can be operated efficiently on a small scale. These firms, which include a number of foreign-owned plants, are competitive and dynamic as contrasted with the integrated steelmakers.

Recent foreign investment in the large integrated plants also appears to be of the type that would help introduce more efficient production techniques and reduce per unit production cost. It might also enhance the allocative efficiency of the integrated steelmakers.

In summary, foreign direct investment may have several positive effects on the U.S. economy, including externalities resulting from technology transfer and the training of labor, creation of investment linkages, and enhancement of allocative efficiency in the part of the industry comprised of large integrated steelmakers. Balance-of-payments impacts are more questionable. In the short run, the substitution of steel produced in the United States for imported steel would reduce the trade deficit. But if it is necessary to import semi-finished steel or raw steel to be finished in the United States, positive impacts on the balance of payments would be thereby reduced. In the long run repatriation of dividends, interest, and royalties would help to negate the positive impact on the balance of payments. Given the need to import foreign technology, it may be anticipated that outward flows consisting of licensing fees and royalties would be substantial.

It is necessary to determine a policy response to the recent inflow of foreign direct investment into the steel industry. The formulation of a response is not independent of potential benefits to the industry and to the U.S. economy.

Perhaps the most important benefit from FDI in steel has been in the transfer of technology. Whether FDI takes place in mini-mill operations which are considered the most efficient, low-cost part of the industry or, more recently, in the integrated sector, FDI in the steel industry has been associated with the transfer of technology.

Another benefit has been in the provision of capital for modernization. Because of the recession and foreign competition, for most of the 1980s the integrated producers have suffered losses that have adversely affected their ability to engage in capital formation and modernization. Large inflows of FDI into steel can help the integrated producers achieve greater efficiency.

Because FDI can transfer technology and provide capital resources to an industry which is, to a large extent, technologically obsolete, any potential policy that the United States might adopt could seek to encourage foreign direct investment. However, one problem that has been associated with multinational activity in host countries results from the fact that MNCs frequently do not undertake R and D efforts in the host countries. This has been the case in many developing countries. As a consequence, transfer of technology is limited, and the host does not receive the benefits that could accrue if R and D efforts accompanied the foreign investment activity. Because of this potential problem, the United States should set up an office to monitor the investment activities of foreign MNCs that invest here and should establish criteria that the MNC must meet before it can engage in FDI. Many other countries have established criteria for MNCs operating within their borders. Although we do not recommend the imposition of performance requirements on foreign MNCs, we do believe that some agency should exist to monitor their activities in the United States. As is argued in Chapter 8, performance requirements imposed on MNCs investing in a foreign country can be trade distorting and are impediments to the free flow of international trade.

The need to undertake FDI in steel cannot be separated from domestic content legislation, which has been proposed as an FDI policy response for motor vehicles. As noted above, the Japanese steel producers who have recently engaged in FDI in the United States have been very closely aligned with Japanese auto producers. Their entry into the United States could make them suppliers of steel used in the production of Toyotas, Hondas, and Nissan trucks. If domestic content legislation is enacted vis-à-vis autos, Japanese steel companies could supply Japanese motor vehicle producers operating in the United States and then transfer profits earned back to Japan. Because of this close interrelationship, domestic content legislation cannot ignore the potential impact on foreign firms that supply imports to the industry.

Government Promotion of Capital Formation

As observed earlier, a shortage of capital to undertake modernization has been a major problem of the integrated steel industry. Suggestions to ameliorate this problem have included acceleration of depreciation allowances, tax credits, and loan guarantees. The 1979 Capital Cost Recovery Act shortened the useful life of plant and equipment. In order to gain from accelerated depreciation allowances, however, a firm must show profits. If it continuously experiences losses, it receives little benefit from such allowances. Such has been the case with the steel industry, especially in 1982–1985, when it experienced heavy financial losses.

Public policy measures may be used to help supply capital in a situation in which market imperfections exist. Market imperfections occur when there is market failure, and market failure occurs when the social benefits or costs are different from private benefits or costs. Private sector calculations need not necessarily bring about socially desirable outcomes. Public policy involving intervention in the marketplace may be used to bring about a solution that enhances social optimality.

For many reasons, market imperfections are a frequent occurrence in capital markets. Expected returns may occur so far into the future that privately functioning capital markets fail to supply funds. Thus, lenders may prefer projects with short-term, immediate payoffs to projects with payoffs occurring further off into the future. That is to say, the social rate of discount may be different from the private rate of discount. Lenders may incorrectly perceive investments by small firms to be riskier than investments by larger firms. In addition, capital markets may have a tendency to perceive a depressed industry or firm to be riskier than one that is earning profits. The perception of excessive risk may make the cost of obtaining private sector funding prohibitive. This was true in the case of Chrysler Corporation; federally guaranteed loans were used to bail out the firm which at present is earning profits. Federally guaranteed loans were also provided to Lockheed Corporation

The steel industry is most likely one where the market cannot effectively allocate capital resources. The time horizon for payoffs from investing in modernization of the steel industry would be far off into the future, and the increasing market share of imports combined with a decline in domestic steel consumption increases the riskiness of the investment. The OTA study of the steel industry indicates that firms in the industry favor projects that have returns in the short run. Moreover, investment does not occur in projects that are geared to renewal of the industry's technological foundations. Even though the industry's debt-to-equity ratio increased somewhat during the 1970s, the ratio was much smaller than that of the Japanese steel industry. Given the high proportion of equity financing, the industry faces the necessity of investing where the payoff is high because shareholders require a more immediate return on equity. However, only long-run profitability can achieve, once again, international competitiveness.

During the past few years public sector loans and loan guarantees have expanded in the United States in order to assist ailing industries and to attract new investment.[68] In effect, loan guarantees help to reduce the cost of capital to the firm because default risk is eliminated. Such guaranteed loans could be very useful in aiding ailing firms in the steel industry. Before extending loan guarantees, the government could establish certain priorities and targets for the industry. These would include estimates for future consumption, estimates for the amount of future capacity considered necessary, the role of imports, and the respective roles of integrated producers and mini-mill operations in domestic production. Given the decline in steel intensity in gross national product, estimates for desired capacity are important. Because the cost of new greenfield investments is so high, in the future brownfield investments will likely occur. In other words, modernization will probably take the form of rounding out existing facilities as a way of reducing the cost of production. It has been pointed out that, because the costs of brownfield expansion are high ($700 to $800 per ton) even these investments will not occur unless cost-price relationships are significantly altered.[69]

If the government were to offer reduced interest loans, either directly to the firm or through some sort of development corporation, it would in effect be subsidizing the firm. Accelerated depreciation allowances and increased investment credits to the industry are also a possible solution. Economic theory suggests that a subsidy occasions less of a welfare loss to society than protection because it does not raise consumer prices. It can be shown that the cost to society of subsidizing investment in the steel industry is similar to trade protection but that consumer prices are unchanged and that the transfer of wealth from consumers to producers is avoided.

Antitrust Legislation

In the area of antitrust the amendment of government policy might be helpful to the steel industry. Section 1 of the Sherman Act prohibits agreements that are in restraint of trade among the several states or with foreign nations. The Clayton Act prohibits acquisitions where the effect may be to lessen competition or create a monopoly. In the antitrust climate prevailing in the United States, firms that form joint ventures involving collaboration on R and D activities or pooling of technical information might be scrutinized by the Federal Trade Commission or the Justice Department or both. Similar problems might be encountered by firms seeking to form a merger in order to rationalize existing means of production and create more efficient and cost-competitive companies. Prior to the merger of National Steel Corporation and Nippon Kokan K.K., U.S. Steel Corporation had announced a plan to merge with National, but this plan was dropped because of fear of objections by the Justice Department. A merger between LTV corporation and Republic Steel Corporation was given approval by the Justice Department only after the companies agreed to sell two steel plants. Therefore, it is widely recognized in the steel industry that antitrust clearance remains an essential obstacle to mergers and joint ventures.

Because the problem of potential scrutiny by the Justice Department becomes less acute when one of the firms is foreign owned, as was the case in the merger of National Steel Corporation and Nippon Kokan K.K., it becomes simpler for a large domestic firm to merge with a foreign-owned firm. This can occur because antitrust legislation appears to be concerned only with excessive concentration in a domestic industry.

NOTES

1. "National Steel Plan With Nippon Kokan Reflects Japan's Stagnant Home Market," *Wall Street Journal*, October 26, 1984, p. 2.

2. Ibid.

3. Ibid.

4. Hans Mueller, "Trends in Steel Production and Trade," paper presented at the annual meeting of the Eastern Economics Association, New York City, March 1984, p. 5.

5. U.S. Congress, Office of Technology Assessment, *Technology and Steel Industry Competitiveness* (Washington, D.C.: 1980), 65–68.

6. Ibid.

7. Ibid., pp. 68–69.

8. Ibid.

9. Ibid.

10. U.S. Federal Trade Commission, *The United States Steel Industry and Its International Rivals: Trends and Factors Determining International Competitiveness* (Washington, D.C.: 1977), Ch. 6.

11. Mueller, "Trends in Steel Production and Trade," p. 7.

12. U.S. Department of Commerce, Bureau of Industrial Economics, *1984 U.S. Industrial Outlook* (Washington, D.C.: 1985), pp. 18–1 to 18–7.

13. U.S. Congress, Office of Technology Assessment, *Technology and Steel Industry Competitiveness*, pp. 186–188.

14. U.S. Congress, House Committee on Energy and Commerce, *Capital Formation and Industrial Policy* (Part 3), Hearing before a Subcommittee on Oversight and Investigation, 97 Cong., 2d Assessment Session, 1982. Testimony of Joel Hirschman, U.S. Office of Technology, pp. 345–355.

15. Robert Crandall, *The U.S. Steel Industry in Recurrent Crisis* (Washington, D.C.: Brookings Institute, 1981), p. 23.

16. William T. Hogan, S.J., *World Steel in the 1980's* (Lexington, Mass.: Lexington Books, 1983), p. 10.

17. Ibid., p. 109.

18. U.S. Congress, Office of Technology Assessment, *Technology and Steel Industry Competitiveness*, pp. 9–11.

19. Ibid., p. 87.

20. Ibid.

21. Hogan, *World Steel*, p. 10.

22. Ibid., pp. 111–112.

23. U.S. Congress, Office of Technology Assessment, *Technology and Steel Industry Competitiveness*, pp. 95–97.

24. Ibid., p. 97.

25. Ibid., p. 18 and pp. 95–97.

26. Crandall, *The Steel Industry*, pp. 19–21.

27. Ibid.

28. Ira Magaziner and Robert B. Reich, *Minding America's Business* (New York: Vantage Books, 1983), pp. 157–158.

29. Crandall, *The Steel Industry*, p. 23.

30. U.S. Congress, Office of Technology Assessment, *U.S. Industrial Competitiveness: A Comparison of Steel, Electronics, and Automobiles* (Washington, D.C.: 1981), p. 59.

31. Crandall, *The Steel Industry*, pp. 89–90.

32. Mueller, "Trends in Steel Production and Trade," p. 9, and U.S. Congress, Congressional Budget Office, *The Effects of Import Quotas on the Steel Industry* (Washington, D.C.: July 1984), p. 24.

33. Crandall, *The Steel Industry*, pp. 89–90.

34. U.S. Congress, Office of Technology Assessment, *Technology and Steel Industry Competitiveness*, p. 54.

35. Peter F. Marcus and Karlis M. Kirisis (World Steel Dynamics of Payne-Webber), "Steel's Survival Challenge," paper presented at the Warren, Ohio, Area Chamber of Commerce, March 21, 1985, p. 8.

36. U.S. Congress, Office of Technology Assessment, *U.S. Industrial Competitiveness*, p. 54.

37. Ibid., pp. 57–58.

38. Magaziner and Reich, *Minding America's Business*, p. 160.

39. "Even If Steel Gets Import Relief Its Anxieties Won't Go Away," *Business Week* (June 25, 1984): 29–30.

40. U.S. Congress, Office of Technology Assessment, *Technology and Steel Industry Competitiveness*, p. 313.

41. Hogan. *World Steel*, p. 124.

42. "Even If Steel Gets Import Relief," p. 29.

43. U.S. Congress, Congressional Budget Office, *The Effects of Import Quotas*, p. 49.

44. "Even If Steel Gets Import Relief," pp. 29–30.

45. U.S. Congress, Office of Technology Assessment, *U.S. Industrial Competitiveness*, pp. 72–73.

46. U.S. Congress, Office of Technology Assessment, *U.S. Industrial Competitiveness*, p. 111.

47. Ibid., pp. 111–112. Another protective measure was the imposition of the quantitative restrictions imposed in 1976 on specialty steel and stainless steel imports after the ITC had ruled that the increase in imports had impaired domestic firms. The Japanese entered into voluntary agreements to limit imports, and quotas were imposed on other countries. Walter Adams and Hans Mueller, "The Steel Industry," in Walter Adams, ed., *The Structure of American Industry* (New York: Macmillan Publishing Co., 1982), p. 130.

48. U.S. Congress, Office of Technology Assessment, *U.S. Industrial Competitiveness*, p. 112.

49. *Wall Street Journal*, June 13, 1984, p. 3.

50. "Even If Steel Gets Import Relief," p. 29.

51. *New York Times*, August 9, 1984, pp. D1 and D2.

52. U.S. International Trade Commission, *Carbon and Certain Steel Products*, Vol. 1 (Washington, D.C.: 1984), pp. 71–81.

53. Ibid., p. 79.

54. Ibid., pp. 77–78.

55. Crandall, *The Steel Industry*, pp. 93–115.

56. Ibid., pp. 103–107, 111–113.

57. Ibid., pp. 133–139.

58. U.S. Congress, Congressional Budget Office, *The Effect of Import Quotas*, pp. 39–57.

59. Winston Williams, "The Shrinking of the Steel Industry," *New York Times*, September 23, 1984, p. D4.

60. Susan Chira, "Struggle Continues at Wheeling-Pittsburgh," *New York Times*, August 10, 1984, pp. D1 and D2.

61. "Kawasaki Steel to Acquire 25 Percent of U.S. Venture," *Wall Street Journal*, July, 17, 1984, p. 2.

62. Daniel F. Cuff, "U.S. Steel in Korean Import Plan: Pohang Will Supply Plant in California," *New York Times*, December 17, 1985, pp. D1 and D2.

63. "America's Best Managed Factories," *Fortune* (May 28, 1984): 16–17.

64. "Nippon Steel to Assist Wheeling-Pittsburgh in Constructing and Operating Rail Product Plant," *New York Times*, April 20, 1979, pp. 5–6.

65. Ibid.

66. U.S. Congress, House, Hearings, Committee on Banking, Finance, and Urban Affairs, Subcommittee on General Oversight and Renegotiation, 1st Sess. on H.R. 638 and Senate No. 98–18, March 9–10 and April 13–14, pp. 364–368.

67. Adams and Mueller, "The Steel Industry," pp. 84–85.

68. U.S. Congress, Office of Technology Assessment, *U.S. Industrial Competitiveness*, p. 155.

69. Crandall, *The Steel Industry*, p. 117.

5

Internationalization of Motor Vehicle Production and the Role of the United States

The U.S. motor vehicle industry and its counterparts in a dozen other advanced countries face difficult times. During 1973–1975 the first oil price shock hit the industry, contributing to a two-year down-cycle phase and a 33% drop in U.S. production. In 1975–1979 differential wage inflation in major motor vehicle-producing countries, accompanied by wide fluctuations in floating exchange rates, brought about shifts in the competitive position of producers (Table 5.1). Over the period 1978–1982 the American-based auto industry suffered substantial layoffs, a slump in production, inflated operating expenses, and near bankruptcy of at least one of the Big Three producers. Production in the U.S. automobile industry declined 41.5% between the peak year 1978 and 1982.[1] Imports increased in the same period from 17.7% to 27.8% of U.S. sales, prompting calls for protectionist measures directed at reducing imports of foreign-produced motor vehicles. In response, the United States and Japan agreed to a system of voluntary import quotas. Japanese producers also initiated investment in U.S. production facilities. In 1983 and 1984 the U.S. government pressed for and obtained an extension of the import quota by Japanese motor vehicle producers. In 1985 the United States announced it would not seek an extension of the voluntary import quota.

The economic upswing of 1982–1985 restored profitability to the American automobile industry. But at the same time it has led to the removal of the voluntary import quota, exposing the domestic industry to serious competitive challenges over the next several years. These developments have been accompanied by a growing clamor from special interest groups for protection from imports. Important theoretical, policy, and practical arguments have been raised against motor vehicle import restrictions, and the U.S. Congress has fought off political pressures for protection. United Auto Workers (UAW) President Douglas Fraser

Table 5.1
Hourly Compensation Changes, Foreign Exchange Rates, and Index of U.S. Competitiveness in Motor Vehicle Production, 1975 and 1979

Country	Hourly Compensation in National Currency			Unit	Exchange Rate: National Currency Units per Dollar			Index U.S. = 100	
	1975	1979	% Change		1975	1979	% Change	1975	1979
United States	9.60	13.72	43	Dollar	—	—	—	100	100
Canada	7.63	11.08	45	Dollar	1.017	1.171	15	78	69
Brazil	12.95	65.54	406	Cruz.	8.129	25.88	219	17	18
Mexico	36.84	89.25	142	Peso	12.50	22.82	83	31	28
Japan	1,056	1,494	41	Yen	296.7	218.2	−26	37	50
Korea	244	763	213	Won	484	484	0	5	12
France	22.37	38.18	71	Franc	4.282	4,255	−1	54	65
Germany	18.89	25.75	36	Mark	2.455	1.833	−25	80	102
Italy	3,332	6,564	97	Lira	652.4	830.9	27	53	58
Sweden	30.82	49.16	60	Krona	4.142	4.288	4	78	84
United Kingdom	177.7	299.5	69	Pence	45.01	47.12	5	41	46

Source: U.S. Congress, Senate, Issues Relating to the Domestic Auto Industry, Hearings before the Subcommittee on International Trade of the Committee on Finance, 96th Cong., 1st Sess., January 14–15, 1981, Part 1.

has cited the switch in consumer preferences to small cars as the basic reason for the slump in the U.S. auto industry that took place in 1979–1982, not increased sales of foreign-manufactured automobiles. Although union leaders have pointed to poor planning and forecasting among the top echelons at motor vehicle companies as a major cause of the difficulties facing the industry, other observers point to high wage costs as a source of difficulty. For example, in 1979 total hourly compensation of workers in the U.S. motor vehicle industry was $13.72, double the amount earned ($6.85) in Japan (Table 5.1). In that year the Japanese auto workers' compensation was in line with that earned by their counterparts in the United Kingdom, Italy, and Spain (all within a range of $6.36 to $7.90 per hour). Not only was average hourly compensation of U.S. motor vehicle workers double that in Japan, it also was more than double the average wage of a production worker in American manufacturing. Detroit's extraordinarily high wage levels are in part responsible for its problems. In the past, high wages have not been accompanied by high productivity. Moreover, the large drain on Detroit's capital represented by wages is a major cause of the industry's capital formation problems.[2]

Whereas Japan's auto industry enjoys lower direct wage costs per unit of labor input, it is also far less labor intensive than the United States. This suggests that Japan enjoys a far greater labor cost advantage over the United States than is indicated in the previously mentioned comparison of hourly employee compensation. For these reasons American manufacturers have invested heavily in Japan. General Motors owns 34% of Isuzu, Ford owns 25% of Toyo Kogyo, and Chrysler owns 24% of Mitsubishi.

The discussion that follows examines the growth and concentration of production in the motor vehicle industry, the economics of the industry, trade, investment and welfare issues, domestic content and industrial policy proposals, and the prospects for strengthening the competitive position of U.S. producers.

Import competition poses a real challenge, perhaps even threat, to the viability of U.S. motor vehicle producers. Given the critical nature of this industry and its pivotal position in the framework of interindustry linkages, we consider it from the standpoint of incentives and disincentives to foreign investment. We begin the discussion with a review of the status of the U.S. motor vehicle industry within the context of global production and competition. The growing internationalization of the industry mandates that it be considered from a global point of view. The following questions indicate the direction of our inquiry in this and the next two chapters.

1. Why is motor vehicle production highly concentrated in only a small number of countries and firms?

2. Does the pattern of locating motor vehicle production reflect multinational enterprise strategies, barriers to dispersal of production due to foreign investment impediments, or other factors?

3. Does location of motor vehicle production relate to distinct comparative advantage, or does comparative advantage only play a secondary role in the location of production?

4. How do special economic conditions in the motor vehicle industry affect the concentration of production in only a few countries, and the mix between foreign investment versus exports?

5. Are the foreign investment and export alternatives available to MNEs based mainly on economic criteria? Or do other factors have a greater influence in determining whether a motor vehicle producer will produce for export or shift production to the consuming region?

6. World trade in motor vehicles represents approximately 39% of production in the ten leading producer countries. This is well above the export percentage for most manufactured products. Why is this percentage so high? Does this reflect special features in the economics of production, government interference with markets, or MNE control of the market?

7. Will nationalist government policies in developing countries shift the location of production, so that export percentages will come down and domestic content will rise? How quickly could these shifts take place?

BROAD TRENDS IN GLOBAL PRODUCTION

Growth in Production

Since 1940 world motor vehicle production has followed what might be called "the expected pattern." By using world production data converted into five-year averages, these five-year averages may be traced over the period 1940–1982, and the growth in production may be calculated from one five-year period to the next. The results of this analysis are summarized in Table 5.2. The data show that in the first two five-year periods following World War II motor vehicle production increased at rates exceeded only in the very early years when the industry was in its pioneer expansion stage (1900–1924). The period of high growth and pent-up demand (1945–1954) lasted approximately one decade (Figure 5.1). Subsequent to 1955, the growth rate of motor vehicle production has taken on the appearance of a prolonged Kuznets cycle, with the growth rate increasing, declining, and even reaching negative values in the 1980s.

The post-war pattern of production growth exhibited by the motor vehicle industry reflects that of a mature industrial sector. Underlying this pattern are the special economic characteristics of the industry. Before we can proceed with our analysis of global production and trade in motor vehicles, we must consider the economics of this important industrial sector.

Importance of the Industry

The economic importance of the motor vehicle industry in the United States and Canada can be viewed from the perspective of the plant facilities, the workforce, and materials required and utilized in the manufacturing process.

The five major motor vehicle manufacturers in North America operated 323

Table 5.2
Post-War Growth Rate in World Motor Vehicle Production, 1940–1982

Period	Percentage Increase in Production
1940–1944 to	
1945–1949	86
1945–1949 to	
1950–1954	93
1950–1954 to	
1955–1959	29
1955–1959 to	
1960–1964	47
1960–1964 to	
1965–1969	43
1965–1969 to	
1970–1974	31
1970–1974 to	
1975–1979	14
1975–1979 to	
1980–1982	−4

production facilities until 1979–1980 shutdowns, 290 of which were in the United States and 33 in Canada including: 86 car, truck, and bus assembly plants; 51 body-stamping and hardware plants; 23 soft-trim and plastics plants; 22 engine plants; 13 transmission plants; 24 chassis plants; 37 forging and foundry plants; 39 mechanical, electrical, and electronics plants; 9 heater and air conditioning plants; 9 bearing and battery plants; and 10 steel and glass plants.[3] General Motors Corporation operated 173 of these plants, Ford 76, Chrysler 50, American Motors 21, and Volkswagen 3. Between 1979 and 1981, 25 of these plants were closed or were scheduled to be closed. Since 1981 additional plants have been shut down.

Supplier companies located throughout the United States and Canada are critical to the economic viability of the motor vehicle industry. In 1981 there were 32,000 suppliers with 45,000 different plant locations (of which 3,000 were located in Canada). These suppliers provide the industry with raw materials, component parts, machine tools, perishable tools, dies, office equipment, transportation services, and other services. Suppliers have closed a number of plants since 1979.

The workforce employed directly by motor vehicle manufacturers exceeded 950,000 workers in 1978, 65,000 of whom were in Canada. In addition, 1,840,000 workers provided component parts, tools, dies, and services as indicated in the accompanying tabulation.[4] A high percentage (60%) of suppliers employ less than 500 workers.

	Workers
Component parts suppliers	610,000
Raw materials suppliers	225,000
Non-productive materials	225,000
Transportation industry, delivering materials, and shipping vehicles	300,000
Tools and dies, perishable tools, and machine tools	480,000
	——————
Total	1,840,000

A total of 2,790,000 workers were employed in 1978 to produce 13.5 million vehicles. By 1981, 625,000 workers or 22.3% of the 1978 total were unemployed. The concentration of this workforce in a small number of states specialized in motor vehicle production suggests that in these states the almost 2.8 million workers directly and indirectly involved in motor vehicle manufacturing account for a high percentage of economic activity, income generation, and industrial production.

The motor vehicle industry is a large and, in some cases the single largest, consumer of many commodities used by our basic industries. It has been estimated that this industry utilizes the following percentages of commodities consumed in the United States:

Rubber	67
Lead	50
Iron	47
Zinc	33
Machine Tools	20
Steel	19
Aluminum	12
Copper	8
Plastics	6

The impact of any cutback in consumption by the motor vehicle industry in any of the above commodity categories could be drastic with respect to cost levels, profitability, and, ultimately, the competitive strength of producers in that commodity sector. For example, a steel mill might find it difficult to remain open if it were to lose 20% of its basic volume represented by auto production. Similarly, machine tool or perishable tool manufacturers would have to retrench significantly if it were not for the volume of business they obtain for vehicle production changes. This discussion indicates that the motor vehicle industry's economic importance in part derives from the strong backward linkages with other supplier industries and firms.

Economics of the Motor Vehicle Industry

The economic characteristics of the motor vehicle industry are important in understanding the status of the United States as a producer and consumer of motor vehicles. They also play at least a partial determining role concerning the flow of international trade and investment in motor vehicles and component parts. These characteristics include (1) strong backward linkages, (2) oligopolistic and even cartel-like behavior, (3) cost behavior, scale economies, and joint costs, (4) highly differentiated product, and (5) high demand elasticities.

Linkages

The linkages and interindustry relations of the motor vehicle industry can be demonstrated by considering the effect of (1) a $10 billion reduction in consumer purchases of domestic automobiles, and (2) a 10% reduction in automobile imports.

The following analysis, based on a study completed by the Congressional Research Service, Library of Congress, points out the importance of backward linkages and indicates substantial multiplier effects on employment and incomes. The employment and output effects associated with a $10 billion reduction in *consumer demand* for automobiles are summarized in Tables 5.3 and 5.4. In 1983 this reduction was equivalent to 18.4% of demand for autos and 1.1% of total consumer demand. The U.S. economy as a whole would lose 588,500 jobs as a result of a $10 billion reduction in consumer demand. Job losses in industries

Figure 5.1
Kuznets Cycle Pattern in World Motor Vehicle Production, 1945–1985

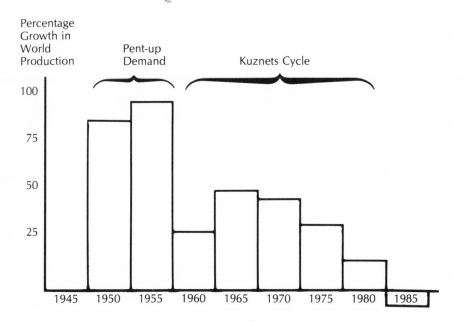

with employment changes of more than one % would total 447,500, and in this group the motor vehicle and equipment industry experiences a job loss of 7.6%. Nine industries would experience employment losses of two % or more. Large employment losses are experienced in the screw machine products and stampings industry and in the miscellaneous electrical machinery and equipment industry (employment reductions of 4 to 5 %). Industries that produce steel, textiles, glass, and rubber experience job losses of 2 to 4 %.[5]

On the output side a $10 billion drop in consumer demand for automobiles translates into a $28.4 billion loss in total output. The motor vehicle and equipment industry experiences an output loss of 13.8%. The screw machine products and stampings industry and the miscellaneous electrical machinery and equipment industry each experience reduced output of 6 to 7 %. Output reductions of 3 to 5 % are recorded in the steel, textile, glass, rubber, and miscellaneous plastics products sectors (Tables 5.3 and 5.4).

The employment and output effects of a 10% reduction in automobile *imports* are summarized in Tables 5.5 and 5.6. The model used in this analysis makes

Table 5.3
Employment Effects of a $10 Billion Reduction in Consumer Purchases of Automobiles, 1983[a] (thousands of persons)

Industry	Base	Cut	Decrease	Percentage Decrease
Agriculture, Forestry, & Fisheries				
Forestry & Fishery Products	112.5	110.9	1.6	1.4
Mining				
Iron Ore Mining	27.8	26.8	1.0	3.6
Chemical & Fertilizer Mineral Mining	15.1	14.9	0.2	1.1
Manufacturing				
Durable				
Lumber & Wood Products	565.6	559.9	5.7	1.0
Wood Containers	15.5	15.3	0.2	1.2
Glass & Glass Products	168.8	165.4	3.4	2.0
Primary Ferrous Metals	621.3	608.7	12.6	2.0
Screw Machine Products & Stampings	303.8	289.4	14.4	4.8

Table 5.3 (*continued*)

Industry	Base	Cut	Decrease	Percentage Decrease
Other Fabricated Metal Products	607.0	598.1	8.8	1.5
Misc. Nonelectrical Machinery	229.0	224.8	4.2	1.8
Misc. Electrical Machinery & Equipment	162.9	155.9	7.1	4.3
Nondurable Plastics & Synthetic Materials	162.1	159.3	2.8	1.7
Paints & Allied Products	56.8	55.9	0.9	1.6
Rubber & Misc. Plastics Products	730.0	707.5	22.5	3.1
Leather Tanning & Finishing	20.5	20.2	0.4	1.8
Fabric Yarns & Thread Mills	452.6	447.3	5.3	1.2
Misc. Textile Goods	118.2	116.2	2.0	1.7
Apparel	1,295.2	1,265.2	30.1	2.3
Misc. Fabricated Textile Products	182.6	176.5	6.1	3.3
Paperboard Containers & Boxes	201.1	199.0	2.0	1.0
Transportation Motor Vehicle & Equipment	848.2	783.6	64.7	7.6
Aircraft & Parts	523.5	517.5	6.0	1.1
Services Wholesale & Retail Trade	16,693.6	16,447.6	246.0	1.5
Subtotal—Selected Industries	24,113.7	23,666.2	447.5	1.9
Other Industries	57,615.7	57,474.7	141.0	0.2
Total	81,729.4	81,140.9	588.5	0.7

[a]The selected industry groups are those with a greater than 1.0% change in employment.

Source: Gwenell L. Bass, *An Inter-Industry Analysis of the Sensitivity of Industrial Output and Employment to Changes in the Demand for Automobiles*, Report No. 83–40 E, Washington, D.C.: Congressional Research Service, Library of Congress, February 24, 1983, p. 6.

Table 5.4

Output Effects of a $10 Billion Reduction in Consumer Purchases of Automobiles, 1983[a] (millions of 1972 dollars)

Industry	Base	Cut	Decrease	Percentage Decrease
Agriculture, Forestry, & Fisheries				
Forestry & Fishery Products	3,167.2	3,130.6	36.6	1.2
Mining				
Iron Ore Mining	1,184.8	1,134.8	50.0	4.2
Nonferrous Metal Mining	2,080.2	2,045.4	34.8	1.7
Coal Mining	7,467.0	7,379.7	87.3	1.2
Stone Clay Mining & Quarrying	3,630.4	3,593.0	37.4	1.0
Chemical & Fertil-izer Mineral Mining	605.7	598.9	6.7	1.1
Manufacturing				
Durable				
Wood Containers	335.0	330.4	4.6	1.4
Glass & Glass Products	5,689.2	5,515.5	173.7	3.1
Primary & Fer-rous Metals	31,499.1	30,516.4	982.7	3.1
Nonferrous Metals	25,803.7	25,367.0	436.8	1.7
Screw Machine Products & Stampings	11,371.5	10,633.4	738.0	6.5
Other Fabricated Metal Products	19,540.2	19,074.5	465.8	2.4
Engines & Turbines	5,781.4	5,672.9	108.5	1.9
Misc. Nonelectri-cal Machinery	7,085.4	6,915.6	169.7	2.4
Electric Lighting & Wiring Equipment	5,319.6	5,221.1	98.5	1.9
Misc. Electrical Machinery & Equipment	4,782.7	4,468.5	314.1	6.6

Table 5.4 (*continued*)

Industry	Base	Cut	Decrease	Percentage Decrease
Nondurable				
Fabric, Yarn, Thread Mills	18,575.3	18,303.6	271.7	1.5
Misc. Textile Goods	6,251.6	6,115.7	135.9	2.2
Misc. Fabricated Textile Products	5,968.1	5,745.3	222.8	3.7
Paperboard Containers & Boxes	9,621.0	9,519.1	101.9	1.1
Chemicals & Products	32,270.1	31,839.1	431.0	1.3
Plastics & Synthetic Materials	14,268.0	13,984.1	283.9	2.0
Paints & Allied Products	3,602.0	3,538.6	63.5	1.8
Rubber & Misc. Plastics Products	27,657.1	26,748.3	908.8	3.3
Leather Tanning & Finishing	1,099.2	1,083.1	16.1	1.5
Transportation				
Motor Vehicles & Equipment	70,378.8	60,698.9	9,679.9	13.8
Transportation & Warehousing	88,489.9	87,497.9	992.0	1.1
Services				
Wholesale & Retail Trade	267,813.9	262,785.9	5,028.0	1.9
Auto Repair & Service	32,703.9	32,391.9	312.0	1.0
Subtotal—Selected Industries	714,045.7	691,852.9	22,192.8	3.1
Other Industries	1,780,940.9	1,774,693.2	6,247.7	0.3
Total	2,494,986.6	2,466,546.1	28,440.5	1.1

[a]The selected industry groups are those with a greater than 1.0% change in output.

Source: Bass, *An Inter-Industry Analysis of the Sensitivity of Industrial Output and Employment*, p. 7.

the simplifying assumption that a 10% reduction in imported automobiles coming into the United States has the effect of producing an increase in domestic production of automobiles of equal dollar value.[6] A 10% reduction in automobile imports amounts to approximately $1,560 million. Assuming a one-to-one correspondence between a change in domestic sales, production, and level of imports, in 1983 employment and output in the motor vehicles and equipment industry increases by 10%. Employment and output gains of 3.0 to 4.5% are experienced in the screw machine products and stampings and in the miscellaneous electrical machinery and equipment industries. Industries producing steel and textiles enjoy employment and output gains of at least 2%. Total employment increases by 137,000 persons within those industries that experience changes in excess of one % (Tables 5.5 and 5.6).

Oligopoly Industry

Whether viewed from a national or international market perspective, the motor vehicle industry is a strongly oligopolistic industry. Very few producers operate in each national market, and the aggregate number of viable independent motor vehicle firms globally totals fewer than 30. According to a recent United Nations study, concentration levels in producing countries are no lower than 56% for the top two firms, 68% for the top three, and 75% for the top four.[7] *The industry* reflects an increasing tendency toward international cartelization. This is evidenced by the increased links between companies located in different countries, taking the form of financial investments by U.S. companies in Japanese firms,[8] sharing of costs in the development of new models, and co-production agreements. A number of motor vehicle manufacturers now operate via an international web of joint production arrangements and other forms of cooperative financial, marketing, and production activities.

Increasingly, motor vehicle manufacturers are displaying multinational enterprise behavior. Trade in autos is determined primarily by production location decisions, and not by changes in consumer taste and income.[9]

In the motor vehicle industry employment and output levels exhibit wide swings over the business cycle, whereas prices remain relatively insulated from recessionary influences. As a result, there are high social costs in periods of recession.

Cost Behavior and Scale Economies

Scale economies are a crucial factor in the production of motor vehicles. There are substantial per-unit cost penalties in producing below *minimum efficient scale*. Estimates of minimum efficient scale published over the past seven years are summarized in Table 5.7.[10] They suggest that (1) any production activity of less than 200,000 units per year will be accompanied by substantial cost penalties and (2) optimal scale is higher for small cars than for large cars.

Based on the information contained in Table 5.7, foreign manufacturers are likely to achieve cost savings when annual production in the United States

Table 5.5
Employment Effects of a 10% Reduction in Imports of Automobiles, 1983 (thousands of persons)

Industry[a]	Base	Cut	Increase	Percentage Increase
Mining				
Iron Ore Mining	27.8	28.5	0.8	2.7
Nonferrous Metal Mining	55.1	55.6	0.5	1.0
Manufacturing				
Durable				
Glass & Glass Products	168.8	171.5	2.8	1.7
Primary Ferrous Metals	621.3	633.9	12.6	2.0
Screw Machine Products & Stampings	303.8	317.4	13.5	4.5
Other Fabricated Metal Products	607.0	615.1	8.1	1.3
Engines & Turbines	106.7	108.4	1.7	1.6
Misc. Nonelectrical Machinery	229.0	232.7	3.7	1.6
Misc. Electrical Machinery & Equipment	162.9	167.8	4.8	3.0
Nondurable				
Misc. Fabricated Textile Products	182.6	186.6	4.0	2.2
Transportation				
Motor Vehicles & Equipment	182.6	932.8	84.5	10.0
Subtotal—Selected Industries	3,258.1	3,394.7	136.6	4.2
Other Industries	78,471.3	78,585.7	114.4	0.1
Total	181,729.4	81,980.4	251.0	0.1

[a]The selected industry groups are those with a greater than 1.0% change in employment.
Source: Bass, *An Inter-Industry Analysis of the Sensitivity of Industrial Output and Employment*, p. 15.

Table 5.6
Output Effects of a 10% Reduction in Imports of Automobiles, for Selected Industries, 1983 (millions of 1972 dollars)

Industry[a]	Base	Cut	Increase	Percentage Increase
Mining				
Iron Ore Mining	1,184.8	1,217.0	32.1	2.7
Nonferrous Metal				
Mining	2,080.2	2,100.7	20.5	1.0
Manufacturing				
Durable				
Glass & Glass				
Products	5,689.2	5,783.4	94.2	1.7
Primary Ferrous				
Metals	31,499.1	32,136.4	637.4	2.0
Screw Machine				
Product				
Stampings	11,371.5	11,887.8	506.4	4.5
Other Fabricated				
Metal				
Products	19,540.2	19,800.4	260.2	1.3
Engines &				
Turbines	5,781.4	5,873.4	92.0	1.6
Misc. Nonelectri-				
cal Machinery	7,085.4	7,199.9	114.6	1.6
Misc. Electrical				
Machinery &				
Equipment	4,782.7	4,925.0	142.4	3.0
Nondurable				
Misc. Fabricated				
Textile				
Products	5,968.1	6,098.6	130.5	2.2
Transportation				
Motor Vehicles &				
Equipment	70,378.8	77,391.6	7,012.8	10.0
Subtotal—Selected				
Industries	165,361.4	174,404.2	9,042.8	5.5
Other Industries	2,329,625.2	2,333,182.8	3,557.6	0.2
Total	2,494,986.6	2,507,587.0	12,600.4	0.5

[a]The selected industry groups are those with a greater than 1.0% change in employment.
Source: Bass, *An Inter-Industry Analysis of the Sensitivity of Industrial Output and Employment*, p. 16.

Table 5.7
Minimum Efficient Scales of Production Estimated for the Motor Vehicle Industry (thousands of automobiles per year)

Production Activity	Toder Study				UN Transnational Center Study
	Mini	Compact	Intermediate	Standard Luxury	
Automotive Assembly	400	300	250	200	200–250
Body Unit-Panel Pressing (metal stamping)	400	300	250	200	1000–2000
Engine & Other Castings	400	400	350	250	100–1000
Frame (chassis)	200	200	200	206	—
Transmission	317	317	317	317	600
Axle Machining & Assembly					500
Painting					250

Sources: Eric J. Toder, *Trade Policy and the U.S. Automobile Industry* (New York: Praeger, 1978), p. 133; and United Nations, *Transnational Corporations in the International Auto Industry* (New York: 1983), p. 73.

approaches or exceeds 500,000 units. Tariffs would make U.S. production economical for at least three and possibly six foreign manufacturers.[11] Foreign producers would face the choice of paying a fixed tariff on home production or absorbing any production cost penalty that might occur if they produced in the United States. It is not altogether clear how a tariff would affect the relative shares of imports among foreign producers. This would depend on the behavior of each firm's production cost curve, the elasticity of demand for each manufacturer's autos, the comparative manufacturing costs at a given scale in different locations, and transport costs.

To retain a wide base of customer loyalty, motor vehicle producers need a range of models. Attempts to overrationalize to achieve larger production volumes and scale economies runs afoul of efforts to achieve marketing dominance. This problem is discussed in the next section, Product Differentiation.

Using data applicable for the mid–1970s, Toder estimated production costs for four different auto model styles, using eight distinct cost components. Based on information provided by a staff of researchers (who interviewed U.S. producers in connection with preparation of a Committee on Motor Vehicle Emissions Report), Toder adds a percentage markup for corporate costs to obtain an estimated sticker price. The results are summarized in Table 5.8. It should be noted that the corporate costs include general and administrative costs, research and development, marketing costs, and dealer markup. The markup varies by type of vehicle, in a purely arbitrary fashion. This is a basic shortcoming in working with *joint costs*. As we will note in subsequent discussions concerning production cost, pricing, and international competitiveness, joint costs (corporate costs) account for a substantial proportion of total costs in the motor vehicle industry (45% to 60%) depending on models produced. The existence of substantial joint costs leaves pricing in the motor vehicle industry subject to arbitrary oligopolist strategy and causes price discrimination with subsequent charges of unfair dump-

Table 5.8
Automobile Unit Production Costs at Optimal Scale

Cost	Type of Automobile			
	Mini	*Compact*	*Intermediate*	*Standard Luxury*
Overall Production Costs	$1,184	$1,660	$1,820	$3,195
Corporate costs	948	1,671	2,201	4,481
Markup (Percent) (Line 2 ÷ Line 1)	80.07	101.87	120.93	140.25
Sticker Price (Line 1 + Line 2)	2,132	3,331	4,021	7,676

Source: Toder, *Trade Policy and the U.S. Automobile Industry*, p. 132.

ing in foreign export markets. In addition, the existence of substantial joint costs raises the question of whether international comparative advantage can be reliably estimated, or in fact if one can with any degree of reasonableness infer that any country or group of countries enjoys a position of comparative advantage.

Product Differentiation

Motor vehicle manufacturers rely on a basic characteristic of imperfectly competitive markets, product differentiation. Various economic and non-economic considerations enter into their motives for this practice, including desire to reduce price elasticity of demand, develop brand loyalty, increase customer loyalty, and avoid cutthroat price competition. Product differentiation is antagonistic toward production and cost efficiency. In fact, American auto makers have reduced their competitiveness by a proliferation of model and style variations. A study by Booz, Allen & Hamilton Inc. asserts that the expansion of auto makers' model-style mixes has added over $1,000 in overhead to the cost of the average car. Added overhead costs narrow the range of potential customers. [12]

Foreign auto producers have prospered because of their ability to produce and sell highly differentiated products. The limited size of their market means that production costs will be high. According to Toder, "We do not expect, for example, that Mercedes-Benz sales in the United States will fall to zero if unit production costs in West Germany are higher than unit production costs in the United States." [13]

Few industries have gone as far as Detroit in their efforts to give the consumers exactly what they want. U.S. car dealers brag that customers can just about design their own sports car, subcompact, or family sedan. With the different combinations of engines, transmissions, and optional accessories, the 1984 Thunderbird comes in more than 69,000 varieties and a Chevrolet Citation over 32,000. Naturally, there is concern over the cost of this approach, especially when foreign competitors take the opposite approach and derive considerable cost advantages. For example, the Japanese car makers have relied on extensive consumer research to determine what types of features U.S. consumers prefer, and have designed their products aimed at broad market segments. The Honda sells only 32 varieties of its popular Accord, including color choices. Because this gives it greater economies of scale, Honda can afford to price below the competition. It can also use the cost savings to improve quality and model features.

Demand Elasticity and the Impact of a Tariff

Demand for motor vehicles is generally considered to be highly elastic to both price and income changes. In an industry subject to pressures of increased import competition and rising market share of foreign-produced autos, there will continue to be support for tariff and other forms of protection. Tariff protection carries important welfare implications. Policies (tariffs) that artificially raise the price of imported motor vehicles reduce net welfare by transferring income from buyers of foreign cars to domestic producers (assuming some inelasticity of domestic supply) and taxpayers (assuming a constant budget revenue amount is raised on each imported vehicle).

If we can assume that the U.S. domestic motor vehicle industry enjoys highly competitive and elastic supply conditions, any increase in the price of imported motor vehicles brought about by a tariff increase will have little effect on the price of domestic motor vehicles.[14] If the market is not competitive, a tariff may raise the price of imports, as well as the price of domestic production. Figure 5.2 depicts some of these relationships more clearly. Introduction of a tariff of $P_{f_0} P_{f_1}$ induces a deadweight loss of ABC,[15] and domestic consumers pay a higher price for imports. In this case we assume perfectly elastic domestic supply as well as perfectly elastic foreign supply. The deadweight loss is greater if the demand for foreign cars is more elastic. If the tariff reduces import quantity demanded to zero, the deadweight loss is greatest. Income transfer takes place with a tariff. In the figure, income transfer from consumers to taxpayers is equivalent to $P_{f_0} P_{f_1} CB$. The greater the elasticity of demand for imports the smaller the amount of income transfer.

Of critical importance to government policies concerning a rising import share of the market is the elasticity of import share: that is, the influence on import share from changes in the ratio of import prices to domestic prices. We examine this relationship in the following section. Toder estimates an elasticity of import share that is quite high and is related to the specific model of U.S. auto involved. Higher elasticities accrue to domestic auto models that are closer substitutes to imports (subcompacts).[16] The relatively high elasticities suggest very strongly that increased import competition can lower domestic motor vehicle prices. In effect, the price elasticities of demand, elasticity of import share, and change in import share relative to change in import price all are mutually interacting variables. A simplified model of these relationships is presented in the following section. As will be observed, induced domestic auto price changes make import share changes smaller.

Figure 5.2
Effect from a Tariff on Imported Autos

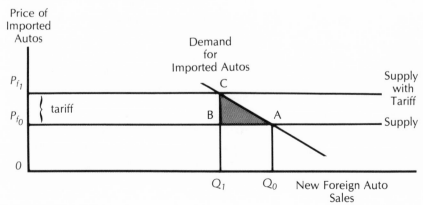

FOREIGN TRADE

Over the period 1974–1984 the motor vehicle industry in the United States has become heavily influenced by foreign trade. Since 1974 demand for motor vehicles has become conditioned by the petroleum crisis and increased concern for fuel efficiency, an inflationary spiral that has made owners of motor vehicles more concerned with cost and operating efficiencies, and an apparent shift in international competitiveness.

Perhaps the most dramatic change in the 1974–1984 decade has been the upward surge in import penetration. The share of imports of automobiles in total sales increased from 5.7% in 1965, to 24.3% in 1970, to 25.4% in 1975, to 35.0% in 1980, and to 38.5% in 1982 (Table 5.9). The growth in imports and the upward shift in import share of the automobile market have been accompanied by fears of deindustrialization,[17] complaints of unfair competition,[18] and proposals for federal legislation requiring minimum percentages of domestic content.[19] More importantly a repercussion effect appears to be developing in the form of investment in U.S.-based production facilities by several foreign motor vehicle manufacturers.

Table 5.9
New Passenger Automobiles, U.S. Factory Sales, Imports for Consumption, Exports of Domestic Merchandise, and Apparent Consumption, 1947–1982

Year	U.S. Factory Sales	U.S. Imports	U.S. Exports	Apparent U.S. Consumption	Ratio of Imports to Apparent Consumption (percent)
1947	3,558,178	1,453	266,795	3,292,836	0.04
1950	6,665,863	21,287	120,285	6,566,865	0.32
1955	7,920,186	57,115	211,614	7,765,687	0.74
1960	6,674,796	444,622	117,126	7,002,292	6.35
1965	9,305,561	563,673	106,079	9,763,155	5.77
1970	6,546,817	2,013,420	285,302	8,274,935	24.33
1975	6,712,852	2,074,653	642,028	8,145,477	25.47
1980	6,399,840	3,116,448	612,723	8,903,565	35.0
1981	6,255,340	2,856,286	545,164	8,566,462	33.3
1982	5,049,184	2,926,407	376,524	7,599,067	38.5

Source: U.S. International Trade Commission, The U.S. Auto Industry: U.S. Factory Sales, Retail Sales, Imports, Exports, Apparent Consumption, Suggested Retail Prices, and Trade Balances With Selected Countries for Motor Vehicles, 1964–82, USITC Publication 1419, August 1983, p. 2.

The discussion that follows considers the potential impact of a ten % tariff on motor vehicle imports into the United States. This analysis is necessary to set the stage for a discussion later in this chapter concerning the welfare effects of foreign trade in motor vehicles and barriers to that trade. The proposed domestic content legislation is considered in the next chapter. Some of the statistical measures in this chapter and related welfare effects will be useful in our subsequent evaluation of the domestic content proposal.

Tariffs and Domestic Demand

The United States is probably the most open market in the world insofar as trade in motor vehicles is concerned. International comparisons of tariff and non-tariff barriers to trade in motor vehicles are made in a later chapter, where we compare trade, investment, and industrial policy alternatives in dealing with the auto import problem facing the United States. The analysis that follows is restricted to automobiles, for many complexities would exist in attempting to deal with diverse motor vehicles products (autos, trucks, vans) that display different demand elasticities and market share characteristics.

An increase in the tariff raises the cost of imported automobiles sold in the United States. Tariffs affect the relative prices of domestic and imported automobiles, through various mechanisms and response effects. For example, the extent to which the ratio of import price to domestic price will increase depends on the response of domestic producers (oligopolistic response coupled with supply elasticity), on the ability of foreign manufacturers to absorb higher costs without increasing prices (depending on their ability to price discriminate), and on exchange rate effects. The imposition of a ten % tariff by the United States on imported automobiles would be expected to have the following general effects: (1) to increase the domestic automobile share of the market; (2) to increase the price (absolute and relative) of imported automobiles; and (3) to provide greater incentives for domestic production of automobiles by foreign producers.

The preceding discussion has avoided consideration of the welfare implications of an increased tariff duty. Trade policies that raise the price of imported automobiles reduce welfare by diverting some buyers to commodities considered less valuable, and by forcing other buyers to pay higher prices for imported automobiles. If the market for automobiles is highly competitive, an increase in the price of imported automobiles caused by a tariff may not affect the price of domestic autos. On the other hand, if the market is not competitive, a tariff will raise the price of imports and also lead to an increase in domestic automobile prices.

Focusing on the U.S. market for imported automobiles, we can express the demand relationships in the generalized format:

$$D_f = f(P_f, P_d) \qquad (4.1)$$

Similarly, the demand for domestically produced automobiles will take the format:

$$D_d = f(P_d, P_f) \tag{4.2}$$

Figure 5.3 reproduces the demand for foreign automobiles from Equation 4.1 at various levels of P_f with P_d held fixed. Underlying the slope of the demand curve for foreign automobiles is the elasticity of import share and substitutability of demand between foreign and domestic automobiles. In Figure 5.3, Q_{f_1} and P_{f_1} represent the quantity sold and the selling price before the tariff increase. Q_{f_2} and P_{f_2} represent the quantity sold and the selling price after the tariff increase. The tariff-induced price change is $P_{f_1} - P_{f_2}$. The shaded area *LMN* represents the tariff deadweight loss. This loss will be greater with a flatter (higher elasticity) demand. The deadweight loss is greatest if the tariff reduces U.S. imports to zero. The tariff also produces an income transfer or redistribution in the form

Figure 5.3
Welfare Effects from Tariff on Imported Autos

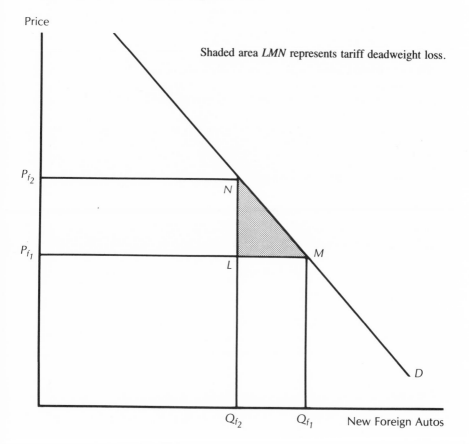

of tariff revenues paid to the U.S. government. The area $P_{f_1}P_{f_2}NL$ measures the income transfer from U.S. purchasers of foreign cars to U.S. taxpayers.

The deadweight loss will be greater if the elasticity of import share is high. Where domestic car price is a function of foreign car price, measurement of welfare loss is more complicated.[20] Where there is high substitutability between imports and domestically produced cars, the availability of foreign cars constrains domestic auto prices.

Our objective in the following and final section of this chapter is to estimate the potential welfare effects from imposition of a tariff on automobile imports. For this reason we now estimate the effects on market share from a ten % import tariff on autos. Our analysis is as follows:

1. Elasticity of import share calculations provide us with an initial effect change in market share between domestic and imported automobiles. The elasticity of import share calculation is as follows, with an assumed ten% tariff and full (ten %) increase in price of imports:

$$^{\mathcal{E}}ms = \text{Percent change in} \atop \text{import share} \quad \div \quad \text{Percent change in} \atop \text{price ratio of imports to} \atop \text{domestic autos}$$

Given an elasticity of import share of 5.0, a ten % price increase of imports will reduce the ratio of imports to domestic autos by 50%. Consequently, with an assumed initial market share of 2.5 million imports and 7.5 million domestic, or an initial ratio of 0.333, the ratio would shift to 0.167, and the market share would be 1.43 million imports and 8.57 million domestic autos. The related elasticities and ratios of imports to domestic autos are summarized in Table 5.10 below.

2. Given a change in market share, domestic producers enjoy a market share anywhere from 7.54 million units to 8.75 million automobiles (Table 5.11). Domestic producers will increase prices based on an upward sloping supply curve and/or oligopolistic tendencies in pricing their product. In our analysis we assume a supply elasticity for the domestic industry of 0.5. That is, for every one % increase in quantity produced there will be a related one-half % increase in supply price. Therefore, given an elasticity of import share of 2.0 and domestic share of the market at 7.88 million units, the supply price of domestic producers rises from $8,000 to $8,200.

3. Given the fact that an elasticity of supply of 0.5 results in raising supply prices of domestic producers by anywhere from no change to $560 (Table 5.11), we can recompute market share based on alternative elasticities of substitution. We use the elasticity of substitution relationship below:

$$\text{Elasticity of} \atop \text{substitution} = \frac{\text{Percent change in } Q \text{ of imports}}{\text{Percent change in } P \text{ of domestic}}$$

Table 5.10
Elasticity of Import Share and Related Ratio of Imports to Domestic Autos

Price Increase of Ten %		Price Increase of Five %	
Elasticity of Import Share	*Ratio of Imports to Domestic*	*Elasticity of Import Share*	*Ratio of Imports to Domestic*
5.0	0.167	5.0	0.250
2.0	0.267	2.0	0.300
1.0	0.300	1.0	0.316
0.5	0.316	0.5	0.325

Given an elasticity of import share of 5.0 and a market share of 8.75 million units, supply price rises to $8,560, or seven %; with an elasticity of substitution of 2.0, imports recapture 200,000 units of the market at the expense of domestic producers.

Several observations are in order concerning the analysis summarized in Table 5.11. Two alternate assumptions made concerning prices of imported autos are that the full effect of the tariff is realized in a ten % higher price of imported autos. The second is that the price of auto imports increases by only half of the tariff (five %). In addition, elasticity of import share exerts considerable leverage on market share with a ten % tariff. The range of effects is from an increase of market share for domestic producers of as little as 40,000 units (five % price increase and low elasticity of import share), to an increase of 1,020,000 (ten % price increase and high elasticity of import share). Furthermore, elasticity of substitution influences the extent to which the price increase of domestic autos exercises a ''reversal influence'' on domestic market share. A high elasticity of substitution brings about a larger reversal or loss of domestic market share. These reversals range in amount from as little as no change in units to as much as 200,000 units. Finally, we have made an effort to use a range of elasticity values that is relevant to the real world. They are in line with other statistical and econometric analyses of auto market demand and import share. The final quantity shares of the market enjoyed by domestic producers range from as high as 8.52 million units to as low as 7.54 million units. A reasonable estimate would be somewhere closer to the midpoint, or slightly in excess of 8.0 million units. In effect, a ten % tariff increase would expand the market share of domestic producers from an estimated 7.5 million units to 8.0 million units annually.

WELFARE IMPLICATIONS

Shift in Equilibrium and Market Share

We are now ready to make use of the market share and elasticity estimates in the preceding discussion to develop a measure of the potential welfare effects

Table 5.11
Market Share Effects from Import Tariff," Assuming Different Elasticities of Import Share, Elasticity of Substitution, and Price Effects in U.S. Automobile Market (Price of Imported Autos Increases Ten % [$8,800])

	Revised Quantity	Revised Expenditure	Elasticity of Substitution 0.5		Elasticity of Substitution 1.0		Elasticity of Substitution 2.0	
			Final Quantity	Final Expenditure	Final Quantity	Final Expenditure	Final Quantity	Final Expenditure
Elast. of Import Share 5.0								
Domestic	8.57	73,359	8.520	72,931	8.470	72,503	8.370	71,647
Imports	1.43	12,584	1.480	13,024	1.530	13,464	1.630	14,344
Total	10.00	85,943	10.000	85,955	10.000	85,967	10.000	85,991
Elast. of Import Share 2.0								
Domestic	7.88	64,616	7.853	64,398	7.827	64,181	7.774	63,746
Imports	2.12	18,656	2.146	18,889	2.173	19,122	2.226	19,677
Total	10.00	83,272	10.000	83,287	10.000	83,303	10.000	83,423
Elast. of Import Share 1.0								
Domestic	7.70	62,216	7.688	62,123	7.677	62,030	7.654	61,844
Imports	2.30	20,240	2.311	20,341	2.323	20,442	2.346	20,645
Total	10.00	82,456	10.000	82,464	10.000	82,472	10.000	82,489
Elast. of Import Share 0.5								
Domestic	7.59	61,024	7.584	60,983	7.577	60,927	7.565	60,830
Imports	2.41	21,209	2.416	21,258	2.422	21,319	2.434	21,420
Total	10.00	82,233	10.000	82,241	10.000	82,246	10.000	82,250

Price of Imported Autos Increases 5% ($8,400)

Elast. of Import Share 5.0								
Domestic	8.00	65,920	7.970	65,673	7.940	65,425	7.880	64,931
Imports	2.00	16,800	2.030	17,052	2.060	17,304	2.120	17,808
Total	10.00	82,720	10.000	82,725	10.000	82,729	10.000	82,739
Elast. of Import Share 2.0								
Domestic	7.70	62,216	7.688	62,123	7.677	62,030	7.654	61,844
Imports	2.30	19,320	2.311	19,416	2.323	19,513	2.346	19,706
Total	10.00	81,536	10.000	81,539	10.000	81,543	10.000	81,550
Elast. of Import Share 1.0								
Domestic	7.59	61,024	7.584	60,983	7.577	60,927	7.565	60,830
Imports	2.41	20,245	2.416	20,290	2.422	20,348	2.434	20,448
Total	10.00	81,269	10.000	81,273	10.000	81,275	10.000	81,278
Elast. of Import Share 0.5								
Domestic	7.54	60,320	7.54	60,320	no change	no change	no change	no change
Imports	2.46	20,664	2.46	20,664	no change	no change	no change	no change
Total	10.00	80,984	10.00	80,784	no change	no change	no change	no change

^aFigures may not add up due to rounding.

Note: Model starts out with total sales volume of 10 million units, and continues with that volume after the tariff is imposed. The initial price per auto is $8,000.

143

from a tariff increase. Welfare effects are measured from the standpoint of the effects on each of the two submarkets (Figure 5.4). Our analysis is based on a four-step series of market influences:

1. An original equilibrium exists with domestic producers selling 7.5 million units and foreign imports taking 2.5 million units.

2. A ten % import tariff is levied, which raises the price of imported autos to $8,800. In Figure 5.4a we move from equilibrium point 1 to point 2. In Figure 5.4b we move from equilibrium point 4 to point 5. The demand for domestic autos shifts from D_1 to D_2 as a result of the increased price of foreign imports.

3. The increased production of domestic autos forces supply price to increase along the moderately upward sloping supply curve SS. As a result, the new equilibrium position in the domestic auto submarket is at point 6.

4. With an increase in supply price of domestic autos to $8,200, the demand for foreign autos shifts to D_{f_2}. A new equilibrium in this submarket, at point 3. At this point foreign imports are at 2.173 million units and domestic autos 7.827 million units.

Welfare Loss on Import Submarket

In this section we summarize welfare loss effects as the tariff increase compresses the share of foreign imports. The deadweight loss is measured in Figure 5.4a as follows: It is the area below the D_0 curve and above the original price level, and between the original and final quantities. On the diagram this is one-half the length IX multiplied by the price increase ($8,800–8,000). Calculations of total deadweight loss and loss per car are summarized in Table 5.12. In the worst case, the total deadweight loss is $408 million, or $40.80 per car sold in the United States. At an $8,000 price level, this represents a burden on the consumer of one-half of one %.

The annual loss to consumers of U.S. domestic automobiles resulting from price increases is far more significant than deadweight losses related to imports. In the worst case the price impact is $560 on domestic autos, aggregating $4.77 billion (Table 5.13). This would take effect if the highest elasticity of import share and a full ten % price increase of imports take place. This might not be the most realistic possibility. A midrange estimate might be a price increase on domestic automobiles of $200 to $240, with an aggregate welfare burden of $1.5 to 2.6 billion per year.

With regard to imported automobiles, there is a second welfare impact, namely, the transfer (redistribution) from auto purchasers to U.S. taxpayers of the amount of tariff revenues. In the case illustrated in Figure 5.4, an import quantity of 2.173 million and tariff revenue of $800 per unit yield, a redistribution of $1.738 billion (Table 5.14). The potential tariff redistribution effect ranges between $812 million and $1.947 million, with a probable midpoint value of $1.1 billion. The potential transfer effects reflected in Table 5.14 are considerably larger than the related deadweight loss. The ratio of transfer loss to deadweight loss ranges

Figure 5.4
U.S. Market for Automobiles

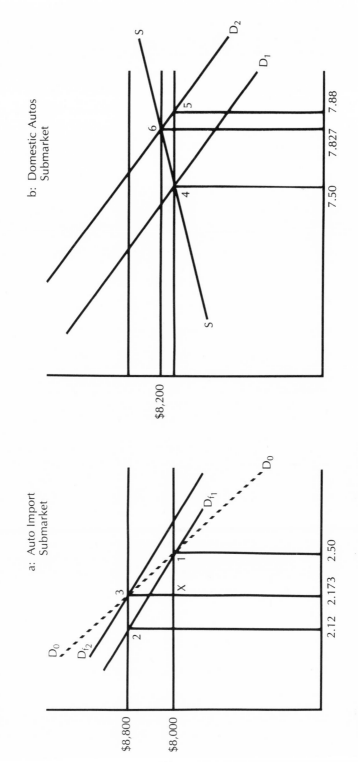

Elasticity of import share = 2.0; elasticity of substitution = 1.0.
Source: Data from Tables 5.9 and 5.10.

Table 5.12
Annual Product Market Welfare Loss (Deadweight Loss) from 10% and 5%
Import Price Increase with Alternative Elasticity of Import Share and Elasticity
of Substitution Values

Elasticity of Import Share Elasticity of Substitution	Annual Product Market Welfare Loss (Deadweight Loss) (in mil. dollars)	Loss Per Car (in dollars)
10% Import Price Increase		
5.0		
0.5	$408	$40.80
1.0	388	38.80
2.0	348	34.80
2.0		
0.5	141	14.14
1.0	130	13.08
2.0	109	10.96
1.0		
0.5	75	7.54
1.0	70	7.08
2.0	61	6.16
0.5		
0.5	33	3.36
1.0	31	3.12
2.0	26	2.64
5% Import Price Increase		
5.0		
0.5	94	9.40
1.0	88	8.80
2.0	76	7.60
2.0		
0.5	37	3.78
1.0	35	3.54
2.0	30	3.08
1.0		
0.5	16	1.68
1.0	15	1.56
2.0	13	1.32
0.5		
0.5	8	0.80
1.0	8	0.80
2.0	8	0.80

Source: Calculations derived from Table 5.11, based on areas outlined in Figure 5.3 and Figure 5.4.

Table 5.13
Annual Loss to Consumers of U.S. Domestic Automobiles from Price Increase of 10% and 5% of Imported Automobiles

Elasticity of Import Share / Elasticity of Substitution	Change in Domestic Price (in dollars)	Change in Welfare Domestic Auto Buyers (thousands of dollars)
10% Import Price Increase		
5.0		
0.5	$560	$4,771,200
1.0	560	4,743,200
2.0	560	4,687,200
2.0		
0.5	200	1,570,600
1.0	200	1,565,400
2.0	200	1,554,800
1.0		
0.5	80	615,040
1.0	80	614,160
2.0	80	612,320
0.5		
0.5	40	303,360
1.0	40	303,120
2.0	40	302,640
5% Import Price Increase		
5.0		
0.5	240	1,912,800
1.0	240	1,905,600
2.0	240	1,891,200
2.0		
0.5	80	615,040
1.0	80	614,160
2.0	80	612,320
1.0		
0.5	40	303,360
1.0	40	303,120
2.0	40	302,640
0.5		
0.5	nil	nil
1.0	nil	nil
2.0	nil	nil

Source: Calculations derived from Table 5.11, based on areas outlined in Figure 5.3 and Figure 5.4.

Table 5.14
Comparison of Annual Losses to Consumers of Domestic and Imported Automobiles from 10% and 5% Import Price Increase (thousands of dollars)

Elasticity of Import Share — Elasticity of Substitution	Consumer Loss from Domestic Auto Price Change (1)	Loss From Import Price Change		
		Total Consumer Loss (2) = 3 + 4	Deadweight Loss (3)	Transfer to Taxpayers from Tariff (4)
10% Import Price Increase				
5.0				
0.5	4,771,200	1,592,000	408,000	1,184,000
1.0	4,743,200	1,612,000	388,000	1,224,000
2.0	4,687,200	1,652,000	348,000	1,304,000
2.0				
0.5	1,570,600	1,858,200	141,400	1,716,800
1.0	1,565,400	1,869,200	130,800	1,738,400
2.0	1,554,800	1,890,400	109,600	1,780,800
1.0				
0.5	615,040	1,924,200	75,400	1,848,800
1.0	614,160	1,929,200	70,800	1,858,400
2.0	612,320	1,938,400	61,600	1,876,800
0.5				
0.5	303,360	1,966,400	33,600	1,932,800
1.0	303,120	1,968,800	31,200	1,937,600
2.0	302,640	1,973,600	26,400	1,947,200
5% Import Price Increase				
5.0				
0.5	1,912,800	906.000	94,000	812,000
1.0	1,905,600	912,000	88,000	824,000
2.0	1,891,200	924,000	76,000	848,000
2.0				
0.5	615,040	962,200	37,800	924,400
1.0	614,160	964,600	35,400	929,200
2.0	612,320	969,200	30,800	938,400
1.0				
0.5	303,360	983,200	16,800	966,400
1.0	303,120	984,400	15,600	968,800
2.0	302,640	986,800	13,200	973,600
0.5				
0.5	nil	992,000	8,000	984,000
1.0	nil	992,000	8,000	984,000
2.0	nil	992,000	8,000	984,000

Source: Calculations derived from Table 5.11, based on areas outlined in Figure 5.3 and Figure 5.4.

between 100–1 and 3–1. This reflects the competitive nature of deadweight loss as compared with transfer loss. The larger the deadweight loss, the smaller the amount of transfer loss. In no case does the total of deadweight loss and transfer loss have a value as large as $2.0 billion. A probable midpoint combined value of the two might be around $1.3 billion.

The welfare effects from imposition of a ten % tariff on foreign-produced automobiles may be summarized as follows:

1. The probable range of welfare loss on the import side of the market would be $0.9 billion to $2.0 billion (deadweight loss plus transfer loss) with a midpoint value of $1.3 billion.
2. The probable range of welfare effects on the domestic automobile side of the market would be from almost a zero cost to as high as $4.7 billion, with a midpoint value of $1.7 billion.
3. The combined welfare costs from a ten % import duty would have a midpoint value of approximately $3.0 billion. This represents approximately 3.6% of the estimated $83 billion of expenditures on automobiles (Table 5.11) and translates into a $300 average increase in the price of automobiles purchased in the United States.

Welfare Implications of Labor Market Adjustment Costs

This section presents estimates of the potential increase in value of production in the domestic automobiles sector resulting from imposition of a ten % tariff. A tariff increase will lead to increased domestic production and employment of additional workers. Several sources of data reflecting job loss (unemployment) in the domestic auto industry are used to arrive at an estimated 260,000 job losses.[21] Next a simulation analysis is used, based on various alternative distributions of unemployed auto workers, including the categories and assumptions concerning wage levels found in Figure 5.5.

Three alternate scenarios for providing employment for auto workers may be constructed:

Scenario 1: Best Case. Very favorable business conditions. Ninety % of unemployed auto workers find suitable jobs or are reemployed by auto producers. There are minor transition problems and low adjustment costs. There is only small gain from tariff-induced automobile production because workers are nearly fully employed.

Scenario 2: Moderate Case. Moderate to favorable economic environment. Seventy % of unemployed auto workers find suitable jobs or are reemployed by auto producers. There are moderate transition problems and moderate adjustment costs. There is moderate gain from tariff-induced automobile production.

Scenario 3: Worst Case. Sluggish economic environment. Fifty % of unemployed auto workers find suitable jobs or are reemployed by auto producers. There are substantial transition problems and high adjustment costs. There is considerable gain from tariff-induced automobile production.

Figure 5.5

Three Scenarios under Which Tariff on Auto Imports Provides Additional Employment for Auto Workers

I. *Best Case:* Strong Domestic Economy, with 90% of unemployed auto workers (260,000) reemployed or finding jobs elsewhere.

No Import Tariff	10% Import Tariff
234,000 find jobs	
117,000 reemployed in autos	58,000 return to auto industry
117,000 employed in other	(with $749,070,000 wages)
industry (65% earnings)	
26,000 leave auto industry	
10,000 drop out of labor market	10,000 return ($369 million wages)
16,000 take marginal jobs	4,860 return ($107,600,400 wages)
(40% earnings level)	Wages gain—$1,225,670,400

II. *Moderate Case:* Semi-strong Domestic Economy, with 70% of unemployed auto workers reemployed or finding jobs elsewhere.

No Import Tariff	10% Import Tariff
182,000 find jobs	
91,000 reemployed in autos	
91,000 employed in other industry	45,000 return to auto industry
(65% earnings)	with $581,375,000 wages)
78,000 leave auto industry	
13,000 relocate	
13,000 never work again	
17,000 drop out of labor	17,000 return ($627.3 million wages)
market temporarily	
35,000 take marginal jobs	10,860 return ($240,440,400 wages)
(40% earnings level)	
	Wages gain—$1,449,115,400

III. *Worst Case:* Weak Domestic Economy, with 50% of unemployed auto workers reemployed or finding jobs elsewhere.

No Import Tariff	10% Import Tariff
130,000 find jobs	
65,000 reemployed in autos	
65,000 employed in other	32,500 return to auto industry
industry (65% earnings)	(with $419,737,500 wages)
130,000 leave auto industry	
26,000 relocate (50% earnings)	
26,000 never work again	
26,000 drop out of labor	26,000 return ($959.4 million wages)
market temporarily	
52,000 take marginal jobs	14,360 return ($317,930,400 wages)
(40% earnings level)	
	Wages gain—$1,697,067,900

Note: The number of workers who return to the auto industry is 72,860, based on producing 14 vehicles per worker per year, and an increase in production after tariff of 1,020,000 domestic autos. The wages gain is incremental, based on differential between other employment and auto industry employment.

Figure 5.5 summarizes the employment and wages effects under the assumption that the maximum possible increase in domestic production indicated in Table 5.11 takes place, namely, 1,020,000 units. Based on a worker productivity of 14 vehicles per worker per year, an increase in domestic auto production of 1.02 million units will generate additional employment of 72,860 workers.[22] The annual salary of the auto worker is estimated at $36,900.[23] Working with simulations wherein the additional employment is spread across various strata of reemployable workers, and utilizing marginal gains in income per worker, we find that incremental wages generated in auto production range between $1.225 billion and $1.697 billion. A midpoint probable wage increment of $1.5 billion appears to be a reasonable estimate.

It must be concluded that the positive welfare effects in the form of reemployment of workers in automobile production are half as large as the accumulation of welfare costs from imposition of a ten % tariff. This comparison does not consider multiplier effects on U.S. domestic employment, which could be in the range of 2.5 to 2.8 relative to the direct employment effect in auto production. In addition, this does not consider the potential positive effects on the market for capital goods. The abandonment, closing, or temporary mothballing of automobile and parts plants represents an underutilization of capital goods and loss of productivity of high material value.

NOTES

1. Gwenell L. Bass, *An Inter-Industry Analysis of the Sensitivity of Industrial Output and Employment to Changes in the Demand for Automobiles* (Washington, D.C.: Congressional Research Service, Library of Congress, February 4, 1983), p. 3.

2. U.S. Congress, Senate, *Issues Relating to the Domestic Auto Industry*, Hearings Before the Subcommittee on International Trade of the Committee of Finance, 96th Cong., 1st Sess., January 14–15, 1981, part 1, p. 5.

3. Prepared statement by James E. Harbour, manufacturing management consultant, Berkeley, California, as printed in U.S. Congress, House of Representatives, *To Determine the Impact of Foreign Sourcing on Industry and Communities*, Hearings Before the Subcommittee on Economic Stabilization, Committee on Banking, Finance, and Urban Affairs, 97th Cong. 1st Sess., April 24, 1981, Serial No. 97–12, 1981, pp. 12–13.

4. Ibid., pp. 14–15.

5. Bass, *An Inter-Industry Analysis of the Sensitivity of Industrial Output and Employment*, pp. 7–13.

6. This is a tenuous assumption. It implies that the domestic car is a perfect substitute for the imported automobile. It also implies that no imported parts and components are used in the production of the domestic automobile.

7. United Nations, *Transnational Corporations in the International Auto Industry* (New York: 1983), pp. 70–71.

8. This pattern was followed by the U.S. electronics companies in responding to Japanese competition in the television and VCR product lines. See Jack Baranson, *The*

Japanese Challenge to U.S. Industry (Lexington, Mass.: Lexington Books, 1981), p. 102.

9. Eric J. Toder, *Trade Policy and the U.S. Automobile Industry* (New York: Praeger, 1978), p. 29.

10. Minimum efficient scale is a very specific term in the nomenclature utilized by industrial economists. That is, according to Pratten's definition, "the minimum scale above which any possible subsequent doubling in scale would reduce total average unit costs by less than 5%." D. B. Rhys, "European Mass-Producing Car Makers and Minimum Efficient Scale," *Journal of Industrial Economics* 25 (June 1977): 315.

11. These include Toyota, Nissan, Volkswagen, Renault, Honda, and Volvo.

12. John Koten, "Giving Buyers Wide Choices May Be Hurting Auto Makers," *Wall Street Journal*, December 15, 1983, p. 33.

13. Toder, *Trade Policy and the U.S. Automobile Industry*, p. 144.

14. This is based on the assumption of competitive pricing based on marginal cost. To the extent that oligopolist pricing prevails, this assumption must be relaxed.

15. A deadweight loss is the loss to motor vehicle purchasers from higher prices, not offset by a rise in income to sellers or taxpayers. In economic parlance, it is the loss in consumer surplus from a cutback in the quantity consumed.

16. Toder, *Trade Policy and the U.S. Automobile Industry*, p. 80. Here Toder takes as his measure of elasticity the ratio of dLog (Sale) to dLog (Price) where (Sale) is the ratio of import to domestic new car sales and (Price) is the ratio of imported to domestic new car prices.

17. Leon Taub, "The De-Industrialization of the United States," in U.S. Congress House of Representatives, *Status of the Economy* Hearings, Subcommittee on Economic Stabilization, Committee on Banking, Finance and Urban Affairs, 98th Cong. 1st Sess., May 26, 1983, Serial No. 98–28, pp. 44–63.

18. The International Trade Commission instituted an investigation on June 30, 1980, upon petition for import relief by the International Union, United Automobile, Aerospace, and Agricultural Implement Workers of America (AUW). The investigation was instituted pursuant to section 201(b) 91 of the Trade Act of 1974 (U.S.C. 2251(b) 91) to determine whether motor vehicle products are being imported into the United States in such increased quantities as to be a substantial threat to cause serious injury. The UAW has repeatedly made vocal claim of unfair competitive practices. U.S. International Trade Commission, *Motor Vehicles and Certain Chassis and Bodies Therefor*, USITC Publication 1110, December 1980. A counterview regarding unfair competition can be found in Baranson, *The Japanese Challenge to U.S. Industry*, pp. 14–17, describing government-industry relations. Baranson notes: "Government industry relations in Japan have contributed immeasurably to the degree of cooperation and consultation among government, industry, and the banking community and this helps to define common objectives of particular sectors." (p.14).

19. The domestic content legislative proposals were initiated in Congress in 1983. See U.S. Congress of House of Representatives, *Fair Practices and Procedures in Automotive Products Act of 1983* (H.R. 1234), Report 98–287, Part 1, June 30, 1983.

20. For a detailed discussion of the interrelation between elasticities and welfare effects, the reader should refer to Toder, *Trade Policy and the U.S. Automobile Industry*, pp. 38–42.

21. Organization of Economic Co-operation and Development (OECD) (Paris: 1983),

pp. 24–25. See also U.S. Department of Commerce, *1983 Industrial Outlook*, pp. 30–31.

22. This is based on data published in U.S. International Trade Commission, *Motor Vehicles*, p. A–38.

23. This is based on dividing wages paid to production workers by number of workers for 1979–1980 and estimating salary earnings increments between 1980 and 1984 of $5,400 (yearly) rate. Source: USITC *Motor Vehicles*, pp. A–38 and A–39.

6

Domestic Content and Alternative Policies for Automobiles

From 1981 to 1985 the U.S. auto market operated under conditions of a voluntary export restraint (VER) applied by Japan and allocated to specific Japanese producers by the Ministry of International Trade and Industry (MITI). Shortly before the voluntary quota expired in April 1985, the United States announced it would not ask the Japanese to renew the quota limit (1.85 million units) for another 12-month period. Before the end of that month, the Japanese authorities indicated their plan to allow Japanese producers to expand annual motor vehicle exports to the United States by 24.3% (approximately 2.3 million units).

Early in 1985 the United States had three basic policy alternatives with respect to auto imports. First, it could ask that the voluntary quota be continued, preserving the status quo in market share. Second, it could take the liberal approach it did pursue, namely, allow the voluntary quota to lapse. Third, it could take a more restrictive approach, which would have involved either a surcharge on auto imports, a sharp reduction in the voluntary quota, or enactment of a version of the proposed domestic content legislation. In this chapter we consider several of these alternatives.

By opting for a more liberal course, the United States was hoping to achieve the impossible—a free, competitive market in automobiles. In effect, the action taken by the United States will accelerate income shift effects as well as other adverse effects. Income shift effects follow from the changing locus of world manufacturing activity. The growing concentration of auto and other manufacturing production in Japan has tended to shift a large share of world income to that country. The willingness of the United States to allow the voluntary quota on autos to elapse will accelerate this income shift.

WELFARE IMPLICATIONS OF ALTERNATIVE POLICIES

Important economic welfare effects follow from each of the three alternative policy directions that the United States can take with respect to auto imports. By identifying the welfare effects that stem from the policy alternatives and by estimating the possible magnitudes of their effects, we indicate which we consider to be second best, third best, or inferior approaches.

We compare the economic welfare effects from (1) a restrictive policy, (2) a moderate policy (renew VER), and a (3) liberal policy (remove VER). The projected auto market shares in the United States in 1990 under these alternatives are presented in Table 6.1. The table notes outline some of the assumptions and approaches used in making these estimates. Based on the market share estimates, we make economic welfare evaluations. The principal factors that determine the welfare evaluations (shown in Table 6.2) focus on effects from changes in import share, in U.S. production by foreign firms, and in output by domestic producers.

Economic welfare costs to the United States are projected as greatest in the case of the original domestic content proposal and in the case of removing the VER. In each case we consider these to be fourth best alternatives (as compared to free trade—which is first best). In the case of the domestic content proposal, this relates to substantial import cutbacks that would take place if this legislation were enacted, inability of foreign firms to maintain U.S. production, and related surge increase in demand for domestic autos (Table 6.2). The effects from the original domestic content proposal are discussed in detail later in this chapter. In the case of removing the VER, this relates to the resulting large increase in auto imports, negative incentive for U.S. production by foreign firms, and large costs to the U.S. economy in the form of income shifts to other countries (auto exporters) and the difficulties faced by marginal firms in the United States.

The 1985 quota allocations to Japanese auto producers issued by MITI in April 1985 are indicated in Table 6.3. These allow for a 24.3 % increase in exports to the United States, a number that confirms our earlier expectations that removal of VER would represent a fourth best policy approach.

Table 6.4 specifies in slightly more detail the nature of the economic welfare costs for each of the five policy approaches. For example, in the case of the original domestic content proposal, these are redistributional (to U.S.) firms, price level (increases), deadweight loss, and negative employment effects (inability of foreign frims to expand U.S. production).

Of the five alternatives described in these tables, the revised domestic content proposal is preferred. The more moderate position taken in this content proposal provides a balanced effect in terms of market share. It also avoids the extreme economic welfare costs associated with the remaining four alternatives, such as international income shifts and undesirable employment effects in the United States.

From the point of view of the economic welfare costs the least desirable alternative is removal of VER (a step actually taken by the Reagan Administration in April 1985). Economic welfare costs resulting from this approach include substantial income shifts from the United States to Japan (in the order of $33.35 billion per year by 1990, equivalent to the income earned by approximately one million workers with annual incomes of $33,000.[1] The negative employment effects are substantial when we consider the full GNP value of the auto production that is shifted to foreign supplying countries, as well as the multiplier effects related to the auto industry. Additional negative employment effects follow from the lack of incentives for investment in domestic production in the United States by foreign suppliers. The loss of this investment suggests that the negative employment effects will be larger.

Another policy alternative, Congressman Dingell's proposal for a "Made in America Act" applicable to the auto industry (H.R. 1050), was introduced in Congress in February 1985. The proposal calls for an overall limit to auto imports of 15% of market, the market share of foreign suppliers to be allocated by the Secretary of Commerce. Violations of these limits will carry a penalty of $2,000 for each new imported motor vehicle made by that manufacturer. The economic welfare costs from this proposed legislation are considerable. They include a substantial redistributional effect on income (to domestic auto firms), a dead-weight loss, significant price level increases, and (loss of) tax revenue effects as foreign manufacturers transfer prices to the United States and shift income back to their respective home countries.

COMPETITION, FAIR AND UNFAIR

Trade and Investment Restrictions Applied to Autos

The United States has more consistently endorsed and adhered to the principle of free trade than its trading partners, especially in the case of motor vehicles. In general, the United States sanctions departures from free trade when the benefits to the global economic system outweigh the costs. This was the case both when the United States supported the formation of the Common Market in Europe and when the question came up of extending trade preferences to developing nations.

The United States may now have to make a choice between free trade and fair trade. Particularly in the case of world trade and investment in motor vehicles, the U.S. component of the global industry is being discriminated against. At the same time, U.S. willingness to maintain open domestic markets leaves American producers defenseless at home as well as overseas.

In Europe, American auto manufacturers face substantial import duties and have invested hundreds of millions of dollars to produce locally, providing significant employment and balance-of-payments benefits to host countries. In the developing nations American firms are extended little leeway; they must conform to local content trade barriers and rigid performance requirements when they invest in local producing facilities. At home, a flood of automobile imports

Table 6.1
Projected Auto Market Share in the United States, under Alternative Policy Action Assumptions—1990

Number of Units (million)	Restrictive Policy						Moderate Policy		Liberal Policy	
	Original Domestic Content Proposal[a]		Revised Domestic Content Proposal[b]		Proposal of Congressman Dingell "Made in America Act"[c]		Renew VER[d]		Remove VER[e]	
	1		2		3		4		5	
	Mill	%	Mill	%	Mill	%	Mill	%	Mill	%
1. Imports	1.0	8.1	1.5	12.1	1.8	14.5	2.6	21.0	3.8	30.6
Japanese	0.5		1.0		1.5		2.1		3.3	
Other	0.5		0.5		0.3		0.5		0.5	
2. Foreign-Owned U.S. Production	0.9	7.3	1.7	13.7	2.1	17.0	1.8	14.5	1.2	9.4
Subtotal Non-U.S. Market Share	1.9	15.4	3.2	25.8	3.9	31.5	4.4	35.5	5.0	40.0
3. Domestic Production	10.5	84.6	9.2	74.2	8.5	68.5	8.0	64.5	7.4	60.0
4. Total U.S. Market	12.4	100.0	12.4	100.0	12.4	100.0	12.4	100.0	12.4	100.0
Remarks	Fourth Best Harsh effects on imports & local assembly		Second Best Moderate incentive for shift to U.S. production		Third Best Forced compression of import & substantial incentive to local assembly		Third Best Small incentive for U.S. production		Fourth Best Imports squeeze domestic firms Weak incentive for U.S. production	

[a] The original domestic content proposal provides that foreign producers who are unable to meet the percentages of domestic content reduce production and sales by 25% in the subsequent year. This "harsh effect" will leave imports down and U.S. production of foreign firms constrained. The discussion later in this chapter under "Effects of Domestic Content Legislation" summarizes the assumptions and analyses underlying Column 1 projections. In this scenario domestic production by U.S. motor vehicle firms is the highest, but negative welfare effects are substantial on the side of reduced imports and constrained foreign firm production in the United States.

[b] The revised domestic content proposal offers several advantages over the original proposal. First, it does not have the sharp impact on foreign suppliers which the original proposal does. In 1990 import projections are down by only one-fourth from 1984. Second, there are much greater incentives for foreign-owned production in the United States. This production is expected to command at least 15% of the market by 1990. Finally, domestic production by U.S. firms is able to perform well, with a projected 74% of market share.

[c] The proposed H.R. 1050, introduced in the 99th Congress, 1st Session, on February 7, 1985, by Congressman John D. Dingell, referred to as the "Made in America Act," provides for a limit on imports of 15% of new motor vehicles manufactured or assembled within the United States. This amount is to be allocated among foreign producers by the Secretary of Commerce in a manner that insures equity to the greatest extent possible, and avoids creating competitive disadvantages. Should it be found that any producer exceeds such allocation, the Secretary shall issue an order of violation, with a $2,000 penalty for each new imported vehicle. In effect, this legislation provides a less flexible control of the U.S. market than the original domestic content proposal. An important difference is that foreign suppliers will not be faced with an immediate domestic content requirement and therefore will be able to enjoy a continued import share of 15%. They will also have strong incentives to produce locally in the United States over and above their import quota. In this case, no domestic content rules will be invoked. Therefore, the 1990 market share is projected to be high—31.5% of the U.S. market.

[d] Renewing the VER will permit imports to hold to a level of 21% of the U.S. market by 1990. Together with foreign-owned production, imports will account for over 35% of market share.

[e] Removal of the VER is probably one of the worst alternatives from an economic welfare point of view. Domestic production will fall precipitously, to 60% of market share. Imports will expand to at least 30% of market share. There will be little incentive for foreign producers to expand U.S. production.

Table 6.2
Economic Welfare Costs Associated with Alternative Policy Approaches

Welfare Effect	Restrictive Policy			Moderate Policy	Liberal Policy
	Original Domestic Content Proposal	*Revised Domestic Content Proposal*	*Proposal of Congressman Dingell "Made In America Act"*	*Renew VER*	*Remove VER*
	1	2	3	4	5
Effect from Change in Import Share	Large import cutback. Increase cost to U.S. consumer*	Moderate cutback in imports due to domestic content*	Moderate cutback due to "Made in America Act"*	Continued expansion in imports as VER allows yearly increments*	U.S. auto market subject to large increase in imports. Domestic industry placed in position of instability*
Effect from Change in U.S. Production by Foreign Firms	Foreign affiliates unable to expand U.S. production*	Moderate incentive for increased U.S. production	Artificial incentive to expansion in U.S. production by foreign firm*	Uncertainty concerning continuation of VER causes overinvestment in U.S. production facilities by foreign firms*	No incentive to increase U.S. production by Foreign firms*

160

Effect on United States from Change in Output by Domestic Producers	Surge increase in demand that U.S. producers are unable to satisfy*	Moderate increase in demand for domestically produced autos	Moderate increase in demand for domestically produced autos	Continued application of VER permits domestic firms to maintain profitable share of market	Large costs to U.S. economy in form of income shifts will place marginal firms in difficult position*
Total Negative Factors[a]	3	1	2	2	3
Economic Welfare Designation	Fourth Best	Second Best	Third Best	Third Best	Fourth Best

[a]The asterisk indicates that the economic welfare effect is decidedly negative. The number of asterisks in the column determines the economic welfare designation, with one asterisk equivalent to second best, two asterisks third best, and three asterisks fourth best.

raises a serious threat to the long-term stability of domestic producers. The negotiation of a voluntary import quota in 1981, whereby Japan agreed to limit its exports of passenger cars to the United States to 1.68 million units during the year beginning April 1, 1981, provided temporary but uncertain stability in market shares.[2] In the period 1981–1985 the voluntary quota was extended, with the last extension providing for imports of 1.85 million units in the year ending April 1985 (compared with 1.68 million the prior year). In April 1985 the Reagan Administration lifted VER, and the Japanese government proposed an increase of 24.3% in exports to the United States during 1985.[3]

In Japan the automobile market is still severely restricted. Although Japan's commodity tax is levied on all automobiles sold domestically, it discriminates against larger imported cars. The tax is 17.5% for smaller (domestic) cars but 22.5% for larger (imported) cars. It is applied to imported cars after including transportation costs. The commodity tax is rebated on Japanese cars that are *exported*. Other Japanese taxes that favor smaller cars are the biannual road tax which ranges from $94 to $125 per year for small cars and $337 to $613 per year for large cars. Other "cost factors" that operate as non-tariff barriers include Japanese safety and environmental standards and inspection of imports ($200 for a full-day inspection). In addition, American auto producers face severe distribution problems in Japan (high cost of land), an exclusive dealership system, and the unsuitability of American cars to Japanese driving conditions. Investment in Japanese industry (including motor vehicles) is monitored carefully and is subject to control. American corporate ownership of Japanese automobile producers is presently limited to Ford's 25% stake in Toyo Kogyo, General Motors' 34% ownership of Isuzu, and Chrysler's 24% stake in Mitsubishi.[4]

Clearly, then, in auto trade, the United States faces unfair trading relationships where the access of American automobile producers to foreign markets is re-

Table 6.3
Allocation of Export Quotas by MITI to Japanese Auto Manufacturers, 1984–1985

Year Beginning April 1	1984	1985	Percentage Increase
Toyota	551,792	617,000	11.8
Nissan	487,040	545,000	11.9
Honda	372,338	425,000	14.1
Mazda	173,468	226,000	30.3
Mitsubishi	122,612	208,000	69.6
Subaru	76,250	106,000	39.0
Isuzu	49,500	120,000	142.4
Suzuki	17,000	53,000	211.8

Source: The Economist (May 4, 1985): 76.

Table 6.4
Economic Welfare Costs Associated with Alternative Policy Approaches Vis-à-Vis the Automobile Market in the United States

Economic Welfare Effect	Original Domestic Content Proposal	Revised Domestic Content Proposal	Proposal of Cong. Dingell "Made in America Act"	Renew VER	Remove VER
	1	2	3	4	5
From Change in Import Share	Redistributional (to U.S. firms) Price level Deadweight	Redistributional (to U.S. firms) Deadweight	Redistributional (to U.S. firms) Price level Deadweight	Market Share Employment	Market Share Employment
From Change in U.S. Production by Foreign Firms	Employment		Tax revenue (from transfer pricing)	Tax revenue (from transfer pricing)	Employment
From Change in U.S. Domestic Output	Price level				Income shifts Employment

stricted by trade and investment controls. Trade is not only free but also unfair. Therefore, the United States has but one logical choice, and that is to restore fairness in world auto trade through some form of tariff or quota limitation on automobile imports, or domestic content requirement. Two arguments have been used against the adoption of such policies, one theoretical and the other practical. The theoretical argument focuses on the doctrine of comparative advantage which holds that international trade is determined by cost advantage. In turn, this cost advantage is controlled by resource endowments in each country (land, labor, and capital). The practical argument focuses on estimates of cost advantages by foreign (particularly Japanese) automobile producers and on how these can be reconciled with the theory of comparative advantage. Isn't the American consumer hurt by trade restrictions when foreign producers enjoy significant cost advantages?

Theoretical Arguments

Theoretical arguments against the United States protecting domestic automobile producers focus on the doctrine of comparative advantage. Free trade advocates maintain that U.S. domestic resource allocation will be made inefficient if automobile imports are restricted. They point to the lower wage costs in Japan as support for their position that Japan enjoys a comparative advantage over the United States.

There are serious flaws in this argument. Comparative advantage cannot be relied on as a rationale for trade policy in general, and applying comparative advantage to the automobile and the motor vehicle industry sectors in particular presents some problems.

The past several decades have witnessed the rapid growth of the transnational corporation. It now dominates world trade, and the adequacy of and reasonableness of the theory of comparative advantage must be reconciled with its preeminent position in world trade and investment. The transnational corporation challenges the validity of comparative advantage in the following areas: (1) growth in importance of intrafirm trade; (2) increased role played by intraindustry trade; and (3) the general problem of oligopolistic indeterminacy.

The theory of comparative advantage is based on the assumption that world trade consists of market transactions between buyers and sellers who are independent of each other. By contrast, a growing part of world trade takes place within one and the same enterprise or between affiliated enterprises (parent and foreign subsidiary, or two or more sister subsidiary companies). It has been estimated that 45% of total world trade consists of intrafirm trade.[5]

Probably the most dynamic component in world trade during the post-war period has been the internal trade of the industrial countries. The industrial nations account for four-fifths of world exports of manufactured products, and seven-eighths of this total is in the form of their trade with one another. Within this industrial product trade of the industrialized countries, exchange of the same kind of products constitutes a growing proportion. Herbert G. Grubel and P. J.

Lloyd estimate that this intraindustry trade accounts for 80% of the growth in total trade of the ten largest industrial countries.[6]

Transnational enterprises, in their domestic markets, function as oligopolists. The oligopolistic model does not fit into the framework of comparative advantage. Basic assumptions in the theory of comparative advantage include immobility of factors internationally and perfectly competitive markets. Neither of these assumptions has any validity in the real world.

Practical Arguments

On a practical level, the United States faces the possibility of a gradual absorption of its domestic auto market by foreign producers. These producers are protected at home by unfair trading rules.

The Japanese production cost advantage over the United States is concentrated on one type of productive resource—labor—and in the area of financial cost advantages. Discussions of Japanese cost advantages rarely extend beyond consideration of the labor input. Other productive costs relating to land, capital, transportation, and energy are largely ignored. From the standpoint of relative cost, the Japanese cannot be expected to enjoy an advantage with respect to land (relative scarcity), transportation (long distance for imports of raw materials and exports of vehicles), or energy (all imported). The only resource input that remains questionable is capital, although we know that the Japanese maintain artificially low capital costs by compressing interest rates in local capital markets. In short, although the Japanese auto makers enjoy relatively low labor costs, they suffer from high energy, transport, and land costs, and perhaps also capital costs. Hence, labor cost advantages do not automatically translate into comparative advantage. Based on high costs of other resource inputs, Japan could very well be in a position of comparative disadvantage with respect to trade with the United States in automobiles.

The Japanese economy is essentially a closed system. Although most industrial nations conduct a high proportion of intraindustry trade, Japan does not.[7] It has a relatively small percentage of intraindustry trade, 20%. The structure of Japan's trade is heavily oriented toward importing raw materials and exporting manufactures. Within this closed system, one industrial sector may subsidize another sector (for export). A closed system permits Japanese auto manufacturers to engage in price discrimination with impunity. As noted later in this chapter, Japanese auto manufacturers use high transfer prices in exporting to the United States. For these reasons, the United States could shift from third best to second best by enacting a domestic content requirement.

The Japanese Cost Advantage

One of the principal arguments given in support of the United States maintaining an open market for automobile imports is the substantial cost advantage of Japanese auto producers. It is contended that American consumers benefit from the competition from low cost imports and that if that competition were interrupted the consumer would be affected adversely.[8] The following discussion seeks to determine (1) how large the Japanese cost advantage in automobiles may be, and (2) what cost elements are most important in providing the advantage for Japanese producers.

Any discussion of international cost advantage must be fairly open-ended in order to avoid omitting considerations important to the overall analysis. For this reason, in comparing Japanese and American automobile production costs attention must be given to (1) static-dynamic analysis, effects of production growth on cost behavior; (2) importable cost advantages should production be shifted to the United States; (3) real versus financial cost advantages; (4) two-way cost advantages; and (5) cost advantage versus pricing policy.

Most of the analysis and discussion concerning cost advantages accruing to Japanese automobile producers is of a static nature, indicating the extent of cost advantage at some point in time, without considering how processes or mechanisms influence relative cost behavior. Our summary of cost advantage shown in Table 6.5 is of this static type. Unfortunately, the literature ignores the cost advantages that might accrue from differences in output growth rates. Japanese motor vehicle production has grown rapidly in the past two decades. During 1972–1982 production nearly doubled, and in the decade prior to that Japanese production increased sixfold. The high growth rates in these two decades doubtless permitted rapid gains in overhead cost economies, scale economies, and external cost benefits for the industry as a whole. Given the high penetration achieved in world markets, these cost advantages were well utilized. Japanese automobile producers invested growing profits in ways that enhanced their global competitive position.

Table 6.5 outlines six different estimates of cost advantage reportedly enjoyed by Japanese auto manufacturers. The total cost advantage per vehicle ranges between $1,500 and $2,073. The cost advantages are ascribed to various cost elements including labor costs, other costs (depreciation, taxes, and interest), lower taxes and tax rebates, management practices, an undervalued yen, and a cost disadvantage related to shipping, landing, and port costs. In only one case (management and business practices) is a cost component of the type that could be imported into the United States, should Japanese auto producers shift their production to the United States (Column 6). This tends to support the view that domestic content might cause foreign producers to lose part of their cost advantage if they are required to produce in the United States to serve this market.

An important distinction can be made between real versus financial cost advantage. Real cost advantages include labor and other direct (physical) costs of production, whereas financial costs include taxes, interest on borrowed funds, and artificial exchange rate levels. Low interest costs and exchange rate advantages account for a considerable part of the estimated cost advantage in at least three of the six estimates shown in Table 6.5. The Japanese government has maintained a relatively controlled financial system which it can be argued is designed to promote the competitiveness of export industries. Low interest rates are sustainable as long as the government also maintains controls on international lending and foreign investment flows. Analysis of the interest cost advantages of Japanese auto producers over American on a per car basis indicates a median dollar cost advantage per car (1981–1982) of $160 for Japanese producers.[9] This represents approximately ten % of the cost advantage generally attributed to Japanese producers.

Two of the six cost estimates in Table 6.4 attribute a considerable part of the Japanese cost advantage to taxes. In one case there is a $1,200 cost advantage related to the forgiveness of domestic commodity taxes on exported cars, and in another there is an estimated $650 advantage that is derived from calculations presented in Table 6.6.

In congressional testimony, John Nevin, chairman of Firestone Tire & Rubber Company has noted that a U.S. small car would carry about $1,550 of tax-related costs if sold in the United States.[10] Property and corporate income taxes paid by U.S. manufacturers account for $440 of the tax burden, and the remaining $1,100 is attributable to employee-related tax costs (social security, unemployment taxes, and employee income taxes and other payroll taxes paid on wages). A comparable car would carry a tax burden of $1,245 if built and sold in Japan (income and commodity taxes). The Japanese car would incur a tax burden of only $920 if sold in the United States. This is due to international trade rules that permit rebate of indirect taxes but not direct taxes. As a result, a Japanese-built car would qualify for a $575 rebate of Japan's commodity tax when exported and would incur only $250 in tariffs and duties when it entered the United States.[11]

The estimated Japanese cost advantage has been criticized as too high for several reasons, including:

1. Selection of the operating year is important because of the high cyclical volatility of costs and revenues.

2. National averages conceal individual firm advantages and disadvantages. For example, General Motors is acknowledged to have lower costs than all other U.S. producers.

3. Production of auto parts may be less labor intensive than production of cars. Extension of labor savings to the suppliers may overstate cost advantages.[12]

In summary, financial cost advantages exceed real cost advantages by a factor of almost 2 to 1. This is based on the following summary and recapitulation of real and financial costs.

Real Cost Advantages		*% of Total*
Labor	$1,100	
Management	100	
Subtotal	1,200	
Cost of import duty and transportation to United States	400	
Net real cost advantage	800	27%

Table 6.5
Estimates of Cost Advantage of Japanese Auto Imports Versus U.S. Domestic Production

Source of Information	Total Cost Advantage	Basic Elements in Japanese Cost Advantage						
		Lower Labor Hourly Wages	Unit Costs Fewer Hours Per Car	Other Costs (depreciation, taxes, interest)	Taxes	Mgmt. & Business Practices	Under-valued Yen	Cost Disadvantage
	(1)	(2)	(3)	(4)	(5)	(6)	(7)	(8)
Gomez-Ibanez Harrison	$1,650	$ 825	$ 825					
Testimony of J. Harbour	1,500	420	1,060	420				400[a]
Testimony of V. Adduci	1,800	550 (2–3)			650	600		
Fair Practices & Procedures in Automotive Products Act 1983	1,875				1,200[b]		675[c]	
Domestic Content Legislation & U.S. Auto Industry CBO Study	2,073	1973 (2–3)					500[d]	400[a]
Testimony of Mr. Elder	1,600						1,600[e]	

[a] Shipping expenses and duty on entry into U.S. market.

[b] Refers to forgiveness of domestic commodity tax on cars exported.

[c] Based on estimated 20–25% undervaluation of yen. Range of values is $600–750, with the midpoint at $675.

[d] Based on devaluation of the yen since 1981.

[e] Based on a 20% undervaluation of yen.

Sources: J. A. Gomez-Ibanez and D. Harrison, Jr., ''Imports and the Future of the U.S. Automobile Industry,'' *American Economic Review* 72 (May 1982): 321–322. House of Representatives, *Domestic Content Legislation and the U.S. Automobile Industry*, Subcommittee on Trade of Committee on Ways & Means, August 16, 1982, pp. 27–31. Statement of James E. Harbour, in U.S. House of Representatives, *To Determine the Impact of Foreign Sourcing on Industry and Communities*, U.S. Subcommittee on Economic Stabilization of Committee on Banking, Finance and Urban Affairs, April 24, 1981, pp. 14–16. U.S. House of Representatives, Statement of V. J. Adduci, *Fair Practices in Automotive Products Act*, Subcommittee on Commerce, Transportation & Tourism of Committee on Energy & Commerce, March 2, 1982, pp. 167–169. U.S. Congress, House of Representatives, *Fair Practices and Procedures in Automotive Products Act of 1983*, June 30, 1983, pp. 12–14. U.S. House of Representatives, *Fair Practices in Automotive Products Act*, Subcommittee on Trade, Committee on Ways & Means, September-October 1982, pp. 810–812.

Financial Cost Advantages		*% of Total*
Tax differential	$600	
Interest cost	150	
Currency overvaluation	650	
Subtotal	1,400	63%
Total of real and financial cost advantage	2,200	100%

Although cost advantages are important in evaluating the domestic content proposal, pricing policy can be equally significant. It can be argued that the Japanese ability to capture a large share of U.S. and other export markets stems from the ability to combine international pricing policy with certain of their financial cost advantages. The following factors play a salient role in this respect: (1) price discrimination by Japanese manufacturers between export and domestic markets; (2) availability of substantial tax rebates on Japanese auto exports; (3) the undervalued yen; and (4) ability of Japanese manufacturers to engage in "legal dumping."

Table 6.6
Taxes on U.S. Versus Japanese Vehicles

Tax	Estimated Taxes on U.S. Built Vehicles	Estimated Taxes on Japanese Vehicles	U.S. Cost (Over) Under Japanese
Manufacturers Taxes	$ 900	$ 550	($350)
Employer Taxes	1,050	550	(500)
Subtotal	1,950	1,100	(850)
Importation Taxes	—	150	150
Dealer & Sales Taxes	550	600	50
Total Taxes	2,500	1,850	(650)

Source: U.S. House of Representatives, Statement of V. J. Adduci, President of Motor Vehicle Manufacturers Association, *Fair Practices in Automotive Products Act*, Subcommittee on Commerce, Transportation, & Tourism of Committee on Energy & Commerce, March 2, 1982, p. 168.

The technique used by Japanese auto manufacturers in capturing large chunks of the market for automobiles in North America and elsewhere is demonstrated in Figure 6.1. Japanese firms transfer prices up to the U.S. export market, which results in shifting profits to Japan and reduces the U.S. profits tax burden. As a result, a form of legal dumping is taking place, with the Japanese auto man-

Figure 6.1
Comparison of Pricing Policies of Japanese and American Auto Manufacturers Supplying U.S. Market

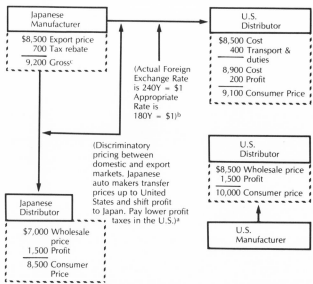

[a]Japanese and U.S. manufacturers obtain similar levels of profit on domestic sales, but the Japanese shift profits on export autos to the parent company via transfer prices, keeping tax liabilities lower in the United States. Japanese manufacturers engage in price discrimination between domestic and export markets.
[b]Japanese producers derive advantages from the undervalued yen. Japanese auto manufacturers get more yen for their dollar export proceeds and therefore enjoy greater home currency profitability.
[c]The Japanese engage in legal dumping where the price to the U.S. consumer is lower than the gross price received by the Japanese producer, except that this results from a combination of pricing policy and export tax rebate.

ufacturer receiving a higher gross (including commodity taxes rebated) than the price paid by U.S. consumers. With the Japanese auto manufacturer transferring prices up to U.S. export markets, a form of price discrimination takes place with wholesale prices in Japan ($7,000) considerably lower than export prices ($8,500). Finally, with an undervalued yen the Japanese exporter receives far more local currency units per dollar of U.S. export receipts. This generates an inflated local currency profit, which in turn facilitates more aggressive reinvestment in production facilities and equipment at home.

In short, the Japanese automobile manufacturer is in a position to employ a combination of financial and economic measures to maximize home currency profit, minimize global tax burden, and discriminate in various ways between the pre-tax and after-tax prices extracted from different market sectors.

BACKGROUND AND RATIONALE FOR DOMESTIC CONTENT

In 1982 sales of American-produced automobiles sank to their lowest level in two decades. Worker layoffs among auto producers and supplier firms reached record highs. At the same time imports of motor vehicles displaced a larger share of the total domestic market. In response to these conditions, legislation was introduced in the U.S. Congress that would impose domestic (local) content requirements for automobiles. Hearings were held on H.R. 5133, the Fair Practices in Automotive Products Act, by the House Committee on Energy and Commerce (March 1982); the House Ways and Means Committee (October 1982); and the House Rules Committee (December 1982). The House passed the amended H.R. 5133 in December 1982, and the Senate introduced parallel legislation two months later.[13]

Rationale for Domestic Content Requirement

Proponents of domestic content legislation cite two primary objectives: (1) to force foreign auto manufacturers to produce their cars and light trucks in the United States, and (2) to prevent U.S. producers from expanding "outsourcing" (buying original equipment and assembled vehicles from abroad). Proponents label domestic content as the first step toward developing an industrial policy that could prevent the "deindustrialization of America."

A more penetrating analysis of the domestic content proposal suggests that it seeks to achieve the following objectives:

1. To force foreign producers that have targeted a share of the substantial domestic auto market to shift from supplying this market with imports to local production, inducing FDI inflows.

2. To prevent the growth of outsourcing, which in part is being imposed on U.S. producers by foreign governments via domestic content and performance requirements.[14]

3. To equalize the competitive position of U.S. producers who face non-tariff barrier restrictions in Japan, substantial tariff duties in Western Europe (11% duty in Common Market countries), and local content laws in numerous developing country markets (see Tables 6.7 and 6.8). The United States is the only automobile-producing nation in the world that has permitted foreign-produced imports to occupy so high a percentage of sales. The 13 auto-producing nations described in Table 6.7 apply tariffs, local content, and other measures to preserve their own domestic auto industry. We should remember that the United States will not be the first to use domestic content requirements. Table 6.8 lists 30 important country markets where domestic content requirements have been in force for some time.

4. To prevent any further erosion of the financial and competitive strength of the domestic motor vehicle industry. Small cars account for over 60% of total unit sales in the U.S.

market. This area is open for further competitive inroads by imports, unless government policy is applied in a clear and definite manner.

5. To assure that domestic auto manufacturers remain sufficiently profitable to be able to finance the substantial capital requirements necessary to assure their long-run stability.

How Domestic Content Works

The domestic content proposal (H.R. 5133 as modified by H.R. 1234) contains six basic provisions.[15]

1. The act institutes minimum domestic content requirements for autos and light trucks sold in the United States. (See Table 6.9 for the percentage requirements.)

2. Domestic content requirements would be calculated as the ratio of U.S. value added to the wholesale price. U.S. value added includes production costs of automotive products sold in the United States (except for export) plus the value of exports of autos and auto products, minus the value of all auto and auto product imports that enter the United States.

3. Domestic content requirements would be applicable to domestic and foreign auto manufacturers producing more than 100,000 units for sale in the U.S. market.

4. A three-year phase-in period would provide for increasing the domestic content requirement each year.

5. Domestic content requirements would be stepped up, based on the number of vehicles sold by the manufacturer (domestic or foreign) in the United States in a given year. Manufacturing firms that sold 500,000 or more vehicles per year would be subject to domestic content requirements of 30% to 90% over the phase-in period.

6. Penalties would be imposed on producers who failed to meet domestic content requirements. A domestic or foreign manufacturing firm that failed to meet the requirements would have to reduce its U.S. sales of vehicles and parts in the subsequent model year. The reduction required would be scaled according to the extent to which the firm failed to meet the domestic content requirements.

Overview of Effects from Domestic Content Legislation

Considerable controversy has arisen concerning the possible effects of domestic content legislation. Political support for domestic content requirements has come from the United Auto Workers (UAW), the AFL-CIO, and major auto supplier industries. U.S. auto makers have reacted in a mixed fashion, generally looking for revisions that ease the adjustment burdens on the industry. Major business groups (the National Association of Manufacturers, Business Roundtable, U.S. Chamber of Commerce) have been opposed to the legislation, as have been consumer groups and foreign automobile manufacturers.[16] The possible effects cited have been in the areas of employment effects, amount of domestic demand, price effects, import share versus domestic production, attainability of domestic content, and reciprocity relations.

Employment Effects

Probably the most controversial point of disagreement centers on how many jobs domestic content legislation would generate. The UAW has estimated at least 700,000 jobs, whereas other estimates actually suggest that jobs could be lost from such enactment.[17] The UAW estimate is based on the assumption that with domestic content the foreign automobile market share would remain at 25%

Table 6.7
Selected National Trade Regulations and Penetration of Markets by Auto Imports from Japan, 1979[a]

Country	1979 Car Industry Sales (thousands)	1979 Japanese Car Import Market Share (percent)	% Protection of Domestic Car Industry
Brazil	830	b	95% local content or 185–205% duty
Mexico	268	b	50% local content
Venezuela	94	b	51% local content or 120% duty
South Africa	213	b	66% local content or 95% duty
Spain	588	b	63% local content and import quota of about $500,000 in car value per country
Italy	1,329	b	11% duty[c] and bilateral import quota restricting Japanese imports to 2,000 cars a year
Argentina	196	1.2%	96% local content or 95% duty
France	1,976	2.2%	11% duty[c] and informal limit on Japanese car share to 3% or less
Germany	2,567	5.7%	11% duty[c]
Canada	1,005	8.2%	14% duty
United Kingdom	1,716	10.8%	11% duty and agreement with Japanese to restrict car market share to 10–11% or less
Australia	458	15.2%	85% local content or 58 percent duty (quota limits import share to 20% of market)
United States	10,510	16.6%	3% duty

[a]Most auto-producing nations have national laws or practices that effectively assure production of parts within their borders. This list does not include all of the regulations and other legal provisions that assure domestic production.
[b]Less than 0.1%.
[c]Effective rate is about 14% because of c.i.f. basis (f.o.b. cost plus insurance and freight) and value-added taxes.

instead of rising to 40%, that the American content of foreign autos sold in the United States would increase to 50% and imports of original equipment by U.S. auto makers would be held down to 10% rather than rising to 20%. The UAW estimates are difficult to justify in light of labor productivity figures in the auto industry.

The Congressional Budget Office has estimated that by 1990 domestic content requirements would reduce imports, permitting an increase in U.S. production of 623,000 units. This would generate an increase in employment in automobile manufacturing of 38,000 workers and in auto-related industries of 69,000.

Table 6.8
Local Content Laws Regarding Auto Trade

Algeria, 25–40% depending on model
Argentina, 90% for cars, 85–95% commercial vehicles
Australia, 85% with a variety of small percentage decreases in special cases
Bolivia, considering 80%
Brazil, 85–100% depending on model
Chile, 15–30% plus stiff tariffs, depending on model
Colombia, 30–45% depending on model
Egypt, announced goal of 100%
India, 40–45%, goal is 100%
Indonesia, 25%
Kenya, 45% (100% of the engine)
Malaysia, 8% cars, 17% commercial vehicles
Mexico, 70% cars, 80% trucks
New Zealand, 30–40% depending on model
Nigeria, 15%
Pakistan, depend on model, must use pistons, tires from local producers
Peru, 30%
Philippines, 62.5% cars, 30–60% commercial vehicles
Portugal, 25%
Singapore, 13%
South Africa, 66% of weight for cars
South Korea, 100% goal, not enforced
Spain, 50%
Taiwan, 60% cars, 32–46% trucks
Thailand, 40%
Tunisia, 20–26% cars, 40–44% trucks
Turkey, 80% cars, 65% trucks
Uruguay, 20–25% cars, 5% commercial vehicles
Venezuela, 70–75% depending on model
Yugoslavia, 50%

Source: U.S. Senate, Issues Relating to the Domestic Auto Industry, Hearings, Subcommittee on International Trade of the Committee on Finance, 96th Cong., January 14–15, 1981, pp. 110–111.

Table 6.9
Domestic Content Requirements under the Fair Practices in Automotive Products Act

Number of Vehicles Sold in the United States	Required Minimum Percentage U.S. Content Requirement		
	Year 1	Year 2	Year 3
Under 100,000	0	0	0
100,000 to 149,999	8.3	16.7	25.0
150,000 to 199,999	16.7	33.3	50.0
200,000 to 499,999	25.0	50.0	75.0
500,000 or more	30.0	60.0	90.0

Source: U.S. House of Representatives, Domestic Content Legislation and the U.S. Automobile Industry, Subcommittee on Trade, Committee on Ways and Means, Analysis of H.R. 5133, August 16, 1982, p. 8.

With foreign retaliation (in non-auto-related industries), employment in U.S. export industries would fall by 173,000, more than offsetting the gain in auto and auto-related employment.

A U.S. Department of Commerce analysis concludes that Japanese auto imports would fall by over one million units in the earliest year that the proposed domestic content legislation became effective. Sales of domestic motor vehicles would increase by 195,000 units, generating about 30,000 jobs in the auto industry. Jobs lost because of reduced employment at U.S. ports where auto imports are unloaded and transshipped, at the Honda and Nissan assembly facilities in the United States, and in Japanese car dealerships in the United States would approximate 23,500, yielding a net gain of 6,500 jobs. Over 130,000 other jobs in the United States related to exports to Japan would become subject to the risk of retaliation by Japan.

Domestic Market

What would happen to total demand for autos in the U.S. market? To answer this central question requires an analysis of the effects on price from domestic content legislation, and in turn the effects of price on domestic auto sales and sales of foreign imports. Will the increase in price resulting from domestic content legislation reduce auto sales by a wide margin?

Price Effects

As proposed in the House version of the legislation, domestic content requirements would be enforced by import restraints. This is likely to raise the prices of domestic and imported automobiles. Supporters of domestic content legislation argue that this is necessary to maintain profitability and to provide the capital funds required for investments in more efficient plant and equipment. Opponents of the proposed domestic content legislation point out that higher prices reduce sales volume and transfer income from buyers to sellers. The CBO estimates that if the domestic content proposal were enacted, the average price of an automobile would rise by $333, or approximately four %. If we were to assume a price elasticity of demand of 2.0, this would translate into a dampening of demand (sales units) of eight %.

Import Share Versus Domestic Production

There is not much room for disagreement in this area. Most analysts believe that the proposed domestic content legislation is likely to depress the import share of the market to 100,000 units per foreign manufacturer. More important is the question of how domestic production will be shared between traditional U.S. producers (GM, Ford, Chrysler) and foreign producers that establish and expand U.S. production facilities to conform to domestic content requirements. Since 1982 foreign producers have increased their capacity to produce autos in the United States and thereby more easily conform to domestic content requirements. Hence, a revised domestic content structure will be required, a subject that is examined in the concluding section of this chapter.

Attainability of Domestic Content

Some critics argue whether the levels of domestic content specified in the domestic content legislation are actually attainable. Evidence on this point is mixed. Volkswagen assembly operations in the United States are approaching 75% content, indicating that at least one of the major foreign suppliers might find the requirements reasonable for its U.S. production activities.[18]

Others maintain that the content requirements are corporate, not model averages. Most foreign car makers sell several different models in the United States. In order to operate at an efficient scale, a U.S. assembly plant must produce at least 150,000 to 200,000 units. Therefore, foreign producers would be limited in the number of models they could efficiently assemble if they were to conform to domestic content requirements.

In 1981–1982, for example, Volkswagen assembled 171,000 Rabbits annually and imported 131,000 Volkswagens, Audis, and Porsches from Germany, the U.S. share produced being 56%.[19] Assuming that the U.S.-produced Rabbits had 70% local content and that the imported vehicles cost the same as the Rabbits, Volkswagen's corporate U.S. content would average 39.2% (70% of 56%). Therefore, local content ratios are unattainable without nearly eliminating imports.[20]

Under the provisions of the Automotive Products Trade Act of 1965, Canadian automotive products are given free entry into the United States (provided there is at least 50% Canadian content). This could provide an incentive for higher volume foreign auto manufacturers to locate in Canada and export to the United States.

Reciprocity Relations

A final point of controversy is whether or not local content requirements violate U.S. treaty obligations. Proponents of domestic content state that over 30 countries utilize such requirements (Tables 6.7, 6.8). The United States would be doing nothing more than providing its industry with a more equal competitive position vis-à-vis producers in other countries. Moreover, domestic content requirements would be providing U.S. industry with the ability to compete more effectively with foreign industry. At the same time the United States would be able to compete more effectively to attract automotive production and assembly operations. Nation states are now making use of various non-tariff barrier (NTB), industrial policy, and fiscal devices to attract a greater share of manufacturing investment and employment within their borders. Supporters of domestic content legislation argue that the rest of the world is in effect stealing from the United States, in one industry sector after another. Considerable amounts of the industrial base are shifting away from the United States, thereby losing tax revenue, employment, and foreign exchange benefits.

Alternatively, opponents argue that the proposed legislation violates provisions of the General Agreement on Tariffs and Trade (GATT). GATT prohibits mixing requirements (specifying certain proportions of domestic and foreign components in a product) and import quotas. Another possible deviation from GATT rules would be a suggested exemption from domestic content requirements for vehicles produced in Canada. This could also be in violation of U.S. obligations under Most-Favored-Nation treatment.

Other arguments employed against domestic content legislation that relate to reciprocity relationships of the United States are as follows:

- Nations with local content provisions tend to be developing countries (true, but their exclusive right to use these requirements has never been negotiated and agreed to by the industrial countries).

- There is not a single instance of a competitive auto industry in any nation that is protected by domestic content requirements. (If we accept the widely preached doctrine that Japan is number one in automobile cost competitiveness globally, Japan is a country that uses means other than domestic content to safeguard domestic auto markets.)

- The U.S. auto market is the world's largest. Therefore, resorting to a domestic content provision would likely be challenged before GATT or invite retaliation by auto exporting nations. (The next section of this chapter discusses an alternative format for domestic content that is much less likely to invite retaliatory treatment or censure by GATT.)

EFFECTS OF DOMESTIC CONTENT LEGISLATION

When fully phased in, domestic content legislation would require that foreign auto producers manufacture 90% of their vehicles in the United States and Canada if they sold more than 500,000 units a year. As observed earlier, there is a wide range of projections concerning employment, market share, and other effects from the domestic content legislation. The pages that follow attempt to answer the following questions: (1) what will the impact of domestic content be on imports and on U.S. production and sales?; (2) will domestic content have an inflationary effect?; and (3) by how much will domestic employment benefit from the domestic content requirement?

Imports and U.S. Production and Sales

The domestic content legislation would compel foreign auto producers wishing to sell more than 100,000 units (cars plus light trucks) in this country to locate their production facilities in the United States. In 1982 seven foreign manufacturers imported 100,000 or more cars and light trucks into the United States, and another ten producers of cars and light trucks imported a smaller volume (under 100,000 units).

These statistics show that foreign auto makers would be differentially affected by a domestic content requirement. High-volume suppliers such as Toyota, Nissan, and Honda would either have to relocate production facilities in the United States or limit imports to under 100,000 units per year, in which case domestic content would not apply. If they built production facilities in the United States, they would need to produce cars with at least 75% domestic content to sell more than 200,000 units. This requirement could not be satisfied simply by assembling cars. Assembly, manufacture of engines and transmissions, and body parts stamping account for under one-half of the work hours required to produce a car.

Anticipating possible enactment of domestic content requirements, in 1984 Nissan announced plans to add car production to its light truck assembly operations at Smyrna, Tennessee. The truck assembly operation began to operate early in 1983. Nissan is to invest another $85 million to equip the plant to produce 240,000 trucks and cars at full capacity. This represents nearly half of all 1982–1983 import sales in the United States. Nissan is the third high-volume Japanese auto maker to decide to assemble cars in the United States. Honda has been building its Accord models at a plant in Marysville, Ohio, and has announced that it will build a second plant in Ohio and has plans for yet another in Ontario. Toyota began joint production with General Motors in Fremont, California, late in 1984. Two other Japanese auto manufacturers, Mitsubishi Motors and the Mazda Motor Company, are now planning production of autos in the United States under joint venture agreements with their partners in the United States (Chrysler and Ford).[21]

Moderate volume suppliers such as Mazda, Subaru, Mitsubishi, and Volkswagen would be in a far less unattractive position than the high-volume suppliers. First, they have a smaller stake in the U.S. market. Second, they face two relatively more attractive options: they can either cut back U.S. sales to 100,000 units and be totally exempt from domestic content requirements, or they can more easily conform with domestic content requirements, which in the 100,000 to 149,999 unit sales range would be 25%.

Low-volume suppliers are largely unaffected by domestic content requirements. They are in a position to displace high-volume suppliers and may be expected to increase U.S. sales volume up to 100,000 units per year. Ten low-volume suppliers were identified in 1982, with imports ranging between 2,193 units (Alfa Romeo) and 71,568 units (Volvo).

Earlier in this chapter, reference was made to the cost advantages of Japanese auto manufacturers compared with U.S. auto producers. Consideration of these cost comparisons is of crucial importance in evaluating the consequences of major relocations of production facilities by foreign auto manufacturers.

Japanese auto manufacturers would lose much of their financial cost advantages as they shifted production to the United States. Tax, exchange rate, and some of the interest cost advantage would disappear. In addition, real cost advantages in the form of lower wage costs would also be cut down considerably. Whether these high-volume suppliers would be able to hold on to their share of the U.S. market (16.84% in 1982) remains to be seen (Table 6.10). U.S. firms are becoming more competitive in the subcompact car market and in production methods in general. Possibly, many of the ten low-volume producers would increase their share of the market at the expense of high-volume and moderate-volume suppliers.

Under the proposed domestic content legislation, high-volume suppliers that failed to meet the domestic content requirements would face an import restriction. In the year following the year in which domestic content requirements were not met, sales would be limited to 75% of the number of units sold in the violation year. A foreign manufacturer selling 400,000 imported units in a given year would be required to reduce its sales of imported vehicles in the United States in the second year to 300,000 units. If in that year domestic content requirements were not met, the sales of imported vehicles in the United States would be limited to 225,000 in year three. Continued failure to meet domestic content requirements in subsequent years would limit import sales in years four, five, and six to 168,800 units, 126,600 units, and 94,950 units, respectively.

The domestic content proposal carries severe consequences for high-volume foreign suppliers, limited problems for moderate-volume suppliers, and substantial market gains for low-volume suppliers.[22] High-volume suppliers would face a mandated cutback in import sales in the United States if they were not able to meet the requirements of the proposed legislation. Alternatively, they might shift a considerable part of their production to the United States. In that case they would lose a considerable part of their cost advantage over U.S. domestic auto manufacturers.

The impact of the proposed domestic content legislation on U.S. market shares is projected in Table 6.11. We start the analysis with a control situation forecast of sales, production, and import expansion between 1982 and 1990–1995. Basic data inputs are derived from projections contained in the *Monthly Labor Review*, U.S. Bureau of Labor Statistics.[23] U.S. market shares for 1982 are based on U.S. International Trade Commission reports and are projected to 1990–1995 by formulating subjective estimates of individual company policies and past achievements in gaining market share. Market shares with domestic content legislation in effect are calculated on the assumption that the full penalty effects will apply upon failure to achieve domestic content percentages. These estimates are adjusted for existing and planned U.S. production capacity.

Without domestic content, imports are projected to displace 30% of the market and to retain that share until 1995.[24] No significant changes are expected for market share among the three categories of foreign suppliers between 1982 and 1990. The 55% expansion in total auto sales (1982–1990) appears high, but it should be remembered that 1982 was a recession year. Therefore, nearly half of the eight-year growth of 4.4 million units that is projected represents an initial (24-month) climb out of a recessionary bomb crater.

With domestic content, high-volume foreign suppliers are affected most adversely, as are moderate-volume suppliers. The three high-volume foreign suppliers are cut back to less than a third of what they would have realized without domestic content and to 54% of their 1982 unit sales. This is due to the 25% cut in unit sales mandated each year whenever domestic content percentages are not attained. It is unlikely that these producers could meet the requirements within a two- to three-year period, and under the original proposal they would have to cut U.S. sales by 25% in each year they failed to meet the domestic content requirements. A three-year series of cuts carries devastating implications from the standpoint of the financial health of the three foreign suppliers. It is assumed that at least two of these three foreign suppliers will be able to accelerate U.S. production because they are now expanding their U.S. production facilities. Therefore, they would experience some recovery in market share between 1990 and 1995.

The four moderate-volume suppliers are expected to meet the 25% domestic content required when 100,000 to 150,000 units are sold in the United States and to remain at a level of 150,000 U.S. sales from 1990 on. This represents a moderate (14%) cutback in sales volume. Only the low-volume suppliers will do better with domestic content. Four may be expected to expand U.S. sales to 100,000 units (Volvo, Mercedes, BMW, Renault), and three to 50,000 units (Saab, Fiat, Isuzu). The remaining foreign suppliers (Peugeot, BL, Alfa Romeo) combined may increase their U.S. sales to 50,000 units.

The devastating impact of domestic content on the three largest foreign suppliers, as well as the moderate decline in sales attainable by moderate-volume suppliers, raises questions concerning the appropriate structuring of the proposed domestic content legislation. This question is covered in the final section of the chapter.

Table 6.10
Market Shares of High-, Moderate-, and Low-Volume Suppliers of Auto Imports to the United States, 1982

Supplier	Imports to United States	Percentage of U.S. Apparent Consumption
High-Volume Suppliers		
(over 250,000 units)		
Toyota	520,727	6.53
Nissan (Datsun)	455,619	5.72
Honda	365,865	4.59
Subtotal	1,342,211	16.84
Moderate-Volume Suppliers		
(100,000 to 250,000)		
Mazda	163,638	2.05
Subaru	150,335	1.89
Volkswagen[a]	126,631	1.58
Mitsubishi (Chrysler)	102,227	1.28
Subtotal	542,831	6.80
Low-Volume Suppliers		
(under 100,000)		
Volvo	71,568	0.89
Mercedes-Benz	62,484	0.78
BMW	50,594	0.63
Renault	37,540	0.47
Saab	18,229	0.23
Fiat	15,973	0.20
Isuzu	15,462	0.19
Peugeot	14,048	0.18
British Leyland	10,313	0.13
Alfa Romeo	2,193	0.03
Subtotal	298,404	3.73
Total	2,183,446	27.37

[a]Includes Audi (45,536 units) and Porsche (13,747 units). Excludes U.S.-produced vehicles. In 1982 VW produced approximately 160,000 vehicles in the United States.

Source: U.S. International Trade Commission, *The U.S. Auto Industry, U.S. Factory Sales, Retail Sales, Imports, Exports, Apparent Consumption, 1964–82*, US ITC Publication 1419, August 1983.

Auto Prices with Domestic Content

Auto price levels control total sales and auto employment in the United States; market share; and consumer welfare. In the past, discussions of domestic content legislation have anticipated that increases in auto price levels will follow such legislation. The reasons are, first, that the substantial Japanese cost advantage

Table 6.11
Estimates of U.S. Auto Market Shares, with and without Domestic Content Requirement, 1982, 1990–1995[a] (mil. units)

Control Situation No Domestic Content Requirement	1982	1990	1995
High-Volume Imports	1.3	2.3	2.2
Moderate-Volume Imports	0.7[b]	1.0	1.0
Low-Volume Imports	0.3	0.4	0.4
Total Imports	2.3	3.7	3.6
Apparent Import Share (pct.)	28.3	30.0	30.0
Total Domestic	5.7	8.7	8.4
Total Sales, Autos	8.0	12.4	12.0
Light Truck Sales	2.4	4.2	4.1
Total Auto and Light Truck Sales	10.4	16.6	16.1
H.R. 5133 in Effect **No Price Increases[b]**			
High-Volume Imports		0.7[c]	0.9[c]
Moderate-Volume Imports		0.6[d]	0.6[d]
Low-Volume Imports		0.6	0.6
Total Imports and Domestic Production by non-U.S. Firms		1.9	2.1
Apparent Import Share (pct.)		15.3	17.5
Total Domestic		10.5	9.9
Total Sales, Autos		12.4	12.0
Light Truck Sales		4.2	4.1
Total Auto and Light Truck Sales		16.6	16.1

[a]Assumes enactment of domestic content law in 1985, phased in 1986–1989.
[b]Results from adding Volkswagen production in United States to imports from moderate-volume suppliers.
[c]Assumes that two Japanese producers are able to accelerate U.S. production and "bounce back" by satisfying domestic content requirements after 1990.
[d]All four producers are able to meet the 25% domestic content requirement, not exceeding 150,000 unit sales in the United States.

Source: A.J. Andreassen, N.C. Saunders, and Betty W. Su, "Economic Outlook for the 1990s; Three Scenarios for Economic Growth," *Monthly Labor Review* 106 (November 1983): 17; and authors' estimates.

will be mitigated by domestic content requirements, and higher cost domestic production will force up average prices paid by U.S. consumers; and, second, that U.S. suppliers operate on a slightly rising supply curve. As they displace a larger share of the domestic market they will be moving up along this supply curve.

On closer inspection these reasons do not hold up well. First, as we have already noted, a major part of the Japanese auto supplier cost advantage results from financial factors. Therefore, much of the cost advantage is illusory from the standpoint of the real productive resources committed to automobile production. Although the Japanese utilize fewer labor inputs per automobile produced, they may be using much larger doses of other inputs (land, transportation, capital). Second, although U.S. suppliers are operating on a slightly rising supply curve, the development of new production strategies and methods may subject this curve to considerable downward shifting. Downward shifting of cost curves of U.S. automobile producers has already been accomplished. As a result of heavy pruning away of facilities and workers, between 1979 and 1982 Chrysler Corporation was able to reduce its corporate breakeven point to one-half the number of units formerly required.[25] U.S. auto producers have reduced their emphasis on specialized machinery in favor of more flexible automation, available through industrial robots and flexible manufacturing systems (FMS). Shifting to increased use of robots and FMS tends to reduce costs, permits more rapid integration of technological change, and reduces the optimum scale of plant (e.g., from 400,000 to 250,000 vehicles per year).[26] U.S. auto makers are adopting new production methods and strategies, including (just in time) inventory policies, unmanned materials movers, and the construction of gigantic, highly automated megaplants.[27] GM is developing a new small car production system labeled the Saturn project. Saturn involves a whole new production system, abandoning the assembly line, drastically reducing the number of component parts, and using modular construction. If GM succeeds, it could become one of the world's lowest cost producers and force its domestic competitors to revamp their operations at huge cost. In modular construction, parts are first subassembled into fairly large components called modules. This requires less space, fewer workers, fewer parts, and use of industrial robots. The Saturn will use an aluminum engine block requiring 40% less machining. In addition, Saturn will use intelligent robots that can see if a part is in position, calculate how far out of position it is, carry out complex assembly and install interior trim, and make quality control checks on dimensions and tolerances.[28]

U.S. auto producers may well be able to achieve substantial downshifting of costs in the period to 1990, while at the same time achieving a 50 to 85% increase in overall output. Yet, other factors may be expected to place downward pressure on auto prices in the United States in an environment of domestic content requirements. First, the U.S. automobile market will be a slower growth market after 1985. Therefore, competition will be more intense and producers will be required to keep costs low to survive. Second, if foreign suppliers are forced to produce in the United States, cost competition will be closer. Pricing policies and practices will become a more critical variable. Finally, multinational company transfer pricing will be influenced by domestic content. Instead of being free to transfer prices up in the United States, Japanese producers will be under greater pressure to transfer prices down. This will be aimed at increasing the percentage of local content but will have the interesting side effect of facilitating lower selling prices.

A domestic content requirement would have two opposite effects on the sales of new domestic cars. First, by restricting import competition, sales of domestic cars would rise. Second, by opening up the possibility of price increases, demand for new domestic cars would be dampened. Based on the assumption of close to unitary demand elasticity, this analysis is consistent with other analyses of the industry.[29] Under these assumptions, if the prices of new domestic autos increased by $500, sales would be around 9.9 million units in 1990 rather than 10.5 million (Table 6.12). Total sales (domestic plus import) would decline from a potential 12.4 million to 11.8 million units. With imports restricted, sales of domestic autos would be 9.9 million units, up from approximately 8.6 million units of domestic autos that would have been sold if there was no domestic content bill. Domestic auto sales would enjoy a net increase of 1.3 million units with domestic content legislation when the average price increase for domestic autos was $500. A price increase of $1,000 would shrink sales of domestic autos to 9,450 thousand units and total auto sales to 11,350 thousand units. In this case domestic auto sales would enjoy a net increase of 750,000 thousand units.

Table 6.12
New Auto Sales with Domestic Content Requirement, Three Alternative Price Level Assumptions, 1990 (thousands of units)

Sales	No Price Increases	Price Increases of $500	Price Increases of $1,000
Total Auto Sales	12,400	11,800	11,350
Domestic	10,500	9,900	9,450
Imports[a]	1,900	1,900	1,900
Net Increase in Domestic Sales Due to Domestic Content Legislation[c]	1,900[b]	1,300	750

[a]Also includes domestic U.S. production by non-U.S. firms.
[b]Obtained by taking 10.5 million units and subtracting 8.6 million units projected in Table 6.11.
[c]With no price increase we assume all imports are converted into sales due to domestic content.
Source: Table 6.11 and authors' estimates.

Employment and Domestic Content

The domestic content legislation can be expected to increase domestic car sales and thereby create additional jobs. The additional jobs would be related to (1) direct employment increases among motor vehicle manufacturing companies, (2) indirect employment increases among supplier firms (manufacturers of components), and (3) employment increases stimulated by additional income and expansion in aggregate output. This discussion is confined to the first two types of employment increases.

Approximately 716,000 workers were employed in the motor vehicle industry in 1981, and another 1,682,000 were employed in associated (supplier) industries. Thus, for each direct job in automobile manufacturing there are 2.35 indirect jobs in supplier (parts) industries. With a total workforce of 2,398,000, and with 1981 domestic production at 7.8 million vehicles, there is an implied average labor content (direct and indirect) of 523 hours per vehicle.[30] This average must be adjusted to arrive at the specific effects of domestic content legislation on employment.[31] As a result of these considerations, we arrive at an estimated requirement of 225 hours per subcompact vehicle produced. This estimate is above industry studies which indicate that between 150 hours and 200 hours are required to produce a subcompact car.

For purposes of our estimates of employment resulting from the domestic content legislation, it is assumed here that 200 hours are required per subcompact and that a ratio of 2.35 is maintained between direct and indirect employment. This breaks down to 60 hours required directly by automobile manufacturing companies and 140 hours required by the chain of supplier companies. If we take the middle price estimate, domestic content creates 46,000 jobs directly in automobile manufacture and 107,000 jobs in supplier industries, for a total gain of 153,000 jobs. This is a considerably smaller employment gain than is generated through natural growth in sales volume over the period 1982–1990. The employment gains resulting from the proposed domestic content legislation are very modest, and if price increases of new domestic autos reach $1,000 the employment gain is negligible (Table 6.13).

Evaluation

The effects of proposed domestic content legislation on market share contain serious implications for high-volume foreign suppliers. Although it is beyond the scope of this study to explore the possibility of retaliatory effects (trade war), such effects cannot be ignored. Three Japanese auto manufacturers face considerable financial pressures from the introduction of domestic content requirements, even though all three are now engaging in or plan auto production and assembly operations in the United States. From the point of view of large foreign suppliers, the domestic content legislation as now contemplated is too inflexible. Application of declining quota limits represents a harsh penalty that might be reconsidered.

Table 6.13

Increase in Employment under Domestic Content Requirement, with Alternative Assumptions Concerning New Car Prices, 1990[a] (thousands of jobs)

Price Increase	Direct Employment in Automobile Manufacturing	Indirect Employment in Supplying Industries	Total Employment Gain
No Price Increases	67	156	223
Price Increase of $500	46	107	153
Price Increase of $1,000	26	62	88

[a]This table does not provide estimates of the employment effects in the United States from foreign suppliers increasing U.S. domestic content. Moderate-volume foreign suppliers especially will attempt to increase domestic content, and this will have positive employment effects in the United States. These are expected to be substantially smaller than any estimate of employment increase reflected in this table.

Source: Table 6.12 and authors' estimates.

The evidence is less clear with regard to the impact on automobile prices. There are strong reasons for projecting a downward shift in cost levels for U.S. producers. However, oligopolistic pricing policies and practices are difficult to forecast.

The influence of domestic content laws in expanding employment is not likely to be very strong. UAW support for domestic content has been based on the premise that between 700,000 and 950,000 jobs would be created by H.R. 5133. The UAW has derived these figures by using average rather than marginal employment effects, including truck and bus employment in the base estimates. But without domestic content the import share would become very high (35% of the U.S. market), and auto price increases would not follow from enactment of domestic content legislation and exert a dampening effect on the U.S. automobile market. The proposed legislation should be modified to consider potential employment effects in the United States.

An Alternative Domestic Content Proposal

The originally proposed legislation suffers from a number of weaknesses. First, It does not come to grips with the problem of growing offshore sourcing by U.S. automobile manufacturers. Offshore sourcing has been on the increase because of the trend toward a world car and use of standardized parts, and because foreign host countries require U.S. producers to purchase components produced in those countries to meet local content requirements. Second, fear of price and wage inflation in the U.S. automobile industry would offset the benefits of domestic content. Third, retaliatory action by countries exporting automobiles to the United States would be most likely in the case of Japan, where three high-volume suppliers could be severely affected. Fourth, the severe reduction in

U.S. demand for foreign autos would depress economic growth abroad, in turn depressing foreign demand for U.S. products. Fifth, it would have weak employment-creating effects. Finally, the legislation would have an adverse impact on foreign companies already producing automobiles in the United States (Volkswagen effect).

The proposal could be modified to meet these objections. The following three modifications focus on the specifics of H.R. 5133 and H.R. 1234. First, a five-year rather than a three-year period should be used to phase in the domestic content percentage requirements (Table 6.14). This would help mitigate the problems found in the original legislative proposal. The adverse impact on companies already producing in the United States would not come into full force until the fifth year, giving them time to adjust operations by shifting their sourcing of components and perhaps investing in additional U.S. manufacturing facilities. More importantly, the possibility of retaliatory action by countries exporting automobiles to the United States would be lessened. Foreign producing companies would have more time to shift production into the United States. Not until the third year would a 60% domestic content requirement apply vis-à-vis high-volume suppliers as compared with the original proposal where a 60% requirement would become applicable in the second year. Similarly, in the case of foreign manufacturers selling 150,000 to 199,999 units in the United States, in the third year only a 40% requirement would be applicable as compared with 50% in the original proposal. Finally, the foreign repercussion effect would be spread out over a longer (five-year) period, easing the general economic pressures in countries exporting autos to the United States.

A second modification involves changing the percentage requirements somewhat. A comparison of Tables 6.9 and 6.14 is in order. For producers selling between 100,000 and 149,999 units in the United States, the domestic content requirement in the final year would reach 35%, as compared with 25% in the original proposal. This is intended to limit the growth in offshore sourcing by low-volume suppliers, as well as make additional employment-generating contributions. The employment-generating effects probably would be in the neighborhood of 2,940 additional jobs annually. Similarly, in the range of supplying 150,000 to 199,999 units a 60% requirement would replace an original 50% requirement. This would have employment-generating effects of approximately 4,120 additional jobs. Note that Table 6.14 is divided into two components. Table 6.14A provides percentage requirements that would replace those specified in earlier legislative proposals. Table 6.14B provides percentage requirements applicable to production in foreign-owned facilities in operation five years or longer. This is intended to avoid unnecessarily burdening producers who undertook to supply U.S. markets with locally produced vehicles many years before the import flood. It provides a ''Volkswagen effect'' in that the Westmoreland, Pennsylvania, facility would find little difficulty in conforming to the specified percentage requirements in Table 6.14B.

Table 6.14
Alternative Domestic Content Requirements to Be Phased in over a Five-Year Period

Number of Vehicles	Required Minimum Percentage U.S. Content Requirement				
	Year 1	Year 2	Year 3	Year 4	Year 5
A. Applicable to all automobile production sold in United States except for that covered in B below.					
Fewer than 100,000	0	0	0	0	0
100,000 to 149,999	10	15	20	25	35
150,000 to 199,999	20	30	40	50	60
200,000 to 499,999	25	35	45	60	75
500,000 or more	30	45	60	75	90
B. Applicable to production in foreign-owned facilities in operation five years or longer.					
Fewer than 100,000	0	0	0	0	0
100,000 to 149,999	0	0	10	15	20
150,000 to 199,999	10	15	20	25	30
200,000 to 499,999	15	20	25	30	40
500,000 or more	25	30	35	40	50

A third modification involves substituting a countervailing tariff duty for the 25% per year import quota cutback as a penalty for non-compliance with the percentage requirements (Table 6.15).[32] Earlier in this chapter the 25% import quota cutback was viewed as an extremely harsh measure. Shifting to a countervailing tariff duty would soften the pressures on foreign suppliers and should assist in avoiding retaliatory action by exporting nations. In addition, the foreign repercussion effects would be less extreme.

Two technical features of the countervailing tariff should be elaborated on. First, the duty should be scaled, according to the extent to which the automobile manufacturer fails to meet the percentage content requirement. If the following scale were applicable (Table 6.15) and GM attained only an 86% level of domestic content (with 90% required), the countervailing duty that this company would be required to pay on $40 billion of U.S. sales would be illustrated as indicated in Table 6.16. Both foreign and domestic automobile producers would be subject to the countervailing duty.

The revenues from the countervailing duty would be obtained from domestic producers (GM, Ford, Chrysler), as well as foreign producers. The revenues collected could be remitted to foreign producers on the basis of their purchasing U.S.-made parts and components for installation as original equipment and replacements for foreign-manufactured vehicles. This would be on a dollar-for-dollar basis. For each dollar worth of U.S.-made parts purchased by foreign auto producers, they would receive a remittance of one dollar from the countervailing duties collected from companies not in compliance. The countervailing duty would be applied at the rates indicated in Tables 6.15 and 6.16. The combined countervailing duty and remittance system would act as an incentive for foreign auto producers to use U.S.-produced components and parts. This would permit export of additional U.S. auto parts and components to Japan and other automobile-exporting nations worth $151 million in the first year of phase-in and averaging approximately $300 million per year in the final three years of phase-in (Table 6.17). At the same time it would facilitate foreign company compliance with the domestic content requirements by purchase of U.S. components for assembly into vehicles to be exported to the United States.

Several additional modifications could be introduced to offset the weaknesses found in the original legislative proposal:

1. A stipulation that price stability targets become a quid pro quo, guiding domestic automobile producers in return for the production afforded under domestic content requirements.
2. Mandated investment in higher efficiency assembly and manufacturing operations.
3. A stipulation that wage increases be keyed to productivity gains by the workforce. In this connection, there should be a mandated special annual report to the U.S. Department of Transportation, explaining any executive compensation provisions that might be considered excessive or wasteful.

These requirements would reduce the risks of price and wage inflation.

Table 6.15
Countervailing Duty Applicable to Value of U.S. Sales That Do Not Conform to Domestic Content Requirement

	Countervailing Duty Applicable to that Tranche	Cumulative Rate
First 1% of domestic content not achieved	5%	5%
Second 1% of domestic content not achieved	4%	9%
Third 1% of domestic content not achieved	3%	12%
Fourth 1% of domestic content not achieved	3%	15%[a]

[a]Maximum rate, applies to all other tranches.

Table 6.16
Calculation of Countervailing Duty Where General Motors Corporation with U.S. Sales of $40 Billion Attains Only 86 Percent Domestic Content Where 90 Percent Is Required[a]

First 1% of domestic content not attained	$400 million × 5% −	$20 million
Second 1% of domestic content not attained	$400 million × 9% −	36 million
Third 1% of domestic content not attained	$400 million × 12% −	48 million
Fourth 1% of domestic content not attained	$400 million × 15% −	60 million
Total Duty		$164 million

[a]4% of $40 billion equals $1.6 billion.

Table 6.17
Projected Application of Countervailing Duty and Duties Available for
Remittance to Foreign Auto Manufacturers

Supplier	No. of Vehicles Imported into U.S.[a] 1982	Est. value of Vehicle Imports[b] 1982 ($ million)	Phase-in Period for Domestic Content Year				
			1	2	3	4	5
			Top Number = $ Domestic Content Shortfall Bottom Number = $ Countervailing Duty (mil. dol.)				
Three High-Volume			900	1,500	1,750	2,000	2,000
Suppliers	1,342,211	12,079	119.8	202.2	239.7	277.2	277.2
Four Moderate-Volume			265	415	490	225	150
Suppliers	542,831	4,885	31.53	52.03	62.28	27.05	18.65
Total Shortfall			1,165	1,915	2,240	2,225	2,150
Total Duty Collected			151.33	254.23	301.25	304.25	295.85

[a]We are using 1982 unit figures in our estimate of the volume of imports to the United States throughout the five-year phase-in.
[b]We are using an average value of imported unit of $9,000 throughout the five-year phase-in.
[c]We are assuming the phase-in takes place in 1986-1990.
   Notes: Volkswagen enjoys an exemption from domestic content requirements on U.S.
          production vehicles.
Source: Tables 6.15 and 6.16 and authors' estimates.

NOTES

1. This is based on the following calculation. Over the period 1984–1990 Japanese auto exports to the United States increased from 1.85 million (the limit under the 1984–1985 VER) to 3.3 million in 1990, or 242,000 units per year. This compares with the initial increase in auto exports planned by the Japanese government of 450,000 to 2.3 million units in 1985; *The Economist* 291 (May 4, 1985): 76. If we use a conservative value per auto of $10,000, the 1.45 million increase in imports from Japan by 1990 will have a market value of $14.5 billion, and if the appropriate multiplier for auto production is 2.3, we have a loss in GNP of $33.35 billion a year in 1990. This implies a similar increase in GNP in Japan.

2. Dick Nanto, *Automobiles Imported from Japan*, Issue Brief Number 1B80030 (Washington, D.C.: Library of Congress, August 2, 1983), p. 13.

3. Susan Chira, "Japan Allotments Set on Cars for U.S.," *New York Times*, April 27, 1985, p. 31.

4. At the time of writing, it was announced that under a new broad agreement Chrysler would increase its ownership of Mitsubishi Motors to 24%. In addition, Chrysler would operate under a joint venture with Mitsubishi to sell one-half of the vehicles marketed in the United States, with Mitsubishi distributing the remaining units. *New York Times*, April 22, 1985, p. D8.

5. Lars Anell, *The Developing Countries and the World Economic Order* (New York: St. Martin's Press, 1980), p. 83.

6. Herbert G. Grubel and P. J. Lloyd, *Intra-Industry Trade* (New York: John Wiley and Sons, 1975), pp. 41–42.

7. Among industrial nations Great Britain is in the top-ranking position, with almost 70% of its foreign trade consisting of intraindustry trade. In the case of the United States, Canada, West Germany, and Italy, intraindustry trade is increasing faster than total trade, representing between 42% and 49% of total trade. Japan, with a sharp divergence in the composition of its export and import trade, has a relatively small percentage of intraindustry to total trade (20%).

8. The alleged price gouging of 1983–1984 related to maintaining voluntary quota limits on auto imports by distributors of imported and domestic autos is a different matter. It relates to the pricing policies of distributors, not manufacturers. It also ties in with marketing strategies developed by Japanese manufacturers to achieve sales and profit growth targets (another form of targeting) by upgrading models and equipment provided on auto imports coming into the United States.

9. This is based on an analysis of data available in the annual reports of Japanese and U.S. auto manufacturers.

10. As reported in a summary version in *Financier* 8 (May 1984): 31.

11. The same car would incur tax-related costs of $1,590 if sold in West Germany, $1,735 in Great Britain, and $2,425 in France. The United States is the only industrial nation that does not assess substantial taxes on imported automobiles. *Financier* 8 (May 1984): 32.

12. J. A. Gomez-Ibanez and D. Harrison, "Imports and the Future of the U.S. Automobile Industry," *American Economic Review* 72 (May 1982): 319–323.

13. H.R. 1234, essentially similar legislation, was proposed in the next Congress (98th Congress).

14. According to reports published in congressional hearings, the Big Three U.S. producers and Volkswagen have undertaken over $900 million in investments in auto-producing facilities in Mexico, based on elaborate performance and domestic content requirements established by the Mexican government. U.S. Congress, House of Representatives, Statement of Howard D. Samuel, President, Industrial Union Department, AFL-CIO, *Fair Practices in Automotive Products Act*, Hearings of Subcommittee on Commerce, Transportation and Tourism, Committee on Energy and Commerce, 97th Cong., 2d Sess., March 2, 1982, p. 145.

15. Two acts have been proposed in Congress. In 1982 H.R. 5133 was ratified by the House of Representatives. In the subsequent year H.R. 1234 was introduced. In general, this description of the domestic content proposal is based on H.R. 5133 as modified by H.R. 1234.

16. Dick N. Nanto, *Automobile Domestic Content Requirements*, Issue Brief Number 1B82056 (Washington, D.C.: Library of Congress, August 18, 1983), pp. 4–5.

17. The UAW assumption and arguments are summarized in Nanto, *Automobile Domestic Content Requirements*, p. 5.

18. However, Volkswagen imports nearly as many Audis and Porsches as it produces Rabbits in the United States. This would penalize Volkswagen unless special treatment were extended to longer standing U.S. production facilities.

19. These figures are annual averages for 1981–1982. U.S. International Trade Commission, *The U.S. Auto Industry, U.S. Factory Sales, Retail Sales, Imports, Exports, Apparent Consumption, 1964–1982*. USITC Publication 1419 (Washington, D.C.: August 1983), pp. 27–28.

20. An exception would be if each company were given an import quota that did not apply in the calculation of domestic content. For example, if each foreign manufacturer were given a 50,000 unit exemption, the calculation for Volkswagen would be as follows: $171/(302-50) = 68\%$, and $68 \times 70 = 47.6\%$ local content. The 302 represents U.S. sales, and the 171 U.S. assembly.

21. Susan Chira, "Mitsubishi Motors Greets Maturity," *New York Times*, April 22, 1985, p. D8.

22. Volkswagen has a capacity to produce in excess of 240,000 Rabbits per year in its Westmoreland, Pennsylvania, facility. Under the proposed legislation these cars (now under 75% domestic content) would be limited in sales to 200,000 units. Volkswagen would be forced to operate its plant at less than capacity. It would also have to decide between further cutting its U.S. production or curtailing imports of Audi and Porsche models. Volkswagen would be in the position of being penalized for having a U.S. production facility and would be placed at a comparative disadvantage to other foreign firms.

23. A. J. Andreassen, N. C. Saunders, and Betty W. Su, "Economic Outlook for the 1990s: Three Scenarios for Economic Growth," *Monthly Labor Review* 106 (November 1983): 15–18.

24. This assumes an extension of voluntary import quotas by Japanese suppliers through the 1980s.

25. Chrysler Corporation, *Annual Report for 1982*, p. 2.

26. OECD, *Long-Term Outlook for the World Automobile Industry* (Paris: 1983), pp. 94–104.

27. Charles G. Burck, "Will Success Spoil General Motors?" *Fortune* 108, no. 4 (August 22, 1983): 94–104.

28. Amal Nag, "Clearing Down," *Wall Street Journal*, May 14, 1984, p. 16.

29. U.S. Congress, House, *Domestic Content Legislation and the U.S. Automobile Industry*, Analysis of H.R. 5133, Subcommittee on Trade, Committee on Ways and Means, August 16, 1982, pp. 40–41. See also Lawrence J. White, *The Automobile Industry Since 1945* (Cambridge: Harvard University Press, 1971), pp. 94–95.

30. This assumes 1,700 hours per worker per year. Multiply 24 million workers by 1,700 hours and divide by 7.8 million vehicles to obtain 523 hours per vehicle.

31. These adjustments include differences between average and marginal labor requirements per vehicle; employment of some workers in truck and bus manufacture; employment of some auto workers to make replacement parts, not original equipment; and most of the shift in production to the United States as subcompacts, not a range of model sizes.

32. Under the GATT rules currently in operation there is a question concerning the status of such a duty.

7

Toward a Foreign Investment Policy for the United States

DOMESTIC CONTENT A FORM OF FOREIGN INVESTMENT POLICY

The modified domestic content proposal developed in Chapter 6 would act as an incentive to FDI in autos and would lead to U.S. production of autos by foreign-owned firms of 1.7 million units by 1990.[1] Furthermore, a domestic content requirement could add nearly a quarter of a million automobile-related jobs in the United States and at the same time prevent further erosion of the market share of domestic motor vehicle producers. Selective modification of the domestic content proposal would result in minimal risks of retaliatory action and negative repercussion effects.

Rationale for Domestic Content

Some proponents of domestic content legislation favor its passage because they believe the import or foreign producer share of the market should be frozen for a period of several years until domestic auto producers can achieve cost reduction and introduce new subcompact models. This could be a valid reason for the legislation. However, a more urgent set of reasons exists. Foreign producers of automobiles are not satisfied with the present market share they hold. Japanese manufacturers of minicars have been poised to strike at the U.S. market for some time. In addition, South Korean auto manufacturers are prepared to enter the high stakes game of selling cars in the United States. Hyundai has introduced an all new front wheel drive, and Daewoo (half owned by GM) will follow.[2] Daihatsu Motor Company, one of Japan's most successful makers of minicars, has never sold its product in the United States. However, Daihatsu and its archrival in minicar production in Japan, Suzuki Motor Company, are preparing to distribute their products in the United States.[3] Until recently, the U.S. market has been considered too venturesome for Daihatsu, which ranks eighth among Japan's nine auto makers.[4] Minicar makers are being pushed into the U.S. market by slow growth in sales. (The Japanese market is saturated with minicars.) Of prime importance in Daihatsu's planning is its affiliation with Toyota, which owns 15% of the minicar manufacturer. It is reported that Toyota could play an important role in launching the minicar in the United States, because Toyota operates over 1,100 retail dealerships in this country. Until 1985 the only factor limiting the volume of foreign minicar sales in the United States was extension of the voluntary import quotas imposed by Japan on its own auto manufacturers. With the removal of this quota, the U.S. market could be flooded with inexpensive minicars, creating a second crisis for the domestic auto industry (the first being in 1980–1982).

Immediate Versus Long-Run Need for Investment Policy

The impending risk of foreign auto producers further increasing the U.S. market share offers sufficient justification for some form of domestic content requirement. The modified domestic content proposal combines investment and trade prescriptions for the U.S. economy. On the investment side, foreign producers are being told that they can continue to sell their products in the United States as long as they increase U.S. production and will eventually reach a point where a substantial proportion of U.S. value added is involved. On the trade side, foreign exporters selling their autos in the United States are being informed that they must use a specified proportion of U.S. domestic content to be able to benefit from market expansion opportunities.

Domestic content legislation will insure a minimum percentage of U.S. domestic content. In addition, it is a new and flexible form of foreign investment regulation. However, the domestic content approach suffers from several shortcomings. It is indirect and therefore suffers from being imprecise in its objectives, difficult to project in its impact on foreign business investment, and almost impossible to evaluate as a contributor to the decision of foreign auto manufacturers to establish production facilities in the United States. In this regard, domestic content legislation is a poor substitute for a more explicit foreign investment policy. Nevertheless, domestic content is necessary in automobiles for the following reasons:

1. It will provide a temporary moratorium on import penetration of the U.S. auto market, thus giving domestic producers an opportunity to adjust to the new competition.

2. It will tend to protect the profit margins of domestic producers, aiding them in financing the substantial capital expenditures required to improve their competitiveness. (It is estimated that GM alone will spend $20 billion in the three-year period 1985–1987.)

3. It will accelerate foreign auto manufacturer investment in U.S. producing facilities,

adding to our knowledge and understanding of how domestic content legislation will affect the amount and pattern of inward business investment.

4. It will insure that the domestically owned component of the motor vehicle industry remains large, healthy, and a significant part of the industry. This is necessary for national defense reasons. (The importance of various industry sectors to national defense and the need to protect these sectors from destructive import competition and excessive foreign ownership are discussed later in this chapter.)

5. It will permit the motor vehicle industry to finance technological advance, by providing a more stable and more profitable domestic environment. The motor vehicle industry is now becoming a developer and user of high-tech industrial methods and techniques.[5] The high-tech orientation of industries may well become a key factor in evaluating the merits of permitting (or encouraging) substantial foreign investment and foreign ownership in U.S. manufacturing.

Domestic content legislation does not provide a blueprint for developing a long-run foreign investment and ownership program for the U.S. auto industry and other industries. However, at least for the U.S. auto industry, it does provide the opportunity for developing such a program by creating a temporary moratorium on import penetration while giving U.S. producers greater flexibility and financial strength.

The United States urgently needs a foreign investment policy that will reflect broad national priorities and yet leave most of the details to the free marketplace and competition. Because FDI is often a substitute for international trade, any policy toward FDI that the United States might adopt must be linked to current developments in the area of trade protectionism by its trading partners. The following patterns of interference in the area of international trade and investment make it important that the United States adopt a broad national policy.

1. Global competition in foreign trade is not conducted on a fair basis. The United States is the loser in this case because its markets are the most open of any nation to imports. Increasingly, U.S. industries such as steel, autos, and textiles have found it necessary to lobby for protection as their domestic markets have been eroded by protectionism in the rest of the world.

2. Destructive import competition has the following consequences. Either the U.S. market is saturated with imported goods, driving U.S. producers out of the field, or U.S. producers arrange to produce outside of the United States, or U.S. import restrictions force foreign producers to manufacture in the United States by means of investment in U.S. production facilities.

3. Foreign producers often enjoy unfair advantages, taking the form of government subsidies, a closed home market meaning that U.S. producers cannot sell in the foreign market whereas those foreign producers that enjoy protection at home can sell (or dump) their products in the United States.

4. Industrial targeting permits foreign producers to marshall government and private sector resources to make inroads on the markets of U.S. producers. U.S. producers cannot respond flexibly because foreign producers enjoy home market protection, U.S.

antitrust laws restrict U.S. companies, and enormous indirect subsidies are available to many of these foreign producers.

5. Foreign targeting can also involve FDI in overseas markets. This is particularly relevant when an exporting country is faced with protectionism in one of its overseas markets. At present, the Japanese are investing heavily in the United States as a consequence of fear of increased future protectionism in its major U.S. markets including autos and steel.

CRITERIA FOR A FOREIGN INVESTMENT POLICY

If domestic content is the final word, the U.S. position on foreign investment in the auto industry will be locked permanently into the situation that prevails at the close of a phase-in period. If at that time foreign auto producers own production facilities and produce one-third of the motor vehicles manufactured in the United States, that situation is likely to continue as the foreign ownership and investment position for many years after. This section considers the implications of this scenario from two standpoints: what is desirable and necessary from the U.S. point of view with regard to the foreign investment position, and what considerations and factors that are applied to developing an appropriate U.S. policy toward foreign investment in autos can be used for other industry sectors in the United States?

In the remainder of this chapter, three sets of criteria are employed in considering the appropriate U.S. policy toward foreign investment in the manufacturing sectors: defense essentiality, high-tech trend and application, and performance characteristics.

Defense Essentiality

In light of the shifts that have taken place in the competitiveness of the American auto industry (and other industrial sectors as well), the United States must adopt a coherent foreign investment and trade policy. Such a policy is needed not so much for domestic economic considerations, but for strategic military reasons. The United States is the only guarantor of security for itself and the Free World and cannot allow its industrial base to be partitioned among the Europeans, Japanese, Koreans, and Taiwanese. Although Japan, Europe, and the rest of the world espouse free trade and open markets, they do so from a comfortable position beneath the U.S. strategic security umbrella. American needs go beyond this. Whereas Europe can afford to lose in electronics and Japan can afford to lose in steel because of the strategic role played by the United States, there appears to be a greater need to protect these and other sectors of its industrial core. As Paul Seabury notes, "The American industrial base constitutes the strategic core of Free World defenses."[6]

The past two decades have witnessed dramatic shifts in international specialization and production, the rise of the multinational corporation to a position of economic dominance, and a growing acceptance that the United States is entering a post-industrial society wherein service industries seem to be displacing manufacturing, at least in part. The Smithian "invisible hand" was perceived to be at work, "assigning commodity manufacture location in accordance with the whims of what economists term comparative advantage."[7] The optimists viewing this process argued that capital-intensive and high-tech industries would remain competitive in the United States while labor-intensive industries would seek low wage host nations abroad. Moreover, the service industries were seen as logical replacements for some of the older smokestack industries. The argument of the (optimist) free traders was that it would be scandalous to subsidize industries incapable of meeting foreign competition. There would be no concern if steel and auto production declined. America would retain its unchallenged economic leadership in space technology, computers, and biochemistry. Interestingly, faith in the efficacy of free competition ignored the fact that government subsidization of the innovation process (in space, defense, and related programs) was an essential ingredient.

The reasonableness and logical consistency of favoring secular shifts in industrial specialization would be obvious if the international trading and investment world was one part of a secure global economy. Comparative advantage could guide the diffusion of factories and assembly lines to locations outside the United States. It would not matter where these productive units were located as long as U.S. corporate ownership assured that America would share in the fruits of a growing world production. As has been noted:

The ease with which other nations, such as Japan, gained access to American technology, capital, managerial skills, and markets, and the eagerness with which U.S. based multinationals embraced the logic of economic interdependence, were simply aspects of a larger, mutually beneficial process. . . .

The migration of U.S. capital overseas was defensible when viewed in the context of a Pax Americana, with its worldwide security systems, military bases, and friendly allies. That this process of capital and technology expansion (branded by Marxist-Leninists as imperialistic) had important corrosive effects on the character of the internal American economy was less remarked.[8]

The doctrine of comparative advantage has never been concerned with the external security of nation states. However, a superpower such as the United States cannot afford the luxury of economic efficiency and prosperity (in the form of a globally diffused and dispersed manufacturing sector) when that undermines the industrial base necessary to produce an arsenal of democracy. Soviet strategic planners are under no illusions concerning the top priority of strategic decisions in guiding resource policy and allocation. It is a contradiction to believe that the United States can maintain its position as a first-rate military power with a second-rate industrial base. If the United States could accomplish this feat, it would be a first in modern history.

The U.S. industrial base is being eroded by import competition, the relocation of industrial facilities overseas by U.S. multinational companies, and a general failure by U.S. companies to modernize domestic plant and equipment. With respect to the problem of relocation of production to facilities overseas, U.S. manufacturing MNCs in 1982 allocated 12.3% of their plant and equipment to overseas affiliates. In several industries essential to defense the percentage of plant and equipment investment allocated to foreign affiliates was quite high, for example, nonelectrical machinery 27.5%, transport equipment 18.3%, chemicals 17.5%, electrical and electronic equipment 9.4%, and primary and fabricated metals 8.2%.[9]

An examination of the American manufacturing base should be sufficient to present the problem. Much of America's defense industrial base is old and verging on the obsolete. More than half of the equipment used to produce military hardware is over two decades old. As parts of the industrial base have contracted in size, the lead time required for delivery of parts and subassemblies has lengthened. The defense industrial base must be viewed from the perspective of a needed range of end-product performance, but, equally important, from the point of view of the ability to undertake large-scale and prompt strategic mobilization. In such cases the desired defense industrial base may be quite different from one that is most effective in competing on world markets, or one that is able to maintain supremacy in high-technology areas. The defense industrial base must be flexible, and therefore able to respond to major international crises and conflicts by matching Soviet capabilities across a broad spectrum of materials and weapons needs. It should be relatively free from production bottlenecks and be able to respond to surge demands for supplies and materials.

Table 7.1 outlines the growing dependence of the United States on imports in a number of product categories important to national defense. The level of import penetration into the defense-essential product categories included in Table 7.1 suggests that the United States is drifting to a position where there is or shortly will be an unacceptable level of dependency on foreign suppliers for key items of defense production. The fact the manufactures essential to U.S. defense production can be made more cheaply abroad is no advantage when the strategic and unacceptable risks involved in this position are considered. How secure is the supply of steel from South Korean facilities that are only hours away from Communist armored tank divisions?

There are a number of critical considerations in establishing an FDI policy from the point of view of American defense needs. To what extent, for example, can the United States permit import penetration to wipe out large sectors of productive capacity in defense-essential industries. If industrial sectors essential to defense are protected from import penetration, at the same time U.S. production will be made more attractive and foreign investment may flow into these

Table 7.1
Imports as a Percentage of U.S. Consumption, 1970 and 1981

Imports	1970	1981
Passenger Cars	15.2	27.3
Trucks	4.0	20.0
Steel	13.8	19.1
Nonrubber Footwear	30.1	50.7
Machine Tools	12.1	29.2
Food Processing Machinery	1.0	23.0
Semiconductors	10.9	38.7
Calculating and Accounting Machines	20.0	39.0
Radio and TV Receiver Sets	32.0	60.0
Ball and Roller Bearings	7.0	15.2
Valves and Pipe Fittings	3.2	8.6
Tires and Inner Tubes	5.0	14.8

Source: P. Seabury, ''Industrial Policy & National Defense,'' in C. Johnson, ed., *The Industrial Policy Debate* (San Francisco: Institute for Contemporary Studies, 1984), p. 205.

sectors of U.S. industry. Given these investment inflows, what policy approach can and should the United States take? Should it permit only a limited degree of foreign investment and ownership in some or all of these industries? Should foreign ownership be allowed up to a certain percentage of total, and how is the percentage limit to be set? If the United States decides to exclude any and all foreign ownership in specific U.S. industries, which industries should these be, and what criteria may be used to identify or isolate these sectors?

The Nuclear Deterrent

Many would-be strategists argue that concern over the defense industrial base is misplaced. Given the politics of nuclear deterrence, an outbreak of open hostilities between the two superpowers is unthinkable. This line of reasoning holds that nuclear deterrence makes the United States (and the USSR) capable of avoiding aggression without requiring a war-fighting capability at all. The United States' huge arsenal of nuclear weapons makes the concept of traditional warfare an anachronism. The dominant priorities of defense policy become deterrence rather than maintaining a war-fighting capability. This view colors the thinking of many Americans who contend that the only realistic alternative to peace through deterrence is a short war with a strategic decision within a few days or weeks. The short war scenario postulates that industrial installations are vulnerable. A short war would be over before Detroit and Cleveland could begin to spew out their planes, tanks, and ordnance equipment.

Unfortunately, no one can predict with certainty how long any possible future military encounters or wars would last. Could anyone have predicted the Korean,

Vietnam, or Beirut encounters, much less their duration? The material requirements of war require common sense conjectures, based on intelligence and an understanding that prediction may err by a wide margin. Most significantly, emphasis should be given to the concept of military potential, which focuses on the importance of strength in war and in unsettled confrontational situations.[10] Nations are military powers because they are perceived to be capable of generating superior military strength via a moderate rate of mobilization. Military potential then also includes the capacity to export arms to allies and others under conditions of urgent need.

Although the United States needs an industrial base to produce materials needed for its strategic defenses, the separate defense industries themselves are highly dependent on the military expenditures of the U.S. government. This can be seen in Table 7.2 which presents data on the percentage of output of various industries that are defense related. For example, in 1980 almost 16% of transport equipment production, and, in the aerospace and shipbuilding subsectors, 35% and 47% of output, respectively, were defense related.

The United States depends on a broad industrial base and a wide range of industries to supply the vast quantity of defense materials required by its armed forces. This can be seen in Table 7.3. Nearly $65 billion of industrial output (value of shipments) is reflected in this table. These industrial sectors cover the entire spectrum of manufacturing. The largest supplier industries in terms of value of shipments in 1980 were transport equipment, electrical equipment, fabricated metal products, machinery, and chemicals.

A more specific list of the type of products purchased in the form of national defense goods and services is presented in Table 7.4. Here we can note that in 1981 over $40 billion in durable goods was purchased by the military sector and over $12 billion in nondurable goods. In addition, the purchase of structures required outlays of $3 billion, and services (primarily manpower) $98 billion.

A Defense-Oriented FDI Policy

A six-step analysis, may be set up in formulating a U.S. policy toward foreign investment in the manufacturing sector, based on the industrial needs relating to production of military goods. The six steps are as follows:

1. Identify the key industrial sectors in manufacturing required for normal and surge demand for military goods. Determine the extent of foreign ownership, if any, in these sectors.

2. Prepare an across-the-board inventory of what the current and emerging character of America's industrial plant now amounts to, primarily in relation to survival in a strategic contest between the two rival superpowers. Where defense-sensitive technology is utilized, determine if any is held by foreign-owned companies.

3. Make an estimate of any shortfall that might exist in industrial plant and equipment in all of the industrial sectors and subsectors essential to national defense. Where such shortfalls can be accounted for by a shift to foreign sourcing and imports, evaluate the relative merits of increasing the share of supply from domestic producers.

4. Given the shortfall in plant and equipment, determine how much annual plant and equipment investment will be required in each subsector to remove the shortfall by 1990. Evaluate the relative merits of domestic and foreign ownership of the investment.

5. Make an estimate of the feasibility of industry self-finance. Where there are financing gaps (financing feasibility lower than the amount of annual investment required), provide for the issuance of U.S. government loan guarantees up to a designated percent of the financing gap.

6. Permit domestic companies to bid for these government loan guarantees on a competitive basis.

High-Tech Trend and Application

America's manufacturing industry is experiencing an R&D-oriented metamorphosis brought on by competitive need. The U.S. industrial sector is facing more intensified foreign competition, as well as slower growth in domestic market sectors. As a result, U.S. companies are adopting strategies designed to renew or enlarge their technological leadership relative to the rest of the world. For example, McDonnell Douglas is diversifying into the information systems business, and traditionally specialized motor vehicle manufacturers such as GM are buying stakes in machine vision companies. Another motor vehicle manufacturer, Ford, has acquired a stake in Synthetic Vision Systems Inc.[11]

Table 7.2
Defense-Related Output of Major Industries as Percentage of Total 1980 Production

Industry		Percent
Ordnance		61.1
Transport Equipment		15.9
Aerospace	35.0	
Shipbuilding	47.0	
Electrical Equipment and Components		11.3
Radio & Television Equipment	46.0	
Mining		6.8
Instruments		6.3
Primary Metals		5.8
Iron & Steel	4.9	
Nonferrous	6.7	
Petroleum Refining		5.6
Fabricated Metals		3.3

Source: U.S. Congress, House of Representatives, Hearings on *Military Posture*, H.R. 5968, Department of Defense, Authorization for Appropriation for FY 1983, Committee on Armed Services, 97th Cong., 2d Sess., February 3, 4, 8, 9, 10, March 2–16, 1982.

Table 7.3
Value of Shipments of Defense-Oriented Industries, 1980

SIC Code	Industry	Shipments to Govt. (bil. dol.)	Percent of Total	Total Employees in Industry Sector (thousands)
28	Chemicals & Allied Products	3.087	15.2	124
29	Petroleum & Coal Products	2.893	1.6	117
30	Rubber & Misc. Plastic Products	0.299	3.5	151
3293	Caskets, Packing & Sealing Devices	0.033	2.2	35
33	Primary Metal Industries	1.446	3.6	342
34	Fabricated Metal Products	4.717	9.4	703
35	Machinery, Except Electrical	4.517	4.3	1,383
36	Electrical Equipment & Supplies	15.845	16.5	1,628
37	Transportation Equipment	28.671	39.8	942
38	Instruments & Related Products	2.524	6.5	600
	Total	64.901		6,073

Source: U.S. Department of Commerce, *Statistical Abstract of the United States*, 1982–1983, p. 352.

Table 7.4
National Defense Purchases of Goods and Services, 1977–1981 (bil. dol.)

Purchases	1977	1979	1981
National Defense Purchases of Goods & Services	92.8	111.8	153.7
Durables	22.3	29.0	40.1
Aircraft	6.9	9.1	12.7
Missiles	2.2	3.2	4.6
Ships	3.3	3.7	4.9
Vehicles	1.0	1.7	1.7
Other Durables	8.9	11.2	16.0
Nondurables	5.0	6.6	12.6
Bulk Petroleum	2.9	4.0	9.0
Other Nondurables	2.1	2.6	3.6
Services	63.1	73.8	98.0
Structures	2.4	2.5	3.0

Source: U.S. Department of Commerce, *Survey of Current Business* (November 1982): 13.

During the ten-year period 1972–1982 the United States recognized that its R&D effort was falling behind, both as a percentage of GNP and relative to the efforts of other industrial nations. Leading companies such as the Radio Corporation of America, National Cash Register (NCR), and B. F. Goodrich experienced lost markets and millions of dollars of operating losses because of their failure to manage technology. Moreover, these firms were decimated by competitors with new technologies. In the early 1970s NCR, the leading manufacturer of electro-mechanical cash registers, wrote off over $100 million of inventory. B. F. Goodrich, the leader of bias-ply tire technology, found itself pushed out of the original equipment market by Michelin's radials. RCA was still coming out with new lines of vacuum tubes, after solid state technology had come along.[12] On an aggregate basis the U.S. R&D commitment had slipped. Whereas R&D accounted for 3% of GNP in the early 1960s, it had declined to about 2.2% in the early 1980s. In the same period countries like West Germany and Japan were increasing the R&D portion of GNP to the levels prevalent in the United States.

Increased competition from foreign sources of supply have made U.S. companies realize that, although they may not be in the export marketplace, they are in the international marketplace. Domestic U.S. companies have lost market share in the United States to non-U.S. producers because of the globalization of business, the miracles of transportation and communication (satellites and jumbo jets) that shrink the world marketplace, and the attractiveness of the large and open American market.

In reaction to these problems, in recent years American companies have been increasing their research expenditures faster than the rate of inflation, hiring the best college graduates in engineering and science, setting up new consortia and joint ventures to perform basic research of value to the industry, and forging links with university and academic scientists. Furthermore, industry is now spending more on research and development than the federal government, reversing the decades-long situation of government as the chief patron of R&D.[13]

Competition in the U.S. marketplace resulting from foreign investment inflows and growth in imports has elicited a number of responses. First, U.S. companies have become more aggressive users of R&D, as one aspect of competitive retaliation. They have shortened the R&D technology cycle, making it more difficult for foreign firms to keep pace with U.S. firms. Second, as a result of ITC findings of damage by import competition, the United States has applied import restraints (voluntary import restraints). Thus, foreign company activity has shifted to investment in production facilities in the United States. Third, the U.S. regulatory posture is moderate on the surface. However, trade negotiations with the Japanese and other important trading nations have become more contentious.[14] In a subtle way, the U.S. government has taken the course of negotiating hard on trade matters and applying a much easier policy on FDI. This gives foreign companies U.S. investment as an escape valve. When the United States closes the door to imports, it leaves the door open for foreign investment.

Increased Technology Orientation

Competition from foreign investment and foreign imports has caused many U.S. companies to reevaluate their strategies in defending domestic and global market share. As a result, companies in these industries have become more R&D oriented, seeking to improve their product lines, manufacturing processes, and cost control techniques. The companies that fall in this category often are in mature product sectors where foreign producers are in a position to benefit from lower wages and material costs while utilizing equivalent or even somewhat better production systems. The steel and auto industries are among these industries, as are some of the machinery-producing sectors. With the exception of the automotive industry (Table 7.5, line 3), these mature industries tend to have a low R&D expenditure commitment as can be observed in the table. The automotive equipment, containers, food and beverage, machinery, metals and mining, paper, steel, textiles, and tobacco sectors have in common a relatively low R&D orientation. These industries cover a broad range of product lines, account for a relatively high proportion of total manufacturing employment and value added, and represent a high percentage of foreign trade on both the import and export side of the balance-of-payments accounts. A number of these industrial sectors have been subject to foreign competition in the form of FDI inflows.

During the 1970s the automotive sector would have been placed among those industries as relatively low in R&D (technology) orientation. Today, however, auto manufacturing is oriented closer to R&D. According to the *Business Week* survey of corporate R&D spending, General Motors is the largest single company spender for R&D in the United States. Moreover, the company has developed a different approach toward high-tech manufacturing processes and product development.[15] This explains the strong interest GM exhibited in acquiring Hughes Aircraft in 1985. The Hughes acquisition fits into GM's plans to diversify into defense. Acquisition of Hughes, with its lines of missiles, radar, satellites, and electronic systems, would encourage "free thinking" in research and development in the parent company.[16] As noted earlier, at the General Motors Corporation, often criticized as an unimaginative, traditional manufacturing company, a major new research effort is underway to integrate computers, software, robots, sensors, and telecommunications systems into a highly automated manufacturing process that might lower the cost of producing automobiles and conceivably revolutionize the production process in a range of other industries as well. Table 7.5 identifies fourteen sectors as high tech, with a sufficiently large amount of R&D spending to warrant this distinction. In these sectors the benefits to the U.S. economy from a high-tech orientation can be considerable.

The Technology Stake

The technology lead which American industries once unquestionably enjoyed has been shortened (and in a few cases reversed) because of two factors. First, other countries have narrowed the gap as their economies have grown and as their domestic industries have reached a size permitting large-scale R&D ex-

Table 7.5
R&D Spending in the United States, by Industry, 1982

Industrial Sector	R&D Expenditure (mil. dol.)	R&D Expenditure as Percentage of Sales
Aerospace[a]	2,510	5.1
Appliances	164	2.0
Automotive (cars-trucks)[a]	4,527	4.0
Automotive (parts-equipment)	279	2.4
Building Materials	155	1.3
Chemicals[a]	3,054	2.9
Conglomerates	1,463	2.8
Containers	99	0.7
Drugs[a]	2,990	6.1
Electrical[a]	1,521	2.9
Electronics	1,286	3.7
Food & Beverage	661	0.8
Fuel	2,353	0.6
Information (Processing) (computers)[a]	5,173	7.0
Information Processing (services)[a]	719	5.4
Information Processing (office equipment)	466	6.7
Instruments[a]	766	5.4
Leisure Time[a]	1,024	4.8
Machinery, Farm, Construction	746	3.3
Machinery, Machine Tools, Industrial, Mining[a]	432	2.9
Metals & Mining	231	1.2
Misc. Manufacturing	1,246	2.4
Oil Service & Supply	796	2.1
Paper	272	1.0
Home Care & Personal Products	761	2.4
Semiconductors[a]	642	7.7
Steel	190	0.6
Telecommunication[a]	1,102	1.3
Textiles	68	0.7
Tire & Rubber	485	2.3
Tobacco	19	0.5
Totals	$36.2 billion	2.4

[a]Indicates high-tech sector.
Source: Business Week (July 7, 1984): 64–77.

penditures. Second, the technology cycle (discovery, exploitation, imitation) has shortened considerably. In the 1950s it may have taken ten to fifteen years for the cycle to be completed. Now it may average three to six years. This means that discovery companies have fewer than three to six years to recover their original investment before foreign imitators are breathing down their necks with equivalent, if not superior, products and production processes.

Even though its technological lead may have been narrowed somewhat, the United States continues to derive important benefits from its technology leadership, for example:

1. The development of new products and processes permits a greater growth rate in GNP. In effect, there is an upward shift in industrial production functions.
2. Society can achieve a lower cost of maintaining a large industrial base. For example, corrosion consumes four % of GNP (about $120 billion) annually.[17] The development of new techniques for producing anti-corrosion steel will reduce this cost by a wide margin.
3. Technology strengthens the nation's ability to export and earn foreign exchange.
4. The problem of materials shortages and scarcities is minimized, as technological gains provide more substitute products.[18]
5. A technological lead brings strategic or geopolitical advantages.
6. More rapid growth in employment opportunities is facilitated. For example, it is projected that in 1982–1995 the growth in technology-oriented occupations will be approximately 40%, double the growth rate in all occupations (Table 7.6).[19]
7. Superior technology permits development of more effective and lower cost national defense weaponry.
8. High-tech gains achieved in one industry spill over into other industrial sectors. In effect, this tends to blur the distinctions between non-high-tech and high-tech industries.[20]

There are three areas of government policy toward technology development and utilization, and research and development spending: (1) Policies that promote R&D spending, across the board or in selected industries. Since 1980 private sector R&D spending has been larger than government R&D. The two major federal government agencies responsible for R&D spending are the National Aeronautics and Space Administration (NASA) and Department of Defense. Private sector R&D is stimulated by more generous tax incentives (provided in tax legislation during the Reagan Administration). (2) Policies that influence foreign trade in high-tech knowledge and products. The United States has imposed export controls on high-tech and other products for several decades. In part these are carried out on a cooperative basis with 15 North Atlantic Treaty Organization (NATO) countries under the informal umbrella of the Coordinating Committee for Multilateral Export Controls (COCOM), which is charged with keeping strategic goods out of Communist hands. Headquartered in Paris, CO-COM was created in 1950 to coordinate Western export policies toward Communist countries as a voluntary organization. Without sanctions it has accomplished

Table 7.6
Projected 1982–1995 Growth in Technology-Oriented Occupations (thousands)

| Occupational Group | Employment | | | | Change 1982–1995 | | | | | | |
| | 1982 | Projected 1995 | | | Number | | | Percentage | | | |
		Low	Moderate	High	Low	Moderate	High	Low	Moderate	High
All Occupations	101,510	124,846	127,110	129,902	23,336	25,600	28,392	23.0	25.2	28.0
Professional	16,584	21,545	21,775	22,325	4,961	5,191	5,741	29.9	31.3	34.6
Technology-Oriented	3,287	4,777	4,795	4,907	1,490	1,508	1,620	45.3	45.6	49.3

Source: R.W. Riche, D.E. Hecker, and J.V. Burgan, "High Technology Today and Tomorrow: A Small Slice of the Employment Pie," *Monthly Labor Review* 106 (November 1983): 54.

much in the way of focusing government attention on the technology threat posed by Soviet efforts to obtain modern technology in microelectronics, fiber optics, computers, and lasers. In an accord reached in July 1984, the 15-nation group jointly agreed to impose broad new export controls on the sale of small computers and sophisticated telephone equipment to nations of the Soviet bloc. The NATO allies have also agreed to place new restrictions on the export of industrial robots, printed circuits, electronic grade silicon, spacecraft equipment, and many other advanced technology items deemed potentially useful to the Soviet defense effort.[21] (3) Policies that influence foreign business investment, designed to provide the United States with maximum effective use of high-tech knowledge. These include controls or limits on foreign business investment, limits on foreign company participation in joint industrial research activities, and policies affecting the takeover of high-technology domestic companies by foreign corporations.

Foreign Investment in High-Technology Areas

Foreign multinationals have exhibited five basic motivations for high-technology investments in the United States: to simultaneously develop and launch new high-tech products; to develop market share in an existing high-tech field; to integrate or match several areas of technology; to employ low cost production methods; and to apply rigorous quality controls.

Foreign companies representing a wide range of industries have launched investments to develop and sell new high-tech products ranging from robotics (GM Fanuc), to fiber optics (Siemens and Plessey), and computers (Fujitsu). In most cases the product lines are on the fine cutting edge of new technology. It is important that U.S. industry have access to this new technology, for considerable cost reductions may result. In the case of GM Fanuc, a large U.S. motor vehicle firm (General Motors) provides a sizable ready market for a Japanese-owned machine toolmaker (Fanuc). GM Fanuc sells Fanuc robots in North and South America and to GM plants worldwide. With the GM connection, GM Fanuc may become the top robot vendor in the United States. (Revenues for 1984 were estimated at $70 million, with almost two-thirds of sales to GM.)[22]

Foreign companies have been increasing their U.S. investments in the fiber optics field, where output is growing in excess of 40% per year. Corning Glass Works has set up a pair of joint ventures with Germany's Siemens (1977) to manufacture fiber optics cable, and in 1984 Corning joined with Britain's Plessey Company to form Pless-Cor Optronics to make fiber optics devices in California.[23] Japan has been preparing for this industry breakthrough for almost a decade by sheltering and subsidizing domestic manufacturers. Production capacity for optical fibers and related equipment is projected to grow from $200 million in 1983 to $2 billion in 1990. This is well beyond Japan's own needs and should be sufficient to supply the entire U.S. market. The Japanese strategy in developing and protecting the fiber optics industry has been described as "Another classic case of what we find unacceptable about Japanese industrial policies. They shut us out while they build an export launch pad, often using our patents and technology, then bombard us in our own and third markets."[24] Japanese companies are moving quickly to take advantage of the U.S. boom. NEC Corporation has remodeled a Virginia plant to assemble fiber optics terminals and electronic components. Fujitsu has opened a Dallas plant to assemble terminals. Sumitomo Electric Industries Ltd. and Corning are building a $10 million research center in North Carolina, which could become the hub of full-scale production in the United States after Cornings' basic patents expire in the early 1990s. The Japanese producers basically employ the strategy of selling optical cables to Nippon Telegraph and Telephone (NTT) at two to four times the world price, while selling at low prices in offshore markets. In this way their ability to unfairly undercut other suppliers in markets outside Japan is subsidized by other sectors of the Japanese economy that purchase services from NTT.

Foreign investment in new high-tech sectors should bring favorable results for the United States, except in cases where non-U.S. companies enjoy unfair competitive advantages. In the case of Japanese targeting, companies such as Nippon Electric Company and Fujitsu are able to catch up with and even surpass U.S. producers as a result of subsidies from domestic sources and by operating from a protected home base. The United States should not permit this form of unfair foreign investment, as it should not permit unfair foreign trade practices.

A second pattern of high-tech foreign investment involves foreign investments in the United States in order to develop or increase market share in an existing high-tech field. Illustrations of this type of investment include CFM International, a 50–50 joint venture set up a decade ago by General Electric Company and France's government-controlled SNECMA to make jet engines; and International Aero Engines (IAE) headquartered in Connecticut with engineering offices in Derby, England. The managing partners include United Technologies, Pratt & Whitney Division and Britain's Rolls-Royce Ltd. In the IAE project each shareholder will design, develop, and manufacture parts of a small jet engine. This type of foreign investment is expensive to operate.

Another illustration of a foreign investment in the United States aimed at increasing market share is the offer by the Mineba Company of Tokyo, Japan's largest manufacturer of ball bearings, to buy outright (for $110 million) New Hampshire Ball Bearings Inc. Mineba's offer to pay $65 for each of New Hampshire's 1.7 million shares resulted in their going from $22.50 per share to $55.50 per share in one day (listed on the American Stock Exchange). Previously, New Hampshire's shares were depressed in connection with a drop in earnings in 1984. Mineba reportedly already controls 30% of the American ball bearing market and has a substantial part of the more restricted trade in miniature ball bearings. For this reason antitrust investigation was feared when the acquisition offer was made. New Hampshire also specializes in precision-made spheres used for missile guidance systems and computer components. Members of the bearing trade association (Anti-Friction Bearing Manufacturers Association) have expressed fears that Mineba could dominate the miniature bearing market if it acquires New Hampshire.[25]

Ball bearings are one of the building blocks of industry and play a role extending far beyond their use in sensitive weapons, missiles, and computer systems. A substantial portion of New Hampshire's business is with major military contractors. Under Pentagon regulations, miniature bearings for military equipment must be purchased from domestic manufacturers, which *include foreign-owned American companies*. The Japanese already are major international bearing producers and have been active in penetrating the $1 billion a year market in the United States. In the past two decades Japanese imports have taken over 50% of the U.S. market, and all the major Japanese bearing companies including Mineba have acquired American companies or built plants in this country. (Mineba owns the NME Corporation, a bearing manufacturer in Los Angeles.)

An acquisition such as that of New Hampshire poses two serious problems from the U.S. point of view: it has anticompetitive effects, and it gives a foreign-controlled company an even stronger strategic position in an industrial sector that is highly sensitive from the point of view of national defense needs.[26]

A third pattern of high-tech foreign investment aims at integrating or matching complementary areas of technology. In October 1983, L. M. Ericsson, with a strong lead in switching technology, joined with Honeywell to develop information processing equipment for the U.S. market (PBX systems). This pattern has been repeated many times in the computer and information processing industry. It reflects the difficulty most high-tech companies have in trying to remain competitive in a fast-moving world. The gains from technological linkups have been recognized. Linkups between U.S. and foreign companies aim at getting the jump on competitors in fast-moving technologies, or at least surviving in a tight race. Where such linkups simultaneously bring new technology into the United States and increase competition, this pattern of foreign investment must be viewed in a favorable light.

A fourth pattern involves foreign investment directed at introducing high-technology production techniques that reduce production costs. Perhaps one of the most timely illustrations of this pattern is the steel industry, where foreign steel producers have been setting up mini-mill operations, as well as investing in integrated steelmaking facilities that employ computer-assisted operations. In such cases the import of improved production processes and retention of steelmaking capacity in the United States are positive factors. This is especially the case when one considers that the American steel industry does not enjoy high credits for developing and using modern technology.

A fifth pattern of high-tech foreign investment aims at applying rigorous quality controls. Illustrations of this pattern include the acquisition of Motorola Television by Matsushita Electric in 1974 and Sanyo's acquisition of Warwick's color television assembly plant in Arkansas in 1979. When Matsushita took over the Quasar plant in 1974, it found a quality level of 150 defects for every 100 finished sets and a high rate of claims under warranty.[27] Application of productivity and quality control techniques employed in Japan proved to be the correct solution, and the preshipment defect rate went down to three or four per hundred. Similarly, Sanyo inherited a high product defect rate in the Warwick television plant, but reduced it from 30% to less than 5% in two months. The success of foreign investors in improving the efficiency of operations in American production systems is noteworthy. However, it is difficult to accept the inevitability of a "cultural difference" in explaining this phenomenon of improved efficiency and productivity. American management should be able to achieve similar improvements by implementing "purchased managerial expertise" in lieu of a massive sellout of U.S. ownership.

To summarize the foregoing, high-tech foreign investment in the United States tends to have favorable competitive and efficiency effects. However, in cases where foreign companies operate from a highly protected domestic market environment, and where direct or indirect (high home country price structure) subsidies are invoked, the unfairness of competition indicates that competitive inequalities must be rebalanced.

Appropriate Policy Toward FDI in High Tech

The future health and viability of America's industry depend critically on a dynamic high-tech sector. A high level of R&D spending, and resulting new processes and products, will permit high economic growth, cost control and reduction, improve international competitiveness, create jobs, and stimulate advances in productivity. Rapidly growing output in new product lines (fiber optics, robotics, computers, microprocessors) will permit sharp reductions in cost levels as firms move down along the learning curve and as they achieve scale economies. We have already referred to the transformation taking place in GM's production planning and control. Repetition of this pattern across wide sectors of industry could bring the United States into a mini-industrial revolution.

America's ability to maintain its high-tech leadership depends on continued free international trade and investment, but it is also being affected by the changing flow and pattern of world business. Technology acquisition by U.S. and foreign companies comes through three basic sources: internal development, purchase of developed technology, and licensing.[28] The competitive strength of U.S. exporters and foreign investors is based heavily on successful R&D development. For example, between 1972 and 1980 the overall trade balance of the United States for R&D intensive products improved from $11 billion to $52.5 billion; in the same period the trade balance deteriorated for non-R&D intensive products from −$16 billion to −$33.5 billion.[29] Equally important, the U.S. external balance on royalties and licensing fees improved in the period 1972–1981 from $1.8 billion to $5.3 billion. Inasmuch as licensing often precedes foreign investment, the U.S. foreign investment position is heavily dependent on R&D activity. Clearly, the United States relies on R&D-intensive products to maintain a strong position in world markets (domestic and foreign).

The global exchange of R&D knowledge is an important support for the continued expansion of the world economy. U.S. companies derive R&D knowledge from foreign sources in the same way that foreign-based companies obtain R&D information in the United States.[30] Technology transfer takes many forms, and foreign business investment represents a vital part of this exchange process.

Foreign business investment in the United States can have three technology-oriented effects: (1) Technology adding—transfers new or better technology into the U.S. industrial process. Examples include foreign investment in steel mini-mills and the GM Fanuc joint venture; (2) technology absorbing—transfers U.S. technology to foreign firms or locations for implementation and use. Examples include the numerous acquisitions of small high-technology firms in the Silicon Valley and Massachusetts[31]; and (3) technology neutral—no direct effect on technology transfer.

Foreign investment that contributes technology to the United States should be encouraged because it expands the base of knowledge available and can exert important technology upgrading effects. Technology-absorbing foreign investment can be both positive and negative. Positive influences apply when the U.S. owner of the knowledge is able to negotiate favorable royalty or licensing fee returns from the foreign investor. This is not likely to be a widespread condition inasmuch as the U.S. holder of the patent, copyright, or process may prefer to exploit the information in the U.S. domestic market with which that firm is familiar. Negative influences apply when the foreign firm attempts to make use of the knowledge without (adequate) compensation.

In this connection in 1984, IBM dealt several Japanese competitors a powerful blow to their efforts to move into computer systems. IBM filed a suit against Hitachi Ltd. for allegedly stealing IBM software. The suit resulted in heavy fines for Hitachi and forced Hitachi and Fujitsu Ltd. to divert large amounts of time and money to rewrite old programs and develop new software that did not infringe on IBM's copyrights.[32] In addition, IBM decided to stop disclosing the source code, the description of the operating system software on which all applications programs must run. This decision put these companies in a tight bind. Without the IBM source code, experts claim the Japanese companies may find it impossible to develop their own operating system. IBM is using this opportunity to move aggressively in the Japanese market. Japan's concern is reflected in MITI's proposal to change Japan's copyright law to enable the Ministry to force a company to license software to its Japanese competitors if MITI deems it in the national interest.

IBM's fast-moving aggressive thrust is taking the form of selective investments in specialty technology firms in the communications and computer equipment fields. Recently, IBM purchased 22.7% of Rolm Corporation, a communications equipment maker, and a 20% share of Intel Corporation, a large chip maker.[33] In addition, IBM is developing joint venture manufacturing agreements with computer companies around the globe. Finally, IBM is laying the groundwork to capture a share of the lucrative telecommunications business. IBM owns 33% of a joint venture with Aetna Life & Casualty Company and Communications Satellite Corp-Satellite Business Systems.[34]

What approach should government adopt to protect and promote the high-tech lead of the United States as this relates to inward foreign investment? An essentially free market approach is necessary. Government should encourage innovation, not specific industrial projects. Rather than targeting industries and products, government should "target the process by which new ideas and products are developed—the process of innovation."[35] In short, government should foster an environment in the United States in which innovations, new ideas, and new companies are likely to flourish and in which companies in mature industries can modernize. This includes a strong commitment to basic research, incentives for investors and entrepreneurs, a strong educational capability, and expanding market opportunities at home and overseas.

High on the list of priority policy actions are the following: (1) Increasing government-sponsored basic research. There are long lead times in this area, and it is difficult for private sector firms to achieve a reasonable payback on basic research unless the government shares in the cost. (2) Modifying antitrust laws to permit research and development joint ventures among corporations. (3) Allowing tax policy to play a more positive and central role in the encouragement of U.S. competitiveness in high-tech and other industry sectors. One approach would include providing permanent tax shelter treatment of R&D expenditures. This would include making the 25% R&D tax credit permanent and making permanent provision for R&D tax shelters-limited partnerships that fund specific research projects. In 1983 these partnerships provided $800 to $900 million in development funds.[36] (4) Strengthening patent laws. In the future, infringements in the computer software and telecommunications fields are expected to increase. Foreign companies operating in the United States that have targeted American industrial sectors will be especially tempted to infringe on patents and copyrights. It has been reported that some U.S. companies lose 10 to 50% of potential business through illegal distribution of programs.[37] (5) Streamlining and refocusing U.S. export controls to eliminate unnecessary trade obstacles. (6) Adopting a flexible technology transfer policy. No problems are more complex than those related to technology transfer. First, the R&D generating institutions (academic institutions) should be encouraged in basic research. Second, care must be exercised to protect against wide dissemination of certain critical technologies such as anti-submarine technology, anti-stealth technology, and key technologies that sustain American leadership in microprocessors and computers.[38] (7) Insuring that the appropriate government agency or agencies has proper jurisdiction to deal with other nations of the world in matters relating to technology transfer and foreign investment. For example, the Office of Productivity Technology and Innovation, U.S. Department of Commerce, has as its major responsibility stimulation of U.S. productivity growth and technological competitiveness. It has been active in sponsoring R&D limited partnerships, funnelling money to encourage superior teaching, establishing a center for utilization of federal technology, and helping firms locate technology of potential commercial interest.[39] (8) Making more aggressive use of executive branch initiatives in dealing with unfair competitive practices by foreign companies. This activity could be centralized in the White House Office of the U.S. Trade Representative.

A change is also needed in the relationship between business and government in the United States if American industry is to survive the new global competitive pressures. Until recently, business-government relationships could be characterized as adversarial rather than cooperative, and excessively naive from the point of view of giving U.S. manufacturers support equivalent to that given foreign manufacturers by their respective governments. High-tech industries especially require equivalent support by the government because of the substantial investment required in R&D and related capital equipment. When we consider that the Japanese government is putting up $450 million to facilitate development of fifth-generation computer know-how by its own industry, we can appreciate the need to rebalance the competitive position of U.S. companies.

In 1983 the U.S. Congress conducted hearings on legislative proposals that would permit U.S. companies to engage in collective research in the early stages of R&D (HR 1952 and HR 3393). This would make better use of limited R&D resources of individual companies and avoid duplication of effort. Joint pooling of research is a hallmark of Japanese industry and is supported with government funds.[40] A statement made by Ronald Myrick of the Semiconductor Research Association at these hearings reflects the need for legislation that would enable joint R&D by U.S. companies.

Foreign high technology companies . . . have been able to capitalize very successfully in recent years on the creative advantages of joint research and development activities— some of them sponsored directly by their government—and all of which have been conducted unencumbered by the type of antitrust law concerns which must now prevail among U.S. companies.

The threat to American technological leadership from foreign targeting practices is further compounded by the escalating costs of research in advanced microelectronics. The United States can no longer afford the duplication of effort and waste of resources that result when many companies attempt individually to advance the frontiers of research in this vital area. In 1982 U.S. semiconductor companies spent an impressive 14 percent of their sales revenues on capital investments and 9.8% on research and development, compared to 7% and 3% for U.S. industry as a whole. Yet we are still being outspent by our foreign competition in Japan where semiconductor companies, supported by government subsidies and other incentives, are spending as much as 20% on capital and 15% on research and development. In short, maintaining U.S. technological leadership requires that we remove any unnecessary obstacles to cooperative research ventures and actively seek to promote such activity.[41]

An illustration of a successful ongoing joint venture in high-tech research and development can be found in semiconductors.[42] The industry has been in existence for only 30 years, and until 1978 it was primarily a U.S. industry with regard to innovations, applications, and demand and supply. By 1982, however, the U.S. share of the industry had eroded to 55%, with Japan occupying 35% of the industry and Western Europe the remaining 10%. In the period 1981–

1982 the Japanese producers of semiconductors apparently gained a competitive advantage, with the Japanese share of the U.S. market growing and the sales of U.S. semiconductors in Japan declining as a share of the market. The reasons for this shift in competitive position include worldwide diffusion of U.S. technology, targeting by Japanese firms, financial support from MITI in the form of loans and research subsidies, and Japanese pooling of engineers and scientists from industry and government.

Despite these pressures, the U.S. semiconductor industry is imaginatively pursuing research and is evolving new technologies and processes. In turn, these new processes have brought a flow of new products.

Faced with increasing competition from abroad, the industry established the Semiconductor Research Cooperative (SRC) to increase research efforts. By pooling funds for priority projects and contracting work to research universities, the industry is increasing semiconductor research in the United States; sharing results among companies, avoiding duplication of efforts; attracting more students to this vital field of study; and improving the quality of education. In 1982 and 1983 SRC expended $5 million and $11 million, respectively. Most of this goes into basic research, an area given lower priority by individual companies (which emphasize applied research).

The companies that participate in this cooperative effort are merchant semiconductor companies (selling components in the marketplace) and companies that manufacture semiconductors, instrument makers, and manufacturers of communications equipment. Companies cooperating in SRC include IBM, Motorola, General Electric, Honeywell (large companies); Central Data Corp., Digital Electronics Corp., Intel, Hewlett Packard (medium companies); and Silicon Systems, Monolithic Memories (small). Several of the cooperating companies are either foreign owned or use extensive licensing arrangements with non-U.S. companies. SRC has entered into contracts with at least 30 private and state universities.

The SRC is considering extending its mission beyond pure research. The industry is in need of automated manufacturing processes, improved product quality, and increased productivity. More specifically, the SRC is considering a program of process definition and advanced design for a four megabit memory chip. This could leapfrog the normal cycle of development.

Another illustration of a joint research effort is the Microelectronics & Computer Technology Corporation (MCC). This joint venture of ten major electronic and computer companies was founded in 1983; the members are Control Data, Honeywell, Sperry, RCA, Motorola, Digital Equipment, Harris, NCR, National Semiconductor Corporation, and Advanced Micro Systems. MCC's initial efforts are to be directed to advanced computer architecture, component packaging, software productivity, and computer-aided design and manufacturing.[43]

Cooperative research efforts may be possible in other industry sectors. To facilitate these efforts, the U.S. Congress must amend the antitrust laws to exempt such activities from the antitrust laws and in effect must declare that American industrial policy supports such activities.

Although modification of antitrust laws is necessary, the United States must also consider how it can most effectively deal with the innumerable cases of foreign government subsidy, protection, and support to home industries. Consideration must also be given to rebalancing the competitive equation in cases where government ownership of industry provides financial and competitive advantages not shared by U.S. companies.

Finally, a key part of developing appropriate policies toward FDI in the United States, especially in the high-tech industry sectors, is the identification of a government unit or office that will have primary responsibility for dealings with foreign governments in matters relating to international trade and international investment. One writer recently proposed that the White House Office of the United States Trade Representative (USTR) be designated to carry out this function.[44]

It is critically important that prompt action be taken to implement such proposals for government restructuring where they will give better focus to issues and problems, and at the same time permit the United States to respond to unfair competitive practices in international trade and investment swiftly and effectively.

Performance Characteristics

A third basis for formulating national policy concerning FDI in the United States is the performance of FDI companies in the U.S. economy. This performance can be considered directly and in comparison with U.S. domestic companies operating in the same industries and product lines.

The activities of FDI investors in the United States have been expanding at a high rate of growth. In 1980–1981 the assets, sales, income, and payrolls of FDI companies grew at rates between 22% and 32%. Employment increased by 15%, and land utilization by over 30%. Investment in plant and equipment jumped 48% in 1981. Foreign trade also experienced a strong growth trend (Table 7.7).

Direct Employment and Tax Contributions

As noted in an earlier discussion, two important contributions made by FDI to the economy of the host country take the form of direct employment and tax effects. The discussion that follows focuses strictly and narrowly on the direct effects in these two areas. Any possible secondary and tertiary multiplier effects from FDI are not taken into account.

Employment generated by FDI in the United States exceeded 2.3 million in 1981 and has been growing at a rate of close to 15% per year. The ten states with the largest amounts of nonbank employment of FDI companies are indicated in Table 7.8. These ten states account for 56.3% of the employment created by FDI firms. The three largest regional concentrations of FDI activity are reflected in the table, namely, the Southeast, East, and Great Lakes Regions. Three states among the top ten (North Carolina, Georgia, and Florida) represent the dominant Southeast region whose 12 states account for 560,000 employed in FDI firms.

Table 7.7
Selected Data of Nonbank Direct Foreign Investors in the United States, All Industries, 1980–1981 (mil. dol.)

Item	1980	1981	Percentage Change 1980–1981
Total Assets	$292,033	$395,032	30
Sales	412,705	503,745	22
Net Income	8,917	11,463	29
Employee Compensation	40,047	52,916	32
Number of Employees	2,033,932	2,343,115	15
Land Owned[a]	9,552	13,134	38
Mineral Rights Owned-Leased[a]	47,785	62,734	31
Gross Book Value of Property, Plant and Equipment	$127,838	$180,005	41
Expenditures for New Plant and Equipment	16,891	25,018	48
U.S. Exports Shipped by Affiliates	52,199	64,060	23
U.S. Imports Shipped to Affiliates	75,803	81,599	8

[a]Thousand acres.

Source: Ned G. Howenstine, U.S. Department of Commerce, "U.S. Affiliates of Foreign Companies: Operations in 1981," *Survey of Current Business* 63, no. 11 (November 1983): 19–34.

Three states among the top ten (New York, New Jersey, and Pennsylvania) represent the second-ranking East region, where FDI in six states generates 547,000 jobs. Finally, the Great Lakes Region includes three other states (Indiana, Michigan, and Wisconsin), and in total the five states account for 378,000 nonbank jobs provided by FDI firms. Clearly, FDI generates a substantial amount of employment in the United States, with over half of this employment concentrated in ten states.

Almost all analyses of the economic effects of FDI agree that the generation of tax revenues represents a clear benefit for the host country. Using the data in Table 7.7 which provides a broad measure of FDI activity in the United States, we estimated the tax revenues generated for federal and state-local governments. At the federal level, nearly $20 billion in tax revenues was generated in 1982 (Table 7.9). This was made up of payroll taxes ($8.0 billion), personal income taxes ($6.0 billion), and corporate profit taxes ($5.6 billion). Revenues generated for state and local governments were considerably higher, over $31 billion. The major source of revenues was sales taxes ($27 billion). Tax revenues at all levels of government probably exceeded $51 billion.

Table 7.8

Major States of Employment of Nonbank U.S. Affiliates of Foreign Direct Investors, 1981

State	Number Employed	Percentage of Total	Cumulative Total (pct.)
California	240,774	10.3	10.3
New York	204,393	8.7	19.0
Texas	172,564	7.4	26.4
New Jersey	131,764	5.7	32.1
Pennsylvania	129,110	5.5	37.6
Illinois	111,850	4.8	42.4
Ohio	97,018	4.1	46.5
North Carolina	86,349	3.7	50.2
Georgia	73,742	3.1	53.3
Florida	69,983	3.0	56.3
Total, 50 States & Territories	2,343,115	100.0	

Source: Ned G. Howenstine, U.S. Department of Commerce, "U.S. Affiliates of Foreign Companies: Operations in 1981," *Survey of Current Business* 63, no. 11 (November 1983): 19–34.

The preceding shows that FDI activity exerts considerable employment and tax revenue-generating power. The only difficulty with this analysis is that there is no basis of comparison to judge whether FDI on a net basis contributes to the U.S. economy. Because FDI activity draws productive economic resources that might otherwise be used by domestic business firms, especially if the economy is operating at or near full employment, it might be asked, "Does FDI have performance characteristics that are superior or inferior to those of domestic firms?" In other words, do FDI firms in electronics or food processing employ productive resources in a manner that generates greater benefits for the U.S. economy than domestic firms? If FDI performs in a more satisfactory manner than domestic firms, perhaps it should be encouraged. If it does not, perhaps it should not be encouraged.

Performance Characteristics Compared

Five performance activities in which foreign-owned affiliates and U.S. domestic companies can be compared are investment in plant and equipment; sales per worker; export position; foreign trade balance; and profitability. First, we consider the comparative performance within separate industry sectors, and then we compare foreign affiliates and domestic companies as a group in each of the five performance activities.

Overall, the comparative performance of foreign and domestic companies in the United States presents a mixed picture. Table 7.10 summarizes the comparative performance in 13 industrial sectors across five activities, for a total of 65 cell comparisons. The overall results are as follows:

Domestic companies superior	20
Foreign companies superior	21
Even	7
Split	1
No information	16
Total	65

On an overall basis foreign-owned affiliates cannot be said to perform better, nor can it be said that domestic companies perform better.

If we focus on individual industries, differences begin to emerge. In five industries foreign affiliates tend to perform better in more activity areas. In four industries domestic firms perform better in more activity areas.

Domestic Firms Superior	*Foreign Affiliates Superior*
Food & kindred	Primary metals
Chemicals	Fabricated metals
Machinery, except electrical	Electrical machinery
Petroleum	Paper and allied products
	Stone, clay, and glass

Table 7.9
Tax Revenues Generated Directly by Foreign Business Investment in the United States, 1982ª

Source of Revenue	Computation	Amount (bil.)
Federal		
Corporate profit (40%)	($14 bil. × 0.40)	$5.60
Employee income tax (10%)	($60 bil. × 0.10)	6.00
Payroll tax (13.4%)	($60 bil. × 0.134)	8.04
Subtotal		$19.64
State & Local		
Sales tax (5%)	($540 bil. × 0.05)	$27.00
State & local income (4%)	($60 bil. × 0.04)	2.40
State corporate income (3%)	($14 bil × 0.03)	0.42
Property (1%)	($200 bil. × 0.01)	2.00
Subtotal		$31.82
Grand Total		$51.46

ªThe methodology used was as follows. The 1981 data in Table 7.7 were extrapolated to 1982 with effective tax rates as indicated.

Table 7.10

Comparative Performance of Foreign-Owned Affiliates in the United States with U.S. Domestic Companies, by Industrial Sector, 1981

Industrial Sector	Investment in Plant & Equipment	Sales per Worker	Export Position	Trade Balance	Profitability	Overall Performance
Manufacturing						
Food & Kindred	Dom[a]	Dom	Dom	Dom	For[b]	Dom 4–1
Chemicals	Dom	Dom	Dom	—	For	Dom 3–1
Primary Metals	For	For	For	—	Dom	For 3–1
Fabric Metals	For	Even	For	—	Dom	For 2–1
Machinery except electrical	Dom	For	Dom	—	Dom	Dom 3–1
Electrical Machinery	For	For	For	Dom	Dom	For 3–2
Textile Products	For	For	Even	Dom	Dom	—
Paper and Allied	For	Even	For	For	For	For 4–0
Rubber & Plastics	For	Even	—	—	—	—
Stone, Clay, & Glass	For	For	—	—	—	For 2–0
Transport Equipment	Dom	Even	Even	—	—	Split
Mining	For	—	—	—	—	—
Petroleum	Dom	Dom	Even	—	Dom	Dom 3–1

[a] Dom indicates superior performance by domestic industry.
[b] For indicates superior performance by foreign-owned firms in the United States.
Source: Tables 1.3 and 1.4.

In the remaining four industrial sectors there is insufficient information, or too narrow an advantage, to make a judgment. In the food and kindred products sector domestic firms enjoy the clearest advantage over foreign affiliates, whereas in the paper and allied products sector foreign affiliates enjoy the clearest advantage over domestic firms.

Examination of the five-activity areas shows that foreign affiliates enjoy clear performance advantages in investment in plant and equipment and sales per worker; that foreign affiliates enjoy a narrow advantage in export position; and that domestic firms enjoy clear advantages in trade and balance profitability. (See Table 7.11.)

Table 7.11
Comparative Performance of Foreign-Owned Affiliates in the United States, with U.S. Domestic Companies, by Type of Activity, 1981

Advantage to	Investment in Plant & Equipment	Sales per Worker	Export Position	Trade Balance	Profitability
Domestic	5	3	3	3	6
Foreign	8	5	4	1	3
Even	—	4	2	—	—

Source: Table 7.10.

Foreign affiliates enjoy distinct performance advantages over U.S. domestic firms in several industrial sectors as well as several activity areas. Foreign affiliates are good performers in primary metals and fabricated metals, sectors that are subject to intense import competition and slow demand growth. Considering that foreign affiliates enjoy a strong export position in these two sectors over domestic firms, it would appear that foreign investment policy should favor the inflow of FDI in these sectors.

Foreign affiliates also enjoy a performance advantage in the electrical machinery sector. This is based on their high level of plant and equipment investment, sales per worker, and export position, all of which are important from the point of view of reflecting differences in resource productivity and comparative advantage. Again it would appear that foreign investment policy should favor the inflow of FDI in this sector.

Foreign affiliates enjoy a very large performance advantage over U.S. domestic firms in the paper and allied products sector. This applies in four of the five activity areas, with foreign and domestic firms approximately even in one activity area—sales per worker. Again, it would appear that foreign investment policy should favor the inflow of FDI into this sector.

TOWARD AN FDI POLICY FOR THE UNITED STATES

The United States lacks a coherent and goal-oriented FDI policy. In part this is due to the tradition of laissez-faire by which government planning or intervention in the working of free market processes is considered undesirable. However, free trade and investment are goals, not reality. All nations of the world have a host of policies that affect the behavior of business, especially on the frontiers of international trade and investment. Until a few years ago the United States could afford the luxury of being unattentive to these matters. Today, the stakes are too high.

Analysis of Industry Sectors

Table 7.12 summarizes the findings of this chapter. In four sectors the performance of domestically owned firms is superior to that of foreign-owned firms; in eleven industrial sectors minimum domestic productive capacity is required to meet potential surge military production needs; and in eight sectors, as a result of high-tech orientation, foreign ownership could be limited or restricted. This analysis is not meant to be final and definitive; rather it suggests the United States' basic need to scrutinize foreign ownership carefully, with a view to insuring that national economic and political interests are given primary consideration.

A Foreign Review Agency

It is recommended here that a federal government agency be given the authority to implement guideline regulations or controls over foreign ownership and investment in U.S. industries. In addition, the same agency may have to coordinate foreign investment regulation with U.S. trade policy. This agency should be jointly responsible to the President and to the U.S. Congress; it should hold broad authority for negotiating tariffs and other related trade agreements; and it should be responsible for advising on the specifics of investment treaties with other nations. (A more detailed discussion of the rationale for and activities of such an agency is presented in Chapter 8.)

NOTES

1. See Table 6.1.
2. Tom Incantalupa, "Korea to Sell Cars in the U.S.," *Newsday*, February 17, 1985, p. 110.
3. Suzuki has supplied GM with 17,000 Sprint models each year. GM owns 5.3% of Suzuki Motor Company (*Newsday*, May 31, 1984), p. 43.
4. "Daihatsu, King of the Japanese Minicar, Steers Its Sights Toward the U.S. Market," *Wall Street Journal*, May 31, 1984, p. 35.

Table 7.12
Industrial Sectors Requiring Maintenance of Minimum Domestic Capacity or Restrictions on Foreign Ownership

Industrial Sector	Performance Characteristics of Foreign-Owned Sector Less Satisfactory Than Domestic Owned	Require Minimum Domestic Capacity for Military Surge Demand	Require Restrictions on Foreign Ownership Due to High Tech
Food & Kindred	X		
Chemicals	X	X	
Primary Metals		X	
Fabricated Metals		X	
Machinery, Except Electrical	X		X
Electrical Machinery		X	
Textile Products			
Paper & Allied			
Rubber & Plastics		X	
Stone, Clay, & Glass			
Ordnance		X	X
Aerospace		X	X
Shipbuilding		X	X
Petroleum Refining	X		
Instruments		X	X
Motor Vehicles		X	
Computers			X
Semiconductors		X	X
Telecommunications			X
Totals	4	11	8

5. OECD, *Long-Term Outlook for the World Automobile Industry* (Paris: 1983), pp. 53–66. "GM Pushes Big Computerization Program—Battle with Japanese Takes a High Tech Turn," *Asian Wall Street Journal*, July 10, 1984.

6. Paul Seabury, "Industrial Policy and National Defense," in Chalmers Johnson, ed., *The Industrial Policy Debate* (San Francisco: Institute for Contemporary Studies, 1984), p. 197.

7. Ibid., p. 198. If U.S. steel, chemicals, and machine tools industries declined and production shifted to other countries, other economic activities would replace them.

8. Ibid., pp. 200–201.

9. *Survey of Current Business*, March 1984, p. 31.

10. In this sense, focusing on war potential is too narrow an approach.

11. Frederick A. Brodie, "GM Seen Buying Stakes in 3 Companies That Make Systems to Let Machines See," *Wall Street Journal*, August 1, 1984, p. 8; "GM Moves into a New Era," *Business Week* (July 16, 1984): 48–54.

12. These cases are described in Richard N. Foster, "Why America's Technology Leaders Tend to Lose," in *Research and Development: Key Issues for Management*, (New York: The Conference Board, 1983), pp. 72–74.

13. Philip M. Boffey, "Industry Takes Dominant Science Role," *New York Times*, July 17, 1984, p. C1.

14. Here we should note that there is a disparity between the rapid pace of the U.S. public policy process. See John Diebold, "The Information Technology Industries," in William R. Cline, ed., *Trade Policies for the 1980's* (Cambridge: M.I.T. Press, 1983), p. 640.

15. Boffey, "Industry Takes Dominant Science Role," p. C1.

16. R. J. Harris and A. Nag, "GM Appears to Be Leading Candidate in Competition to Buy Hughes Aircraft," *Wall Street Journal*, May 8, 1985, p. 2.

17. U.S. Congress, House of Representatives, *Materials Research and Development Policy*, Hearings before the Subcommittee on Transportation, Aviation, and Materials of the Committee on Science and Technology, 98th Cong., 1st Sess., May 15–16, 1983, p. 198.

18. Ibid., p. 8.

19. R. W. Riche, D. E. Hecker, and J. Burgan, "High Technology Today and Tomorrow: A Small Slice of the Employment Pie," *Monthly Labor Review* (November 1983): 54.

20. Ibid., pp. 196–197. For example, a joint effort by the Department of Energy and the American Iron and Steel Institute to develop a sensing device based on laser and fiber optic technology will permit direct measurement of the chemical composition of molten steel at its temperature of 3,000°F. Use of the device would save the iron and steel industry $200 million annually in operating costs.

21. Paul Lewis, "Allies Curb Computers for Soviets," *New York Times*, July 17, 1984, p. 7D; and F. Kemple and Z. Lachica, "Cocom Feuds Over Trade to East Bloc," *Wall Street Journal*, July 17, 1984, p. 35.

22. "Are Foreign Partners Good for U.S. Companies?" *Business Week* (May 28, 1984): 59.

23. Ibid., p. 59.

24. "The Inroads Japan Is Making in Fiber Optics," *Business Week* (May 21, 1984): 176.

25. James LeMoyne, "Mineba's Ball Bearing Bid," *New York Times*, July 16, 1984. p. D1.

26. Structural conditions work to the disadvantage of the United States when in competition with the Japanese. Venture capital markets in the United States encourage formation of a number of small specialized companies, often with a narrow product range. Conversely, MITI provides funds to large, integrated Japanese firms, where a single product is not vital to profitability. See Diebold, "Information Technology Industries," pp. 644.

27. George C. Lodge, *The American Disease* (New York: Alfred Knopf, 1984), p. 20.

28. Mary L. Good, "Licensing—Technology Transfer for Profit," in *Research and Development*, pp. 55–56.

29. Ibid., p. 57.

30. Leon C. Greene, "Capitalizing on Foreign Research and Development," in *Research and Development*, pp. 60–63.

31. Earl H. Fry, *Financial Invasion of the U.S.A.* (New York: McGraw Hill, 1980), p. 3. Fry refers to a warning by Gaylord Nelson of the Senate Committee on Small Business that foreign firms are acquiring U.S. firms at such a fast rate that this could lead to a technology drain for the U.S..

32. "Can Japan Ever Be More Than an Also-Ran?" *Business Week* (July 16, 1984): 103–104.

33. "Reshaping the Computer Industry," *Business Week* (July 16, 1984): 84–85.

34. "How the IBM Juggernaut Will Keep Rolling," *Business Week* (July 16, 1984): 105–106.

35. Ed Zschau and Don Ritter, "Encourage Innovation Instead of Industrial Lemons," *Wall Street Journal*, August 1, 1984, p. 24.

36. Leon E. Wynter, "Congress Is Debating Federal Role in Setting Technological Priorities," *Wall Street Journal*, August 1, 1984, p. 27.

37. John Diebold reports that the Apple Computer Corporation has suffered such losses ("Information Technology Industries," p. 663).

38. George A Keyworth, "Creating a Climate for Industrial Progress," in *Research and Development*, pp. 27–29.

39. Egils Milbergs, "The Federal Government's Role and Its Programs," in *Research and Development*, pp. 27–29.

40. U.S. Congress, House of Representatives, Statement by Doug Walgren in *Research and Development: Joint Ventures*, Hearings of Subcommittee on Science, Research and Technology, Committee on Science and Technology, 98th Cong., 1st Sess., No. 43, July 12, 1983 (Washington, D.C.: Superintendent of Documents, 1984), p. 21.

41. Statement by Ronald Myrick, Semiconductor Research Association, July 12, 1983, in *Research and Development: Joint Ventures*, p. 65.

42. U.S. Congress, House of Representatives, *Possible United States Responses Using Research Joint Ventures*, Hearings of Subcommittee on Investigations and Oversight, Committee on Science Research and Technology, 98th Cong., 1st Sess., June 29–30, 1983, No. 45 (Washington, D.C.: Superintendent of Documents, 1984), pp. 42–51.

43. Peter F. McClosky, "Joint Research Ventures," in *Research and Development*, p. 65.

44. Lodge, *The American Disease*, pp. 246–247.

8

Policy Approaches to Foreign Direct Investment _____

Jean-Jacques Servan-Schrieber, writing in the 1960s, spoke of the challenge posed by U.S. multinationals investing overseas.[1] In the mid–1980s firms in other industrialized countries had matured and were engaging in FDI all over the world. As noted in Chapter 3, multinationals have been increasing the proportion of their FDI that goes into other industrialized countries as contrasted with developing countries. During the 1970s and early 1980s the trend toward inward FDI into the United States has been greatly increased. By the early 1980s, inward FDI into the United States was substantially in excess of outward flows by U.S. multinationals. With much of this investment going into the manufacturing sector, an increasing proportion of American manufactured goods is being produced by multinationals.

This chapter is concerned with the policy response to FDI in manufacturing. The present policy is one of leaving the door open for foreign multinationals to invest freely in the United States, and restraints are relatively rare. In this chapter the "open door" policy is challenged, and measures to protect our basic industrial base from dominance by foreign-owned multinationals are proposed.

THE PRESENT U.S. POLICY TOWARD FDI

Foreign owned multinationals have a fairly easy entry into U.S. markets. The central theme of the Carter Administration's 1977 policy directive concerning international direct investment was that it was U.S. policy neither to encourage nor discourage the inflow and outflow of FDI. Hence, the United States is committed to holding the economy open to the inflow of FDI. The 1977 directive also affirmed that "the United States has an important interest in seeking to assure that established investors receive equitable and non-discriminatory treatment from host governments."[2] In short foreign-owned companies should receive fair treatment from all host governments and international capital flows should be encouraged.

Although the United States does not discriminate against foreign investors, there are a number of exceptions. The United States does have certain restrictions designed to protect our national security and other important interests. Foreign nationals are limited in their ownership share in areas of the economy concerned with national defense, nuclear energy, inland shipping, domestic air transport, domestic radio communications, the production of hydroelectric power, and the exploitation of federally owned lands. Some states also have limited restrictions in areas such as land ownership, banking, and insurance.

The U.S. government has also established the Committee on Foreign Investment in the U.S. (CFIUS) to monitor the impact of foreign investment and to coordinate their implications for U.S. policy. CFIUS monitors the flow of FDI and reviews cases that could have major implications for national interests. It also oversees efforts of agencies, including the Departments of the Treasury, Commerce, and Agriculture, as well as other regulatory and executive agencies in the area of FDI. The existence of CFIUS facilitates coordination among the various executive agencies having the authority to implement federal laws and regulations with respect to FDI in the United States.[3] CFIUS makes a distinction between private FDI and investment by government-controlled entities.

In addition to federal legislation that directly controls foreign investment, a number of laws and regulations exist, especially in the antitrust and securities areas that are equally applicable to both foreign and domestic investors. One area is antitrust legislation that can prevent foreign acquisitions by investors because of their effect on actual or potential competition. In recent years, a number of foreign companies planning acquisitions or mergers have been subject to litigation under Section 7 of the Clayton Act, and the Federal Trade Commission has carefully scrutinized activities when foreign companies have attempted to enter the U.S. market by way of the acquisition route.[4] U.S. securities laws and practices are another area that affect foreign investors. Although such legislation applies equally to all investors, foreign investors find them to be burdensome because they are much more rigorous than those found in other countries.[5]

In addition to direct and indirect control at the federal level, many states have laws that regulate foreign investment. Although these laws rarely bar foreign investors outright, they do impose conditions to establish or operate a venture that applies specifically to foreigners. These include restrictions on land ownership and use, insurance, banking, mining and mineral rights, utilities, commercial fishing and the maritime sectors of state economies, and securities. States can prescribe the terms under which foreigners may hold stock in a corporation, and some states require that the majority of shares of certain companies be held by U.S. citizens.

Because in the early 1970s Americans became concerned about the impact of FDI on the U.S. economy, a number of studies have been conducted, reporting requirements established for foreign affiliates, and a monitoring agency (CFIUS) has been established. Two pieces of federal legislation have been enacted: the Foreign Investment Study Act of 1974, which directed the Secretaries of Commerce and Treasury to undertake a large study of foreign investment in the United States, and the Agriculture Foreign Investment Disclosure Act of 1978, which was enacted to require any foreign person who had acquired land to submit a report to the Secretary of Agriculture.[6]

In addition, the International Investment Survey Act of 1976 was enacted to give the President authority to collect information on international investment and provide analyses of such information to Congress. The President delegated the survey of FDI to the Commerce Department, portfolio investment to the Department of the Treasury, and the determination of the feasibility of establishing a system of monitoring foreign investment in real property to the Department of Agriculture.[7]

From the above, it is evident that federal and state governments both directly and indirectly impose a number of restrictions and regulations on foreign investors. In addition, foreign investors are closely monitored by the federal government and must report substantial amounts of information. Although these laws do provide information concerning foreign investment and restrict unwanted FDI in certain areas, the United States does not have a comprehensive and uniform policy toward FDI. Because many of the laws such as antitrust and securities legislation in the United States can be subject to legal interpretation in the courts, foreign investors may encounter uncertainty when planning an investment in the United States. Furthermore, the wide array of alternative legislation encountered in the 50 states does impose burdens on foreign investors.

FOREIGN GOVERNMENT PERFORMANCE REQUIREMENTS AND INCENTIVES TO FDI

At the same time the United States continues to maintain an "open door" to inward FDI, other foreign governments try to manage investment by foreign-owned multinationals by imposing a wide variety of performance requirements on foreign investors and by offering investment incentives. Although the existence of performance requirements and incentives is widespread in the developing countries, they are also fairly prevalent in many of the industrialized countries. Performance requirements and investment incentives, which in reality are non-tariff barriers imposed against the free flow of international trade and investment, distort trade flows and affect the worldwide allocation of economic resources.

Performance Requirements

Most major trading partners of the United States have imposed some trade-distorting performance requirements on foreign investors. These requirements are more widespread in developing than in developed countries. They can be classified as requirements based on domestic economic considerations, financial performance, manpower performance, balance-of-payments, and other.[8] Performance requirements are imposed to assure that foreign investors satisfy certain domestic objectives. In many cases they are linked to permission to enter the country or to receive investment incentives.

Performance requirements based on domestic economic considerations cover a number of different types, the most prevalent being local content requirements. In some countries, a stated percentage of local content is required for certain specified industries, such as automobiles, whereas in other countries the industry is not specified. The 1977 Benchmark Survey of U.S. Direct Investment Abroad undertaken by the Bureau of Economic Analysis (BEA) of the U.S. Department of Commerce covered 3,540 U.S. parent companies and their 24,666 foreign affiliates and found that 3% of the affiliates were required to utilize a minimum amount of local content, and of these reporting affiliates, 25% stated that the requirement applied only to foreign investors. Another important performance requirement applied to the transfer of technology.[9]

Financial performance requirements including local equity participation require the foreign-owned firm to put up a certain amount of its own capital and limit remittances abroad. A large number of developing countries have local equity participation requirements.

Manpower performance requirements are also imposed in a number of countries. The most widespread involve job creation and the limitation of foreign employees. Some countries impose requirements to train local employees and for management participation. According to the 1977 BEA survey cited above, use of a minimum amount of local labor is the most commonly reported performance requirement. Of the 24,666 foreign affiliates, 8% reported this requirement and 28% of the group that reports this requirement indicated that it was imposed only on foreign investors.

Two other major requirements reported in the BEA Survey were minimum export requirements and maximum import limitations, both of which affected the balance of payments. Two % of the affiliates reported being subjected to minimum export requirements, and 37% of these stated that the requirements were imposed only on foreign investors. Three % reported being subjected to maximum import requirements, and 21% of these stated that the requirements were imposed only on foreign investors. Three % reported they were required to use a minimum amount of local content, and 24% of these reported that the requirements were imposed only on foreign investors.

The BEA survey found that on an average U.S. affiliates were subjected to performance requirements much more frequently in developing than in developed countries. In developing host countries, 29% of U.S. affiliates reported being subjected to performance requirements as opposed to 6% investing in developed countries. In addition, whereas 3% of U.S. affiliates were subjected to minimum export requirements in developing countries, 1% were subjected to such requirements in developed countries.[10]

In general, the proportion of developing countries imposing performance requirements on U.S. affiliates was substantial. With the exception of Argentina, South American countries subjected at least one-third of reporting affiliates to performance requirements, and in Peru and Venezuela, the proportion was 50%. Mexico imposed requirements on 41% of the reporting affiliates. Among the African countries, Nigeria, Egypt, and Libya had such requirements in one-third to one-half of the cases.[11]

It was reported that India subjected 60% of reporting affiliates to such requirements. The percentage reported in Indonesia, Malaysia, and the Philippines was between 27 and 33% of affiliates and in South Korea, 40%.

Performance requirements in Mexico and Canada, the two countries bordering the United States, have been significant for the United States because U.S. investors have made large investments in these countries.

Mexico imposes a number of restrictions on foreign investment. Although Mexico recognizes the need for foreign direct investment, it imposes limitations on foreign equity participation. Under a 1973 law, new FDI involving up to 49% foreign ownership of the capital stock of a Mexican company is permitted. In acquisitions, foreigners are only able to acquire 25% ownership or 49% of the fixed assets of a Mexican company. Foreign investment is excluded from a substantial number of economic activities. Among them are certain activities reserved for the Mexican government, including petroleum and hydrocarbons, petrochemicals, radioactive minerals, the generation of nuclear energy, telegraphic and radio communications, railroads and electricity, and certain mining activities. Activities reserved for Mexican companies prohibiting foreign ownership of their shares include airways, national maritime transportation, radio and television, automotive transportation, gas distribution, and forestry. Minority ownership of shares by individual foreigners is permitted in banking, insurance, and investment. As an exception, 100% ownership is permitted in in-bond processing companies located near the U.S. border which process or assemble foreign raw materials and components for re-exports.[12]

Mexico has performance requirements to affect technology transfer, employment, and minimum local content. At least 90% of a company's employees (excluding top executives) must be Mexican citizens. Because the government is attempting to foster industrialization and employment, import permits are required for many types of foreign-made components and industrial raw materials. Usually, the goal is to maintain 60 to 80% local content.

The Mexican Auto Decree of 1977 encompasses both local content and minimum export requirements. The objectives of the decree were to accelerate the growth of Mexico's automotive industry and to increase Mexico's earnings of foreign exchange. Local content requirements were initially set at 50%, and it was recommended that they go to 75% for autos and 80% for trucks by 1981. If the company fails to meet the recommended local content requirements, it will be required to meet higher export requirements because motor vehicle companies were required to cover 100% of their foreign exchange costs by exports in 1982.[13]

The decree can have a number of trade-distorting effects.[14] Because all four

U.S. auto firms assemble autos in Mexico, the U.S. industry can be adversely affected. U.S. sales of auto parts to Mexico may be reduced, and U.S. sales of motor vehicles to free trade zones may fall. At the same time, the shipments of parts to the United States could increase to the extent that companies would choose to export instead of utilizing a greater amount of local content, and Mexican exports to the United States would rise. It can be anticipated that this decree will have negative impacts on the U.S. balance of payments and on jobs. The government of Mexico has estimated that the decree would raise exports of Mexican auto parts from $650 million in 1979 to over $5 billion by 1983. About 60% of increased Mexican exports would be directed to the U.S. market, resulting in a loss of 86,000 to 115,000 jobs in the U.S. auto and auto parts industry.[15]

Given the necessity of exporting if they fail to meet local content requirements, firms must increase production in Mexican plants. For instance, in 1981 Chrysler de Mexico chose to construct an engine plant with capacity to produce 200,000 four-cylinder engines. It was planned that three-fourths of annual production (valued at about $60 million) will be exported to the United States each year. In January 1984 Ford Motors announced its plan to build a $500 million stamping plant in Hermosillo, Mexico. The plant scheduled to open in late 1986, is expected to produce 130,000 automobiles a year, mainly for export to Canada and the United States. It will hire 3,000 workers. Construction of the plant was motivated by the Mexican Automotive Decree. Another motivating factor was an agreement with Ford by the Mexican government to complete a 211-mile, $23 million natural gas pipeline, the cost of which would be borne entirely by the Mexican government. The gas is to be used in the manufacturing process. Ford already produces four-cylinder engines in a plant located in Chihuahua. Ford uses some of the engines in its Mexican-produced models and ships the remainder to the United States.[16] In this case, an automotive plant that could have been producing in the United States is to be built in Mexico because of the necessity of conforming with Mexico's automotive decree.

Beginning with 1974, Canada's Foreign Investment Review Agency (FIRA) was responsible for regulating the inflow of FDI by examining every proposal for inward FDI to assure the Canadian government that the investment would benefit the Canadian economy before permission would be given to undertake the investment. However, the government of Brian Mulroney, the Canadian Prime Minister elected in late 1984, committed itself to undertake a fundamental change in policy. In conjunction with a desire to reverse economic direction in a sluggish economy with an 11% rate of unemployment, FDI would be welcome. In an effort to reverse direction and to remove the controversial FIRA, the Mulroney government proposed legislation to replace FIRA.[17]

Briefly, FIRA had been responsible for reviewing all new foreign investments and acquisitions to be certain that the investment proposal would provide substantial benefits to Canada. Included in the perceived benefits are the effects on exports and on use of Canadian services, parts, and components. Performance requirements took a number of forms, including the establishment of export targets (exports as a percentage of output or sales), commitment for the further processing of Canadian mineral ores, and procurement in Canada.[18]

These performance requirements had been viewed as trade distorting, and the United States claimed that some recent Canadian policies conflicted with its obligations as a member of GATT. On February 17, 1982, the United States made a formal complaint within the framework of GATT, but the extent to which FIRA activities distorted trade is unclear. U.S. Department of Commerce data indicate that, at least until 1977, the influence of FIRA on U.S. subsidiaries was minor.[19] However, it is believed that the incidence of performance requirements increased considerably after 1977.[20] The Labor Industry Coalition for International Trade (LICIT), a private committee of U.S. companies and labor unions, claimed that the policies impeded the efficient international allocation of resources and were trade distorting.[21]

Because the newly elected Conservative government wishes to actively promote FDI, legislation to replace FIRA with an agency called Investment Canada was passed by Parliament in August 1985. The purpose of the legislation is to encourage and facilitate investment. Only large, direct acquisitions with assets of over $5 million and indirect acquisitions of Canadian businesses by non-Canadians with assests of over $50 million will be subjected to review to ascertain that they offer significant benefits, but for the establishment of new businesses or to undertake small acquisitions, non-Canadian investors will only have to notify the agency of their intentions to invest. The agency will be empowered to carry on activities to encourage investment.[22]

Certain identified activities may be subjected to review. These regulations pertain to specific types of business activity that are related to Canada's cultural or national identification, including the publication and/or distribution of books and periodicals and the production and distribution of films.

A number of factors will be considered in assessing investments that are subject to review to determine if it is a net benefit to Canada. These factors of assessment include the impact of the investment on the level of economic activity in Canada; the degree and significance of participation by Canadians; the effect of the investment on productivity and industrial efficiency; technological development; product innovation and product variety in Canada; the effect of the investment on competition; and the contribution of the investment to Canada's ability to compete in world markets.

The purpose of the proposed legislation is to encourage and facilitate investment. The proponents of this legislation believe that FIRA has sent negative signals to domestic and foreign investors and the investors are convinced that Canada is ambivalent or even hostile to foreign investment. The legislation was proposed to encourage as much investment as possible in order to promote trade and industrial development and to improve international competitiveness in Canada. By exempting new business investments and limiting review to the larger acquisitions, it is estimated that the number of transactions now subject to review will be reduced by 90%.[23]

Investment Incentives

Many countries also offer investment incentives to encourage the inflow of FDI. Investment incentives such as tax credits or subsidies are often linked to the stipulation that certain performance requirements, such as meeting a minimum share of exports, be fulfilled. These incentives distort the decisions of private investors, and jobs, exports, technology, and so on, are shifted toward the host country offering the incentives.

The results of the 1977 Benchmark Survey of the U.S. Department of Commerce which surveyed U.S. firms investing abroad showed that 6,041 or 26% of U.S. affiliate firms that had responded had received one or more investment incentives. Twenty % of the affiliates received tax concessions, 9% received subsidies, 8% tariff concessions, and 5% other concessions. The survey also showed that some host countries gave incentives more frequently than others. Ireland gave incentives to 70% of U.S. affiliates, and South Korea to 53%. Some 40% of affiliates investing in Israel, Taiwan, and Brazil received incentives. A group of countries including Luxembourg, the United Kindgom, Greece, Spain, Sweden, Argentina, Peru, Venezuela, India, Indonesia, and Malaysia granted one or more incentives to between 30 and 40% of U.S. affiliates. Other countries granted incentives less frequently. In Canada, 19% reported receiving incentives, in Japan 9%, and in Hong Kong 5%.[24]

Whereas developing countries imposed performance requirements more frequently than developed countries, an almost equal percentage of U.S. affiliates in developed countries and developing countries received investment incentives (25% as opposed to 27%).

Affiliates engaged in manufacturing received incentives more frequently than affiliates in other industries (41% reported receiving such incentives), and affiliates producing transportation equipment, food products, and electrical machinery were more likely to receive investment incentives than other manufacturing affiliates.[25]

Although the U.S. government does not grant investment incentives, many of the 50 states as well as many localities actively provide investment incentives, including subsidies, tax abatements, and low-interest loans. A number of foreign subsidiaries receive incentives from the states and localities.

FOREIGN DIRECT INVESTMENT AND COMPARATIVE ADVANTAGE

The U.S. government has attempted to pursue a policy of free trade and maintains an "open door" to FDI. With respect to FDI, most foreign countries maintain some combination of performance requirements and investment incentives. In the United States, there are no performance requirements, but the states and localities do extend investment incentives. Robert F.Owen and Rachel McCulloch have pointed out that many host countries pursue a "carrot and stick'' approach to FDI, with the carrot being the foreign investment incentives and the stick being performance requirements. By using a carrot-and-stick combination, host countries attempt to promote national objectives without eliminating investment incentives. The provision of investment incentives helps to offset the burden and detriment that performance requirements impose on the foreign affiliate.[26]

Arguments favoring regulatory practices generally focus on market imperfections. Because FDI does not take place within an environment of perfect competition, the neo-classical analysis that sees nonintervention as the best means to foster economic efficiency is inapplicable. Host country measures to regulate FDI are designed to correct two types of market imperfections—market power and externalities in production.

Performance requirements designed to correct for market power attempt to counteract restrictive practices that arise from the fact that the monopolistic or oligopolistic parent firms are pursuing a global profit-maximization strategy by controlling the activities of the subsidiaries. The most important profit-maximizing practices pursued by MNCs include placing restrictions on exports, limiting the subsidiary's use of the parent firm's technology, and requiring imports of complementary products of components.

Performance requirements have also been developed to help capture the positive externalities created by the MNC in the host country. Host countries, especially less developed countries, often try to attract FDI for the positive externalities the MNC can generate, especially the transfer of technology through training of local workers. Measures setting employment levels for various categories of local employment or requiring that the subsidiary undertake local research and development are designed to increase the benefits the host country can receive by enhancing externalities in production.

Performance requirements are frequently designed to affect the trade of multinationals in the host country and, therefore, are trade distorting. Those that set minimum export targets or maximum export requirements are very clearly trade related. Import limitations or minimum value-added requirements have effects similar to those resulting from quotas that are placed on components and other inputs.[27] Under the GATT trading rules, such quotas would be specifically prohibited, but the rules are less precise when countries use investment policies for achieving similar ends. Because a minimum export requirement raises exports above the level they would otherwise be, the effect is similar to an export subsidy.[28] Although such requirements are inconsistent with both the GATT and the subsidy code, because they are tied in to investment policies, they are hard to deal with.

Other performance requirements more indirectly affect trade or investment; examples are requirements for the transfer of technology, maintaining jobs, and financial requirements.

Performance requirements skew FDI in order to achieve certain industrial policy goals and thereby produce distortions in international trade. Performance requirements, especially those related to trade, tend to shift investment and jobs away from other countries.

Investment incentives used by governments for the purpose of attracting FDI can have trade effects similar to performance requirements. Incentives frequently occur in conjunction with performance or trade requirements such as requirements for local content and minimum export of the product produced.[29] Investment incentives can have trade effects similar to those resulting from the imposition of performance requirements. If they shift investment from one country to another, employment, technology, and other benefits are shifted to countries providing the subsidy away from those countries unwilling or unable to subsidize the investments. Because countries offering the incentives often wind up emulating one another, they may end up transferring revenues to the treasuries of the home countries and to the firms.[30]

When discussing policies for FDI, it is important that investment incentives also be considered because incentives are frequently tied in with fairly specific performance requirements that are trade related. Host countries are making increasing use of investment incentives that are tied in with performance requirements. For instance, Brazil offers tax incentives to enterprises that use a high proportion of local raw materials and permits accelerated depreciation on capital equipment that is locally produced. Brazil also grants incentives based on an investment's location and its possibility for import substitution or export.[31]

To date, substantial progress has been made in achieving reduction in trade barriers. Even so, there is the possibility that FDI policies implemented by host countries would obliterate the gains achieved through reductions in trade barriers. Although these performance requirements and investment incentives may be trade distorting, little has been done to integrate the analysis of tariffs and non-tariff barriers to trade with FDI.[32]

In maintaining an "open door" policy to FDI, U.S. policymakers do not consider the trade-distorting effects of performance requirements in the rest of the world. In addition, they have refrained from taking measures that would offer strong incentives for foreign producers to shift the location of production to the United States. An important consideration is the desire not to interfere with comparative advantage. However, comparative advantage is an elusive concept and must be considered in light of broad trends in world trade and production as well as the increased degree of risk and instability in the world economic system.

Broad Trends in Composition of World Trade and Production

The past decade has witnessed rapid growth of the multinational corporation. Because the multinational corporation has become such a dominating factor in world trade, the adequacy and reasonableness of the theory of comparative advantage must be reconciled with the predominant position of the multinational corporation in world trade and investment. By the nature of its importance, the multinational corporation challenges the validity of comparative advantage in the following areas: (1) growth in importance of intrafirm trade; (2) the increased role played by intraindustry trade; and (3) the general problems of oligopolistic indeterminacy.

The theory of comparative advantage is based on the assumption that world trade consists of market transactions between buyers and sellers who are independent of each other. By contrast, a growing part of world trade takes place within one and the same enterprise or between affiliated enterprises (parent and foreign subsidiary, or two or more sister subsidiary companies). It has been estimated that between one-eighth and one-fourth of total world exports consist of intrafirm trade.[33] In 1974 about 50% of U.S. exports were on an intrafirm basis, while 59% of Canadian, and 29% of Swedish exports were intrafirm transactions.[34] Intrafirm trade is not the only departure from the assumed competitive market model. Multinational corporations play a dominant role in the trade of most primary commodities. Furthermore, the purchase of MNCs from subcontractors has become a growing form of trade in the Far East. In such circumstances, the MNC (the importer) is responsible for design, technology, and financing, whereas the producing enterprises (exporters) deliver the merchandise as agreed.

Probably the most dynamic component in world trade during the post-war period has been the growth of intraindustry trade in developed countries. These countries account for four-fifths of world exports of manufactured products, seven-eighths of which takes the form of trade between these countries. Exchange of the same kind of products constitutes a growing proportion of trade that exists in manufactured goods between developed countries. Grubel and Lloyd estimate that this intraindustry trade accounted for 80% of the growth in total trade of the ten largest industrial countries.[35] Great Britain is in the top-ranking position, with almost 70% of its foreign trade consisting of intraindustry trade. In the case of the United States, Canada, West Germany, and Italy, intraindustry trade is increasing faster than total trade, representing between 42 and 49% of total trade. Japan, with a sharp divergence in the composition of its export (manufactures) and import trade (raw materials), has a relatively small percentage of intraindustry to total trade (20%). Several factors help to explain why a high percentage of trade in some countries is intraindustry trade, namely a highly advanced specialization in production, the large share of trade comprised of components and semi-manufactures, and the need to concentrate on a narrow range of products to achieve long production runs and economies of output.

As the preceding discussion makes clear a large and growing proportion of world trade is accounted for by multinational enterprises, which in their domestic markets function as oligopolists. The oligopolistic model, which entails market power, does not fit into the framework of comparative advantage which assumes perfectly competitive markets and immobility of factors internationally.

One problem with fitting oligopoly into the theory of comparative advantage is the problem of oligopolistic indeterminacy. Most oligopolistic models lead to inderminate conclusions. Two examples should suffice. The firm is concerned with the conflicting goals of maximizing the growth rate of the firm and achieving maximum valuation of the firm's shares (in effect, a goal achieved by profit maximization). In a situation of *managerial capitalism* the aim of management is to accelerate growth. In this regard, shareholder interest would often tend to coincide with management interests. In addition, both parties have an interest in achieving high share prices, so that asset values will increase, capital issues will be facilitated, and cheap takeovers can be avoided. As long as the firm's economic growth does not conflict with the value of shares, shareholder and management interests tend to coincide. That is, when growth of firm and share valuation both coincide, the interests of management and shareholders are not in conflict. After a point however, the firm's growth may need to be financed increasingly out of earnings. Dividends are reduced, and a conflict arises between shareholders and management. Oligopolistic indeterminacy occurs at the point where maximizing the firm's growth rate conflicts with the achievement of a maximum valuation of the firm's shares.

The second problem stems from the fact that many of the products exchanged internationally between oligopolistic multinationals are traded in imperfect markets. Therefore, strong elements of bilateral monopoly are present, with the attendant risks. Such situations exist where a chemical manufacturer in one country buys intermediate products from a competitor in another country. In such cases the negotiated price involves a sharing of economic rent between the parties, the sharing being dependent on the ability of both parties to derive a satisfactory strategic benefit, often regardless of whether supply is emanating from the lowest cost source. The purchaser may have adopted a strategy of reducing currency risk or minimizing the risk of long transportation line breakdowns, with the result that the material required is obtained from a source other than the lowest cost source. To assure a minimum level of capacity operation, the supplier may have adopted a strategy of price discrimination downward, again violating the economic principle of comparative advantage, that is, sourcing in the lowest cost market sector.

PROPOSALS FOR U.S. POLICY FOR FDI

As observed earlier whereas the United States follows a fairly open policy toward inward FDI, most other countries apply various performance requirements for FDI. In a trading situation where the law of comparative advantage is not strictly applicable when dealing with large multinationals, trade and investment policies based on precepts of perfect competition and comparative advantage lose at least some of their applicability. Within such a context, it is necessary to develop a U.S. policy stance toward inward FDI, the objective being not to follow restrictive practices but to protect national interests against further distortions in the international trading situation.

With regard to U.S. policy toward inward FDI, the United States maintains an "open door" to foreign direct investment inflows. Trade and investment are assumed to take place in an environment in which the law of comparative advantage is applicable, a condition we have shown to be questionable when the trading and investing parties are large, oligopolistic multinationals.

Although the United States does favor the free flow of trade and investment, at both state and federal levels there are a number of restrictions and impediments to FDI. When viewed from the vantage point of foreign observers wishing to undertake FDI in the United States, the United States may appear not to follow a strictly open door policy. What policy does exist has evolved in a very piecemeal fashion, with impediments at times flowing from legislation that was never intended to apply to foreign investment. In this section we argue that the United States should adopt a framework for assessing inward FDI in the United States, achieving bilateral and multilateral reciprocity from foreign nations in their treatment of U.S. multinationals, and developing a uniform procedure for monitoring inward FDI. Because it may not be possible for the United States to separate out the subject of FDI in the area of manufacturing from the subject of a strategy for industrial policy in the United States, some of our recommendations may spill over into the area of industrial policy. Because we believe the United States should not shift its industrial base away from basic manufacturing such as steel and automobiles, even though it is becoming more high-technology oriented, some of our policy recommendations will reflect these beliefs.

Macroeconomic Policy and the Widening Current Account Deficit

As noted above, international trade and foreign direct investment can be substitutes for one another, with the amount of inward FDI being affected by policy measures toward international trade. In turn, the policies which countries adopt toward international trade have frequently been an outgrowth of economic conditions. For instance, unfavorable economic conditions preceded the escalation of tariff walls during the Great Depression of the 1930s as countries responded with escalated protectionism. Since the early 1970s, the world economy has been witness to turbulent economic conditions, and any explanation of FDI inflows into the United States during the past decade must be combined with a discussion of macroeconomic conditions.

The 1970s and the early 1980s witnessed a number of events, including the breakdown of the Bretton Woods system and the advent of floating exchange rates; the large increase in petroleum prices; worldwide inflation; the slowdown in growth in productivity, slow economic growth in the industrial economies; two severe economic recessions from which Europe has not yet recovered; the proliferation of non-tariff barriers at the same time that multilateral trade agreements had led to reductions in tariff barriers; and growth in debt burdens in the less developed countries coupled with frequent cases of insolvency. All of these events have helped produce uncertainty and instability in the world economy.

Macroeconomic policies in the United States during the recent past have contributed to world economic instability. In 1980, in an effort to curb double-digit inflation, an extremely tight monetary policy was initiated which was instrumental in producing the largest recession since World War II. At the same time the United States pursued a stimulatory fiscal policy as tax rates were reduced by a cumulative 23% over a three-year period and government spending continued to grow. Although the easy fiscal policy gave a tremendously large stimulus to the economy at a time when the economy had sunk into the worst recession during the postwar period, it produced large budgetary deficits of roughly $200 billion per annum in fiscal years 1983–1984 and 1984–1985, years of economic recovery.

The exceptionally large budgetary deficits have had a number of effects on the world economy and the United States. Domestically deficits proved stimulating to the growth in spending and helped fuel the recovery and domestic spending underwent sustained economic growth. But the export sectors and sectors that compete with imports faltered as the huge budgetary deficits were accompanied by growing trade deficits and a loss of international competitiveness. During 1981–1985 the dollar surged in value against foreign currencies. Although by December 1985 the dollar had declined by 17% in effective terms from its peak values in February 1985, this did not have an immediate impact on international competitiveness.[36]

Several factors have contributed to the relative strength of the dollar.[37] The first has to do with the success of the U.S. government in bringing inflation under control more rapidly than expected and the fact that economic recovery in the United States came earlier than expected and has been stronger than in other industrial countries. The strength of the recovery has also been associated with enlarged inflows of capital to the United States in response to an improved investment climate. Another explanation has to do with the attractiveness of investing in the United States during a period when financial and political uncertainties in other parts of the world have been greatly increased. But of perhaps greater significance have been the differences in fiscal policies in the United States compared with Japan and most European countries. All major industrial countries have been pursuing a fairly restrictive monetary policy, but in the United States during the last few years this has been coupled with an easy fiscal policy whereas in most other countries this has generally been combined with fiscal restraint.

U.S. fiscal policy has created pressures in financial markets and expectations that these pressures would be intensified. Interest rate differentials have been large. Interest rate differentials have attracted capital inflows from abroad and have driven up the external value of the dollar.[38]

Continuation of high real rates of interest is a worldwide phenomenon. Restraint in monetary policy has been a contributing factor, but large public sector deficits and rising public sector debt in comparison to nominal output have caused both savers and investors to be concerned. For if the public sector debts were monetized, they would help to fuel inflation, and even if they were not monetized, the competition for funds would intensify as the recovery progressed. It is believed that either possibility has the potential to produce upward pressure on interest rates.[39] As a consequence, the credit markets have already taken these possibilities into consideration and real interest rates remain high.

The deregulation of financial institutions commencing in 1980 may also have contributed to high interest rates. Now that commercial banks and savings and loan associations in the United States are free to compete for funds by offering attractive interest rate incentives, the cost of funds to financial institutions has increased, thus contributing to the perpetuation of high interest rates.

The relative strength of the dollar has had an adverse impact on U.S. competitiveness in international markets. Many basic manufacturing industries in the United States have found it difficult to compete in international markets, and output, employment, and profits remain low in many manufacturing industries. Relatively high wage rates, low productivity, failure to adopt more efficient productive techniques, and structural changes in the U.S. economy have all contributed to the inability of large segments of the manufacturing sector to compete in international markets. But macroeconomic policies that combine restraint in monetary policy with an easy fiscal policy have also contributed to difficulties which the manufacturing sector faces in competing in international markets. Because exports comprise a substantial part of the demand for U.S. agricultural products, the agricultural sector has also been adversely affected by the strength of the dollar. The difficulties faced by U.S. export sectors have produced a strong demand for protectionism, especially against Japanese imports.

At the same time there has been a growing concern about the large growth of foreign capital into the United States. Between 1970 and 1983, known cumulative foreign investment in the United States rose from $174.5 billion to $781.5 billion. Of those amounts, foreign investments in government securities, stocks, and bonds increased from $153.9 billion to $646.1 billion. In 1983 the total inflow of foreign investment amounted to $81.7 billion, of which $70.4 billion represented portfolio investment. Capital inflows from Japan made up between $25 to $50 billion of the $70.4 billion of inward portfolio investment in that year. In 1984, the inflow of foreign investment reached $97.3 billion, of which portfolio investment represented $74.8 billion. This large influx of foreign capital into the United States has given rise to a growing debate in the financial community concerning the risks of this inflow. Some bankers and economists believe that foreign investment has indirectly had an adverse impact on the trade balance. Henry Kaufman, an economist with Salomon Brothers Inc., a large Wall Street investment firm, has been quoted as saying that "foreign investment has contributed to the strength of the dollar, which has contributed to the strength of the trade deficit." Paul Volcker, chairman of the Federal Reserve Board, has noted that the trade and budget deficits "imply a dependence on foreign borrowing by the U.S. that, left unchecked, will sooner or later undermine the confidence in our economy essential to a strong currency and to prospects for lower interest rates."[40]

Under a system of flexible exchange rates, the mechanism whereby an increased inflow of foreign investment into the United States can affect the value of the currency and the trade balance is as follows. Assuming that the Japanese desire to purchase U.S. securities, they will exchange yen for dollars with which to purchase the dollar-denominated securities that are offering higher interest rates than can be earned in Japan; the price of the dollar rises relative to the yen and contributes to the growing trade deficit with Japan. When the demand for dollars relative to the yen raises the dollar price in terms of the yen, the appreciation of the dollar in terms of the yen makes American goods more expensive in Japan and reduces exports.

Deficits on the trade balance are in effect the counterpart to surpluses on the capital account. Similar mechanisms are involved in creating trade deficits (or current account deficits) and capital inflows.[41] Policy proposals developed to deal with the large inflows of foreign capital should also have an impact on trade deficits under the present flexible exchange rate system.

A national income accounting framework can be used to describe the mechanism whereby current account deficits contribute to capital inflows. It is assumed that a system of flexible exchange rates prevails. An identity relates the national income accounts to the current account in the balance of payments.

(1) $Y - E = S - I_D = X - M = I_F$

where

$Y =$ the current value of the country's net national product.

$E =$ the value of the country's domestic spending.

$S =$ the value of the country's saving.

$I_D =$ the value of the country's domestic capital formation.

$X - M =$ the current account balance (exports minus imports).

$I_F =$ net foreign investment (net increase in claims on foreigners plus international reserve assets).

In the identity, $Y - E = S - I_D$, the difference between what a nation produces and what it spends for all purposes is shown to be equal to the difference between its savings and domestic capital formation.

Savings are equal to the sum of domestic capital formation plus net foreign investment.

(2) $S = I_F + I_D$.

Net foreign investment, I_F, is represented by the difference between exports and imports (the current account balance). If $(X - M)$, the nation's current account surplus, increases, the difference between that nation's net national product minus spending $(Y - E)$ must also increase, which raises the difference between savings and domestic capital formation.[42] Alternatively, if the country has a current account deficit (imports exceed exports), an increase in this deficit means that the deficit of domestic investment over savings must grow, and the rest of the world accumulates net financial claims on this country.

Within this framework, foreign investment must rise as a country develops increasing current account deficits, or as the net foreign investment inflows increase, deficits must increase. The relatively high interest rates prevailing in the United States since 1981 have encouraged large foreign investment inflows which have contributed to the relative strength of the U.S. dollar and the ever widening current account deficit.

In 1984 the current deficit was $101.5 billion. Part of the increase in current account financing was met by a $20.4 billion decline in net new foreign lending and investment by U.S. residents (bank and non-bank), and a large part of the remainder was met by increases in foreign direct investment and other foreign holdings of U.S. assets. Increased foreign portfolio investment contributed to the growth in foreign holdings of U.S. assets.

If the U.S. trade deficits of 1984 magnitude were to continue to grow ($108.3 billion), the current account deficits would rise in response to the trade deficit as well as the growing charges on the mounting U.S. foreign debt. Growing dividend and royalty payments of foreign-owned companies would also contribute to the growth in the current account deficit.[43] As the deficits continue, the foreign debt mountain continues to grow as the United States shifts from a net creditor position to a growing net debtor position.

Some contend that the widening current account deficit poses three major problems.[44] The first is a financial problem of the growing volume of foreign debt as the United States passes from net creditor to net debtor status. The need to attract net capital inflows could have worldwide implications for exchange rates and interest rates.

The second is an economic problem that stems from the leakage of U.S. domestic demand through the trade deficit as imports remain high relative to exports. For instance, in the third quarter of 1984 over two-thirds of the growth in U.S. domestic demand went for increased net imports, and at the same time exports sagged. For 1985 figures of the U.S. Department of Commerce showed that economic growth had declined significantly, the main reason for the slow-down being the drag from the international sector as imports rose and exports declined.

The third problem is the increased momentum to protectionism caused by the trade deficit. Since 1982 trade balances have badly deteriorated in most categories of the manufacturing sector, not only in industries that have had longstanding structural problems, but also in many high-technology industries such as business data processing, semi-conductors, and telecommunications. During the spring and summer of 1985, demand for protectionism, especially against Japanese imports, reached astonishingly high proportions as industry after industry was being hit by sagging output resulting from import penetration and falling exports.

Increasingly, the flow of imported goods has undermined the country's manufacturing industries, and protectionist feelings have been enhanced by weak U.S. export prospects. U.S. export prospects are depressed because foreign markets have not been growing as rapidly as the U.S. market. U.S. firms face restricted access to foreign markets, and the value of the dollar has raised the relative price of U.S. exports. Even though multilateral agreements have produced large-scale tariff reductions, non-tariff barriers including production subsidies offered by foreign governments, dumping, industry targeting, and cartel agreements have contributed to the grievances of U.S. industries.[45]

A Concise Proposal for Macroeconomic Policy

The impact of recent macroeconomic policies on the U.S. industrial sector and foreign investment inflows, including FDI have already been noted. These policies have been instrumental in the loss of international competitiveness of U.S. industries. At the same time they have encouraged massive inflows of foreign investment, including direct investment. Changes in macroeconomic policy can help U.S. industries regain their competitiveness.

It is important that the United States gear its macroeconomic policies to the international needs of the nation. Within the context of this volume, there are several essential ingredients of macroeconomic policies. These include interest rate policy, foreign investment policy, a clearcut balance-of-trade program, and incentives that favor saving and investment.

The United States needs *a low interest rate policy*. Such a policy would help reduce the foreign trade deficit, encourage domestic investment which in the long run should make our industries more competitive vis-à-vis imports and FDI, and assist in reducing the federal budgetary deficit (by lowering the interest service part of budget expenditures). According to the Report of the President's Commission on Industrial Competitiveness, "it is ironic that in the world's richest nation capital cost is a disadvantage for U.S. competitiveness. The high cost of capital has led to low levels of investment by U.S. firms."[46]

Low interest rates would contribute toward a more realistic dollar exchange rate. The 1984 appreciation of the U.S. dollar on the foreign exchange markets is generally recognized as a major factor in the escalation of the U.S. trade deficit from $61 billion in 1983 to $108.3 billion in 1984. (The U.S. trade deficit was only $28 billion in 1981.)[47] According to a Federal Reserve analysis: "The high dollar priced many U.S. tradable goods out of international markets and encouraged a flood of imports into the domestic goods market. Both developments generated pressures for sectoral protection and for greater shielding of the U.S. market against all imports."[48]

An increasingly popular viewpoint is that capital flows play a more important role in altering foreign exchange rates than trade flows. This viewpoint is supported by the fact that capital flows have come to dwarf flows of traded goods. The current view is becoming synchronous with the notion that changes in capital flows establish exchange rates, and in turn the size of the current account and capital account balances of nations.[49] For this reason, we strongly support macro-economic policies that will over time reduce interest rate levels in the United States.

Interest rate levels could probably be reduced over time if the United States conducts an easing of monetary policy that is accompanied by a tightening of fiscal policy to substantially reduce the size of the budgetary deficit, which currently is about $200 billion per year. At the same time it would be necessary to prevent a reoccurrence of inflation. This could be accomplished by introducing a system of worker compensation in which wage payments would be geared to the level of the firm's profits. In other words, we recommend introducing some type of profit control that shares profits with workers in good years, but limits wage increments in poor years. Furthermore, because deregulation and the competitive bidding for funds by U.S. financial institutions may have contributed to high interest rate levels, it may be necessary to reintroduce regulation of the level of interest rates that can be paid by financial institutions.

A somewhat more loose monetary policy would help to lower interest rates, which would probably reduce capital inflows and cause a decline in the international value of the dollar. To avoid too rapid a decline in the price of the dollar, monetary policy should not be loosened too suddenly.

Although the large budgetary deficits have stimulated domestic spending, they have contributed to the high interest rates, and measures must be introduced to significantly reduce budgetary deficits. However, there are dangers in abruptly cutting the size of the deficit. At a time when much of the rest of the world has failed to recover from the last recession, the U.S. budgetary deficits have provided a stimulus to domestic spending and have indirectly contributed to a large growth in imports with positive repercussions on the economies of the rest of the world. Furthermore, the U.S. recovery has begun to slow down, and significantly lowering budgetary deficits could directly depress the U.S. economy and indirectly affect the economies of the rest of the world which are already experiencing slow economic growth. Within this context, a reduction in domestic spending at this time could have severe consequences for the exports of some of the debt-ridden Third World countries, thereby enhancing the possibility that some of these countries would be forced to default on their debt obligations. That is why we urge that, in conjunction with any budgetary tightening that may occur, the Federal Reserve pursue an easy money policy to help reduce the level of interest rates.

In summary, lower interest rates could have a number of effects. First, they would help stimulate domestic capital formation, Second, by preventing a significant reduction in domestic demand, the United States would continue to stimulate economic recovery in the rest of the world. Economic recovery in the rest of the world would also be furthered because low interest rates in the United States would facilitate an easing of monetary policy abroad, thereby lowering foreign interest rate levels. Finally, it is quite likely that capital inflows would taper off in conjunction with lower interest rates and the expansion of profitable investment climates in the rest of the world, thus leading to a depreciation in the value of the dollar and a reduction in the trade deficits.

Macroeconomic policy indirectly implies a foreign investment policy. As noted in the preceding section, we support a low interest rate policy. This is based on the need to curb foreign investment inflows which in the past have contributed to a strong appreciation of the U.S. dollar on the foreign exchange markets, in turn leading to a deterioration in the U.S. balance of trade.

Therefore, the United States must apply a neutral policy vis-à-vis foreign investment flows to avoid unnecessary appreciation of the dollar and excessive fluctuations in foreign exchange rates in general. Application of a neutral policy of this sort implies that the United States will be able to stabilize international interest rate differentials. The differentials in interest rates between nations in large part serve as an incentive for portfolio capital flows. Looking back over the past decade of international monetary experience, wide swings in interest rate differentials can be observed. Understandably, then, the prospects of stabilizing interest rate differentials are not favorable. Nevertheless, the United States must be prepared to take action in this area when necessary. This suggests a more active role for the Federal Reserve in the future. It further suggests international coordination of monetary policy to avoid wide swings in exchange rate relationships.[50]

An important step toward alleviating the wide swings in the value of the dollar was taken on September 22, 1985, when the U.S. Secretary of the Treasury met in New York with finance ministers from the other four countries belonging to the group of five (United States, United Kingdom, Japan, Germany, and France) for the purpose of finding a way to achieve greater stability in exchange rates. It was agreed that there was a need for a co-ordination of monetary policies and enhanced intervention in foreign currency markets to stabilize exchange rates. Since September 22, 1985, there is evidence of greater intervention by the Federal Reserve Bank of the United States. Previously, the Reagan Administration had undertaken little intervention in foreign currency markets and the dollar appreciation was excessive. But, since September 22, the Federal Reserve Bank has intervened substantially by selling dollars on foreign currency markets. From September 22, 1985 to the beginning of December, 1985, the U.S. dollar depreciated by 8% in effective (trade-weighted) terms.

It may be necessary to implement additional measures to avoid wide swings in the international value of the dollar. One such measure would be to use currency intervention to "target zones" for currencies. Such a measure was proposed by President François Mitterand of France. Under this system, the government would select a value of its currency, and fluctuations ranging from 10% to 15% above and below the range would be permitted before the country would be required to undertake currency intervention.[51] Within this context, it may also be necessary to expand the present activities of the International Monetary Fund with respect to the surveillance of exchange rates. It is also very possible that countries will seek to undertake international monetary reform to avoid such wide fluctuations in exchange rates as has occurred during the past five years. Such reform would no doubt move toward the direction of implementing a system that permits greater stability of exchange rates.

The U.S. must adopt a clearcut balance of trade program. The United States cannot sustain the large balance-of-trade deficits of recent years which, in an accounting relationship, are the other side of the investment inflows. As indicated in Table 8.1, these investment inflows have had the effect of reducing the net international creditor position of the United States. The larger part of the reduction in the overall U.S. net investment position has taken place in portfolio investment, reflecting the importance of securities transactions and interest rates in U.S. capital inflows, as discussed earlier. It is projected that at year-end 1985 the net international investment position of the United States will be approximately $400 billion in the red.[52]

The eroding U.S. net investment position has been one of the reasons for the sharp decline in net service receipts since 1981. (Net service receipts declined from $41 billion in 1981 to $17 billion in 1984 and were largely associated with a decline in net investment income from $34 billion in 1981 to $18 billion in 1984.[53] There is a clear connection leading from an appreciation of the dollar caused in part by capital inflows, which to a large extent are associated with high interest rates in the United States, to a growing balance-of-trade deficit, to an impairment of other sectors in the balance of payments, especially net service and net investment income.

The United States must adopt a program in which the balance of trade will be managed. Balance of trade deficits should not be permitted to exceed one % of GNP. The actual measures that must be used to accomplish this target include a mix of macro- and microeconomic policies.[54]

The United States is in an unusual position that mandates a near balancing in its trade accounts. First, it contains the largest national market for commodities in the world. Any significant increase in domestic market share captured by imports will bring about a disproportionate shift in the U.S. foreign trade balance. For example, in 1984 the non-service component of GNP totaled $1,850 billion. Every additional one % of this market captured by imports represents a potential increase of $18.5 billion in the U.S. trade deficit. The massive size of the markets for commodities and goods in the United States suggests that imports will be massive, even if policies directed at controlling the trade balance are moderately successful.

Incentives toward increased saving and investment are necessary. A larger flow of domestic saving is required if the United States is to avoid depending on foreign sources of capital to equilibrate aggregate savings and investment. A larger flow of domestic savings should slow down and reverse the recent U.S. trend toward a net debtor position. Policies that would promote domestic savings

Table 8.1
International Investment Position of the United States, 1981–1984[a]
(bil. dol.)

Year-end	Net Recorded International Investment Position				Cumulative Unrecorded Transactions[b]	Recorded Position Plus Cumulative Unrecorded Transactions[c]
	Total, Net	Net Direct Investment	Other Recorded Portfolio, Net	Gold, SDRs, and IMF		
1981	143.1	122.2	0.6	20.3	− 78.1	65.0
1982	149.5	99.6	26.2	23.7	− 111.1	38.5
1983	106.0	92.6	− 14.1	27.5	− 120.4	− 14.4
1984	35.0	80.0	− 75.0	30.0	− 150.0	− 115.0

[a] Positive figures denote U.S. investment abroad: negative figures indicate foreign investment in the United States. All data except those for 1984 include estimates for gains or losses on assets denominated in foreign currency due to their revaluation at current exchange rates, as well as estimates for price changes in stocks, bonds, or other assets. Other adjustments to the value of assets relate to changes in coverage, statistical discrepancies, and the like.

[b] This item is the statistical discrepancy from the U.S. international transaction account, which is cumulated beginning in 1959 with a base of zero. A positive discrepancy in the international transactions account appears here with a negative sign, on the assumption that it represents a net accumulation of claims by foreigners.

[c] This item is equivalent to the cumulative U.S. current account position plus valuation adjustments (note a).

Source: Catherine L. Mann, "U.S. International Transactions in 1984," *Federal Reserve Bulletin* (May 1985): 285.

include more favorable tax treatment of interest earned on bank deposits, a lower capital gains tax, and lower taxation on earnings from other investment instruments.[55]

Investment in lower cost production processes and new products is required if U.S. industries are to expand exports and remain competitive in domestic markets. A more favorable investment climate in the United States is required to encourage corporate investment and to increase the channeling of corporate cash flows into productive investments.

Policy Approaches to Foreign Direct Investment

As pointed out in Chapter 3, among the reasons for FDI inflows into the United States were size of the U.S. market, fears of protectionism, and exchange rate movements. Since 1983, the U.S. economy has been growing much more rapidly than European economies. Given the growth in the size of the U.S. market relative to markets abroad, FDI flows into the United States would have been expanded.

With regard to exchange rate changes, during the 1970s when the dollar had depreciated significantly, its reduced value in conjunction with a depressed stock market contributed to FDI inflows. But during the 1980s, with the overvaluation of the dollar and increased stock market prices, FDI still continued to flow inwards and showed significant increases during 1983 and 1984. Obviously, the strong recovery of the U.S. economy, which greatly enhanced corporate profitability, encouraged heavy FDI inflows at a time when the dollar was substantially overvalued.

As U.S. manufacturing industries were losing their ability to compete internationally, industries such as steel, textiles, footwear, and autos sought protection. The voluntary restraint agreements that were negotiated in 1985 for steel imports and proposed domestic content legislation for autos are the results of two such efforts. Fear of impending protectionism was especially instrumental in encouraging large inflows of FDI by the Japanese.

Domestic content legislation would be one form of protectionism directly linked to FDI. The fear of protectionism in the United States has been the major factor in the decision of Japanese motor vehicle producers to locate production facilities in the United States. In earlier years fears of protectionism motivated Japanese color television producers to produce in the United States.

Domestic content legislation on autos, if enacted, would directly affect FDI inflows. Although such legislation may be considered inconsistent with the open door approach to international trade, it does offer specific advantages when applied under proper circumstances. In Chapter 6 it was noted that if applied by the United States in the case of autos, a domestic content requirement would have significant beneficial employment and income effects. It was also suggested that a modified domestic content requirement would reduce the risks of retaliation and price inflation. As discussed in Chapter 7, domestic content is one aspect of FDI policy. A carefully planned domestic content requirement applicable to autos would give domestic producers an opportunity to finance technological advance and provide temporary relief from rising international competition. It would also insure that the domestically owned component of the industry would remain healthy and a significant part of the industry. This may be necessary from the national defense standpoint.

The realization that trade and FDI policy measures may overlap and that foreign direct investment is often a substitute for trade makes it imperative that policymakers also focus on FDI. The globalization of international production and the growth of intrafirm trade have altered the nature of international trading relations. When a large and growing part of international trade cannot be governed by the laws of comparative advantage, it is not possible to anticipate that a free trading situation is able to provide the optimum allocation of resources. At the same time, it must be recognized that the imposition of performance requirements and granting of investment incentives only add further impediments to trade. Within this context it becomes increasingly important that the international community begin to recognize the necessity of focusing on reducing the proliferation of performance requirements and investment incentives.

Several organizations have attempted to work on some elements of problems involved in FDI policies. Article 92 of the Treaty of Rome provides that aid given through state resources is not compatible with the Common Market if the aid affects the trade of member states.[56] As a result the Commission of the European Economic Community has set rules limiting the amount of investment incentives allowed. If arrangements proposed by countries are not consistent with the rules, the Commission undertakes intensive country-by-country reviews. Not knowing the size of the subsidy involved in a complex package including expenditure, tax, and regulatory items makes it difficult for the Commission to implement the rules.

The Organization of Economic Cooperation and Development (OECD) deals with policies toward FDI through the Code of Liberalization of capital movements, which covers transactions between residents and non-residents and includes a commitment to liberalize policy on FDI; and the Declaration and Decisions on International Investment and Multinational Enterprises, which is concerned with performance guidelines for MNCs, review and consultation on incentives and disincentives to FDI, and notification of exceptions to national treatment.[57]

The United States has a number of options in developing a policy approach to FDI. The United States can implement some of these options on a unilateral basis. Bilateral approaches involving investment protection treaties such as those developed by several European countries are also possible. Most important is the attempt to deal with the multinational aspects of the issues because, ultimately, international investment issues will have to be tackled in international forums similar to those concerned with trade issues.[58]

One way to counter foreign government actions that impose requirements on FDI would be to retaliate or emulate such actions. The United States may take "unilateral measures," measures that are in conformity with U.S. international commitments, to offset interventionist investment policies abroad. Here the United States would encourage either public or private actions that would obtain compensation for the injured parties in the home countries or impose costs on host governments.[59] Such actions would include making use of the U.S. escape clause" and imposing countervailing duties and other trade remedies. Possible "unilateral" measures have been classified into three types, depending on who holds the right of action. These include a public response, mixed public-private response, and purely private response.[60]

The U.S. government would initiate a purely public response. Section 301 of the 1974 Trade Act, which provides responses to certain trade practices of foreign governments, would be a possible avenue of response to the intervention policies of host governments. "Under Section 301, the President can respond to any act, policy, or practice of a foreign government that is inconsistent with the provision of, or denies benefits to the U.S. under any trade agreement, or is unjustifiable, unreasonable, or discriminatory and burdens or restricts U.S. commerce."[61]

Gary Hufbauer has suggested a mixed public-private response that could be patterned after Section 201 of the Trade Act of 1974 which is concerned with escape clause relief. Under this procedure the private petitioner affected by the performance requirement files a petition for eligibility of import relief in order to facilitate orderly adjustment to import competition. If there is a determination of harm, the President determines what remedy is to be granted, subject to congressional approval. To implement this mixed public-private response, it would be necessary to amend Section 301 of the 1974 Trade Act to provide that the President may take action when a private party demonstrates harm to its interest. The U.S. government could then bring a GATT case, holding that a performance requirement should be treated as equivalent to an export subsidy or that a local sourcing requirement should be treated as equivalent to import quotas. To the extent that it would be determined that these performance requirements hinder U.S. exports, they would involve a denial of national treatment.

A countervailing measure would then be imposed if GATT issued a ruling that the export or sourcing requirement was a violation of the code and if the President decided that relief was appropriate. The countervailing measure could be directed against a broad range of imports from the offending country in order to raise a fund for compensation of the private party.

A third form of unilateral response would involve legislating a private right of action. Such legislation would almost automatically impose reciprocity on foreign investors in the United States. If a host government were to impose performance requirements on U.S. investors, at the instigation of a U.S. petitioner, the U.S. government would impose similar requirements on firms from that country that invested in the United States.

The bilateral approaches that have been proposed would involve investment protection treaties. The United States does have an extensive network of tax treaties, but in negotiating tax treaties, both parties have similar objectives. When it comes to investment incentives and performance requirements, objectives differ, and a country that is trying to attract FDI may not wish to be bound by a treaty. In addition, because countries follow different industrial policies, it would be difficult for the two countries to negotiate a treaty.

A multilateral approach could also offer a solution. Multilateral efforts to reduce tariff rates have been very successful during the post-war period, and in the Tokyo rounds of tariff negotiations, some inroads were made in negotiating a reduction in non-tariff barriers. From time to time, the United States has proposed the establishment of a "GATT for Investment" to protect on a world-wide basis the open flows of foreign investment. The objective of an international investment policy would be to limit the manipulation of international investment flows, especially through performance requirements and investment incentives. The GATT for Investment would prevent governments from manipulating international investment flows. It has been suggested that the GATT for Investment could start by negotiating a standstill agreement prohibiting new government interventions, and later it could negotiate a rollback on existing distortions. Participating countries in the organization would agree on sanctions and police the agreement.[62]

Even though such an organization could be beneficial to the international trading and investing community, it would be very difficult to negotiate a GATT for Investment. Although in the recent past the United States did make some efforts to address the problem of performance requirements and investment incentives, any actions resulting from these efforts have been quite limited.[63] The problem is that at present our negotiating partners are not strongly motivated to limit or reduce their interventionist policies. Unlike reductions in tariffs and even many of the non-tariff barriers, each country imposing performance requirements and establishing investment incentives is doing so to conform to its own industrial policy and attempts to try to affect the location of economic activity to conform to it policies concerning industrial acitivity. Moreover, the less developed countries have been among the most active participants in imposing trade-distorting foreign investment policies, and any attempt to affect these policies would be regarded as a North-South confrontation. Although we strongly believe that the U.S. government should continue to press for multilateral negotiations in the area of investment incentives and performance requirements, we recognize that in reality results from such efforts could not accrue in the immediate future.

Because the FDI inflow into the United States is continuing to grow, it is necessary that the United States adopt a strong FDI policy as far as these investment inflows are concerned. As indicated in Chapter 1, the FDI policy must be complemented by a forceful trade policy that will insure that key American industries be able to retain their competitive balance and financial stability. It is important to complement the FDI policy with a strong trade policy which will assure the continued viability of U.S. industries because of the interrelationship between international trade and FDI when FDI substitutes for international trade, as is the case of Japanese investment in the United States, and when the policies of home country governments distort the free flow of international trade. Finally, the emphasis should be on certain key industries in developing an FDI policy approach for the United States, and it is necessary that the United States adopt a weak version of an industrial policy that would establish some variety of loose framework for the "safe-guarded industry sectors."

We propose that the United States develop unilateral and even bilateral approaches to dealing with the problem of FDI inflows. These approaches include the following:

1. FDI should be channeled into industries where FDI will be beneficial, not harmful, to the United States. Studies of the impact of FDI would be useful in this connection (Chapter 2).

2. An agency should be established to oversee and monitor foreign investment activities, and the Department of Commerce should be reorganized to include international trade and FDI activities.

3. An office such as the United States Trade Representative should also establish a division to work on matters concerning investment policies with a view toward working with foreign governments to establish a GATT for Investment.

4. Unilateral actions such as those under the escape clause should be taken against countries that have trade-distorting performance requirements. In certain circumstances, the United States should attempt to negotiate with other countries on a bilateral basis in an effort to coordinate trade and investment issues and to reduce trade-distorting performance requirements and investment incentives.

5. The overriding concern of U.S. policy should be to leave the world market open for the free flow of FDI between countries before an investment war ensues that would replicate the tariff wars of the 1930s.

6. In the United States, the state and local governments have enacted a whole series of investment incentives in an effort to lure investment into their areas. Foreign MNCs have taken advantage of these incentives and have at times chosen to locate operations where such incentives were offered. As part of an FDI policy, the United States should be prepared to negotiate reductions or eliminate such incentives.

Chapter 7 showed that FDI in 23 industrial sectors would not be beneficial to the U.S. economy. In four of these sectors, the performance of domestically owned firms was shown to be superior to that of foreign-owned firms, eleven sectors required a minimum domestic productive capacity to meet potential surge needs for military production, and in eight foreign ownership should be limited or restricted because of the high-technology orientation of these industries. Although we are not advocating that the United States should adopt a comprehensive industrial policy, there is reason to believe that FDI in certain sectors would not be beneficial either because foreign firms fail to perform as adequately as domestic firms or we wish to protect certain sectors given their high-tech and/or defense-related usefulness. In conjunction with an attempt to designate certain sectors as being unlikely candidates for FDI, we would recommend that some agency of the U.S. government, perhaps the Department of Commerce, undertake studies of different industries to assess the benefits and costs that would accompany FDI in those sectors. In addition to the impacts on employment and tax revenues examined in Chapter 7, these studies would examine the forward and backward investment linkages with other industries, the external economies (or diseconomies) generated by the foreign investment such as the impact on labor training and technology transfer, the potential ability of the investment activity to increase (or decrease) competition in a given industry and thereby raise allocative efficiency, and the overall impact on the balance of payments, taking into consideration the effects on the current account and capital account. Furthermore, because there is little empirically tested knowledge concerning the importance of foreign investment policies as trade-distorting mechanisms, we suggest that the U.S. government also undertake a series of studies to determine the trade-distorting nature of these policies. If it were to become evident that such policies are inherently trade distorting, it would be easier to convince government officials abroad of the necessity of undertaking multilateral negotiations to dismantle some of these measures.

A Foreign Review Agency should be established to implement guideline regulations and controls over foreign ownership and investment in U.S. industries. Another purpose of such an agency would be to coordinate the regulation of foreign investment and the U.S. response to FDI policies of foreign governments, including performance requirements and investment incentives, with U.S. trade policy. As has been extensively discussed in this chapter the foreign investment policies of foreign governments can be just as trade distorting as the escalation of tariffs and the implementation of quotas, subsidies, and other non-tariff barriers. It is expected that the Committee of Foreign Investment in the United States would monitor all FDI inflows into the United States and coordinate its activities with the various federal agencies and regulatory bodies having authority over FDI inflows.

As part of the federal government's commitment to removing trade-distorting investment policies, it is recommended that the duties of the U.S. Office of the U.S. Trade Representative be expanded to incorporate jurisdiction over performance requirements and investment incentives. In its expanded role the USTR would formulate both trade and FDI policy concerns. The fact that FDI and international trade are frequently substitutes for each other makes it imperative that policymaking for trade and investment be coordinated. The U.S. Office of the USTR could assemble data on the FDI policies of other countries and keep abreast of changes that occur. Because these investment policies do affect the location and quantity of international production, they should be as much of a concern to the USTR as are tariffs and non-tariff barriers. We do not believe that it is possible for the USTR to negotiate effectively with foreign governments on all other trade matters without entering into negotiations on foreign investment policies that are instrumental in distorting the volume and pattern of trade.

At present, no one agency or cabinet-level office exists to coordinate trade and foreign direct investment activities. U.S. trade and investment policy mechanisms are highly fragmented and duplicative. Volume I of the *Report of the President's Commission on Industrial Competitiveness* published in January 1985 points out that decisions concerning trade and investment policy mechanisms are split between at least 25 executive branch agencies and 19 congressional subcommittees. Even though many government agencies including the Department of Treasury, Justice, and Defense make policies that exert a strong influence on our international trade, they frequently do not take into consideration the ramifications of their decisions on America's ability to be competitive in world markets.

The Trade Policy Committee chaired by the U.S. Trade Representative and the Cabinet Council on Commerce and Trade chaired by the Secretary of Commerce are two cabinet-level committees concerned with trade policy. Membership in these committees is almost the same (Figure 8.1), with the USTR being responsible for formulating trade policy and Commerce for implementing policy. However, neither cabinet-level committee has the authorization to consider a number of international economic issues that render trade policy effective.[64]

As an outgrowth of all this fragmentation in trade policy, policy officials are forced to spend time coordinating trade policy and little time is spent on designing and implementing it.[65]

It is recommended that the government reassess its policy mechanism concerned with foreign trade and investment. Because of the new global competition, the U.S. Department of Commerce should be reorganized into a Department of Industry, International Trade and International Investment. This executive agency would have a strong role in formulating and implementing policy with a view toward eliminating many of the duplicative trade functions of other agencies. The newly revamped department would be better able to position the United States to face the new global competitiveness which is not only threatening the existence of our basic industries, but even many of our high-technology industries which still appear to have a comparative advantage in world trade.

It has been proposed that the main objective of a U.S. international investment policy should be the limitation and eventual elimination by all governments of the manipulation of FDI. In the long run, the best way to accomplish this objective is to negotiate a GATT for Investment. For the immediate term, however, it is recommended that the United States undertake unilateral and bilateral actions as part of a strong FDI policy.

It is necessary to clarify which unilateral actions would offer the best mechanism for reducing the impact of investment policies by foreign governments. If it were possible to clarify that Section 301 of the 1974 Trade Act does authorize the President to retaliate on investment issues, Section 301 could be used to deal with the FDI policies of foreign governments that affect U.S. interests. However, because Section 301 involves a clearly internal mechanism, it is necessary to know what provision of GATT or other international instrument could be used prior to seeking an international remedy.[66]

Figure 8.1
U.S. Government Trade Relationships

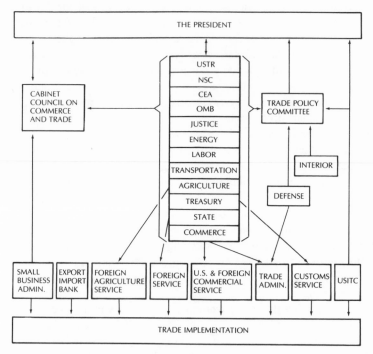

Abbreviations: USTR—United States Trade Representative
NSC—National Security Council
CEA—Council of Economic Advisers
OMB—Office of Management and Budget
USITC—United States International Trade Commission
Source: *Global Competition: The New Reality*, January 1985, vol. 1 (Washington,
D.C.: The Report of the President's Commission on Industrial
Competitiveness, 1985).

In certain cases, bilateral remedies should also be used. When two countries
have an interest, as both a home and host country, a bilateral negotiation between
them may offer a possibility. For instance, it has been suggested that the bilateral
negotiations between the United States and Japan on a whole group of economic
issues may offer a prospect for mutual benefit by linking trade and investment
issues because Japan's exporting and FDI are complementary processes. Because
Japan places severe restrictions on inward FDI, it may be possible to link negotiations on liberalizing Japan's barriers to FDI with negotiations on trade.[67]

The overriding concern of U.S. policy is to leave the world economy open
to facilitate the free flow of investment between countries. To the extent that
investment incentives and performance requirements interfere with the free flow

of international trade, they serve as impediments to an open trading system. Because each nation imposes these investment policies in order to obtain a national advantage, it becomes more difficult to dismantle these mechanisms than to reduce tariffs and the usual non-tariff barriers, the reduction of which provides clear benefits to all participants in the negotiating process. National advantages from investment policies appear relevant for the less developed countries, and it may be extremely difficult to induce these countries to dismantle their policies toward foreign investment. It may turn out that the most one can hope to achieve is a mutual reduction of performance requirements and investment incentives among industrial countries if each of them achieves mutual gain.

Finally, the investment incentives offered by the 50 states and localities in order to affect the location of foreign investment in the United States can also impede free trade. It is suggested here that the United States be prepared to legislate that such incentives be dismantled to achieve uniformity when negotiating a reduction in barriers to FDI.

In conjunction with the development of an FDI policy, it is necessary that the United States develop a strong trade policy. The reason is that foreign governments, particularly Japan, have been involved in targeting their industries for development, and FDI can serve as a substitute for exporting to an overseas market once these countries perceive that the industry is threatened by protectionism abroad. Because the MNC serves a global market, it can initially develop a dominant role in any overseas market by techniques such as downward-transfer pricing. Once entrenched in a given market, the MNC will undertake FDI to maintain its market share. In addition, because the targeted industry in the home country may not have a market of a size sufficient to permit MNCs to enjoy the benefits of economies of large-scale production, the necessity of exporting overseas becomes increasingly acute.

As has been noted earlier, Japan undertook FDI when the targeted industries were threatened by protectionism in the overseas market. Japan undertook production of color television sets in the United States in the early 1970s when threatened by protectionism. Fear of protectionism motivated Japanese production of motor vehicles in the United States during the early and mid–1980s.

During the early 1980s, much rhetoric was heard concerning the deindustrialization of America, and there were dire predictions that the United States was about to become a "nation of hamburger stands." Yet at the same time, there is increasing evidence of tremendous technological change in American industries. The latest technology has been introduced in some of our smokestack industries. A prime example is the U.S. automotive industry which has been involved in widespread technological changes. For instance, as already noted, General Motors has recently introduced highly sophisticated technology into its productive process. Some claim that the automotive industry in the United States has been undergoing an industrial renaissance, with the de-maturity of the industry proceeding rapidly.[68]

It has been argued that several of America's industries have recently been undergoing a process of de-maturity. These industries have begun to arrest and even reverse the maturation process. The main characteristic of a mature industry is the stable nature of its technology and the relative ease with which this technology can be copied. The product has become standardized, and only minor technological changes occur. However, because the design concepts are standardized, the productive unit has become vulnerable to changes in market prices, technology, and relative prices. Thus, when a diversity of consumer tastes develops, as toward more fuel-efficient and better handling automobiles, those producers who can best perceive changing demand preferences develop competitive advantages. Thus, a de-maturing industry is one that moves away from the standardized product, increases the diversity of the product's technology that is to be offered in the market, and increases the competitive visibility of the product.[69] In some U.S. industrial sectors the "life cycle" of maturity and decay have been reversed. In addition to the automotive industry, de-maturity has been occurring in industries like steel, textiles, and even footwear. Air jet looms have been revolutionizing the textile industry. As shown in Chapter 4, mini-mills have introduced new technology in steelmaking, and the trends toward jogging and other leisure sports is having a revolutionary impact on the footwear market.

Because industries are able to undergo a process of de-maturation and more creatively integrate the workforce into the productive process, there is a strong likelihood that U.S. industry can regain its domestic and international competitiveness. There is evidence that, given appropriate conditions, industries do not have to go through a process of maturity and decay. It is necessary that the federal government realize that mature industries (sunset industries) as well as newer (sunrise) industries be supported. For reasons outlined in Chapter 7, it is crucial that industries in addition to high-technology industries be supported.

NOTES

1. Jean-Jacques Servan Schrieber, *The American Challenge* (New York: Atheneum, 1965).

2. U.S. Congress, Senate, Committee on Foreign Relations, *U.S. Policy Toward International Investment*, Hearings before a Subcommittee on International Economic Policy, 97th Cong., 1st Sess., 1981, p. 86 (Testimony of Joseph E. Conner, Labor-Industry Coalition for International Trade).

3. Ibid., pp. 237–238 (Testimony of Robert D. Hormats, Assistant Secretary, U.S. Department of State).

4. Canada, Foreign Investment Review Agency, Policy, Research, and Communications Branch, *Barriers to Foreign Investment in the United States*, 1982, pp. 22–26.

5. Ibid., p. 27.

6. Ibid., pp. 51–52.

7. Ibid., p. 52.

8. U.S. Congress, Senate, *U.S. Policy Toward International Investment*, p. 81 (Testimony of Joseph E. Conner).

9. Ibid., pp. 207–210 (Statement of Raymond J. Waldman, Assistant Secretary for International Economic Policy, U.S. Department of Commerce).

10. Ibid.

11. Ibid., p. 209.

12. Ibid., pp. 454–457 (*Investment Policies in Seventy-Three Countries, A Survey Submitted by Price Waterhouse, and Co.*).

13. Ibid., p. 38 (Testimony of Joseph E. Conner).

14. Ibid., p. 61.

15. Ibid., p. 60.

16. *New York Times*, January 11, 1984, Section D.

17. "Canada's New Economic Clout," *New York Times Magazine*, February 17, 1985, pp. 63–65 and 69.

18. U.S. Congress, Senate, *U.S. Policy Toward Foreign Investment*, p. 81 (Testimony of Joseph E. Conner).

19. Rachel McCulloch and Robert F. Owen, "Linking Negotiations on Trade and Foreign Direct Investment," in Charles P. Kindleberger and David B. Audretsch, eds., *The Multinational Corporation in the 1980's* (Cambridge: M.I.T. Press, 1983), p. 340.

20. Ibid., p. 341.

21. U.S. Congress, Senate, *U.S. Policy Toward Foreign Investment*, p. 63 (Testimony of Joseph E. Conner).

22. Canada, Statement of the Honourable Sinclair Stevens following the tabling of the Investment Canada Bill, December, 7, 1984, and Canada, News Release, "Government Introduces Legislation to Encourage Investment in Canada," December 7, 1984. A direct acquisition is the acquisition of control of a Canadian business either by acquiring its voting interests or assets or by the acquiring of the Canadian parent in Canada. An indirect acquisition is the acquisition of control of a Canadian business by acquiring control of its parent outside Canada.

23. Ibid.

24. U.S. Congress, Senate, *U.S. Policy Toward Foreign Investment*, pp. 203–206 (Statement by Raymond J. Waldman).

25. Ibid.

26. McCulloch and Owen, "Linking Negotiations on Trade," p. 336.

27. Ibid., pp. 336–337.

28. A.E. Safarian, "Trade Related Investment Issues," in William R. Cline, ed., *Trade Policy in the 1980's* (Washington, D.C.: Institute for International Economics, 1983), p. 613.

29. Ibid.

30. U.S. Congress, Senate, *U.S. Policy Toward Foreign Investment*, p. 59 (Testimony of Joseph E. Conner).

31. Safarian, "Trade Related Investment Issues," p. 621, and U.S. Congress, Senate, *U.S. Policy Toward Foreign Investment*, p. 14 (Testimony of C. Fred Bergsten, Senior Associate, Carnegie Endowment for International Peace).

32. U.S. Congress, Senate, *U.S. Policy Toward Foreign Investment*, p. 232 (Testimony of Robert D. Hormats).

33. Kathryn Morton and Peter Tulloch, *Trade and Developing Countries* (New York: John Wiley and Sons, 1977), p. 203.

34. Ibid.

35. Herbert Grubel, and P.J. Lloyd, *Intra-Industry Trade* (New York: John Wiley and Sons, 1975), pp. 37–40.

36. International Monetary Fund, *IMF Survey*, December 9, 1985, pp. 374–375. It may be anticipated that a country's trade balance will worsen for a short while following

a decline in the price of its currency. This expectation arises because the relevant price elasticities are very low in the short run. However, it may be assumed that eventually price effects will have the expected outcome. Because the time path of the movement of the trade balance is similar to a "J" tilted to the right, the effect has been called the "J-curve effect." Richard E. Caves and Ronald W. Jones, *World Trade and Payments: An Introduction* (Boston: Little, Brown, 1984), p. 464.

37. International Monetary Fund, *1984 World Economic Outlook* (Washington D.C.: 1984), p. 19.

38. Ibid., p. 19.

39. Ibid., p. 5.

40. "Foreign Capital Growth in U.S. Causes Concern," *New York Times*, March 31, 1985, pp. D1 and D2.

41. Peter H. Lindert and Charles P. Kindleberger, *International Economics* (Homewood, Ill.: Richard D. Irwin, 1982), p. 269.

42. Ibid., pp. 269–271.

43. Morgan Guaranty Trust Company of New York, *World Financial Markets* (March/April 1985): 4.

The balance-of-payments impact of FDI is complex. Whereas the initial capital inflow represents a balance-of-payments inflow, subsequent to the initial investment, income produced by the foreign investment can represent a current account outflow. These investment income outflows include dividend payments, interest, and royalties and fees. Furthermore, balance-of-payments repercussions include the impact of reducing imports of the finished product, the increased importation of components, and the impact of exports of the product.

44. Morgan Guaranty, *World Financial Markets*, pp. 2–3.

45. "Economic Growth Fell to 1.3% in First '83 Period," *New York Times*, April 1985.

46. *Global Competition—The New Reality*, Report of the President's Commission on Industrial Competitiveness, Vol. 2, January 1985, p. 30.

47. Catherine L. Mann, "U.S. International Transactions in 1984," *Federal Reserve Bulletin* (May 1985): 277–282.

48. Ibid., p. 285.

49. Nicholas D. Kristof, "Cash Flows Count More Than Goods," *New York Times*, May 12, 1985.

50. Ronald I. McKinnon, "Currency Substitution and Instability in the World Dollar Standard," *American Economic Review* 72 (June 1982): 320–333. Ronald I. McKinnon, *An International Standard for Monetary Stabilization* (Cambridge: M.I.T. Press, 1984).

From the end of World War II until the 1970s, the theory of exchange rate adjustments and the balance of payments was centered on the current account. But, in the 1970s, the focus shifted, and most of the theoretical work on exchange rate determination and the balance of payments was focused on the capital account. It is only within the past few years that attention has begun to be focused upon the link between the determinants of the current account and the capital account. See Anne O. Krueger, *Exchange Rate Determination* (Cambridge: Cambridge University Press, 1982), p. 54.

51. "Democrats Seek Currency Intervention Policy," *New York Times*, April 25, 1985, p. D5.

52. *The Economist* (May 12, 1985): 72.

53. Mann, "U.S. International Transactions in 1984," p. 285.

54. These include interest rate policy, domestic content for automobiles, variable tariff duties, and others.

55. *Global Competition—The New Reality*, p. 29.

56. Safarian, "Trade Related Investment Issues," p. 630. Some exceptions are allowed, including aid for regional development, to remedy a serious disturbance in a state or to promote a project that is of common European interest.

57. Safarian, "Trade Related Investment Issues," p. 631.

58. U.S. Congress, Senate, *U.S. Policy Toward Foreign Investment*, pp. 143–159 (Testimony of Gary Clyde Hufbauer, Deputy Director, International Law Institute, Georgetown Law Center).

59. Safarian, "Trade Related Investment Issues," p. 633.

60. U.S. Congress, Senate, *U.S. Policy Toward Foreign Investment*, p. 151 (Testimony of Gary Clyde Hufbauer).

61. Ibid., p. 152.

62. U.S. Congress, Senate, *U.S. Policy Toward Foreign Investment*, pp. 1–18 (Testimony of C. Fred Bergsten).

63. Ibid., pp. 1–18, 143–159 (Testimonies of C. Fred Bergsten and Gary Clyde Hufbauer).

64. *Global Competition—The New Reality*, pp. 37–38.

65. Ibid., p. 39.

66. U.S. Congress, Senate, *U.S. Policy Toward Foreign Investment*, p. 251 (Testimony of Robert D. Hormats).

67. McCulloch and Owen, "Linking Negotiations on Trade and Foreign Direct Investment," p. 351.

68. William J. Abernathy, Kim B. Clark, and Alan M. Kantrow, *Industrial Renaissance: Producing a Competitive Future for America* (New York: Basic Books, 1983).

69. Ibid., especially pp. 15–29 (Ch. 2).

9

Toward the Future

This work investigates only the beginning of a very long narrative. The United States has entered a period in which global competition for industries has intensified and will continue to intensify. The competition is between all nations, not only large industrial nations such as the United States and smaller yet efficient ones such as Japan. It is also between industrial nations and developing nations and between capitalist and socialist nations. All are entering the battle. The real war for a larger share of world production has only just begun.

This book provides partial and limited insight into the forms this global battle has taken, and recommends policy approaches the United States must consider if it is to survive this global battle and retain a significant share of world manufacturing capacity. Although specific policy measures are recommended, an understanding of the broader picture is more important than the specific policy recommendations. This is because once a nation such as the United States permits its industrial base to begin to grow smaller, the erosive forces that will be set in motion will be difficult to slow or reverse.

The major theme underlying this work is that the world has entered a global battle, and the battle is for supremacy in manufacturing. At present Japan and the United States are the leading contenders, but other nations and regions are and will enter into this battle. Within a very short time Western Europe, the Soviet Union, Mainland China, Brazil, Mexico, and other newly industrializing nations will be engaged in an intense struggle for a larger share of world manufacturing production.

Until recently, it was possible to argue that the battle was simply for a larger share of world export markets. That statement is no longer valid. The battle has become one aimed at maximizing world manufacturing share, not world exports. There are several reasons for this change. First, trade issues can no longer be separated from investment issues. When Japanese auto makers increase U.S.

market share and then establish local assembly operations in the United States
to more firmly "lock up" the recently gained manufacturing market share, we
have a refocusing of corporate and national priorities, namely, to control a larger
share of world production and markets in that line of manufacturing. Second,
although world export markets have displayed minimal growth in recent years,
world manufacturing output continues to grow. Third, control of a larger percentage of world manufacturing offers nations a more strategic position than
control of a larger percentage of world exports.

FIFTEEN ROUNDS

The global battle for world industrial production is only warming up. Only
the first two rounds have been played out in what promises to become a fifteen-
round fight for the world championship in manufacturing.

The United States has just about lost the first two rounds. Round one consisted
of a battle for supremacy in textiles and consumer electronics. Japan, Hong
Kong, and Taiwan, by gaining a dominant share of world production in these
product lines, were the big winners.

Round two is not quite over, but it appears that the United States will lose
this round too unless Washington policymakers act decisively and without delay.
In round two, Japan, Korea, and several other countries are taking a large and
growing share of world production in steel and motor vehicles. This book focuses
on the policies the United States needs to adopt in order to recover in the last
moments of this round.

Round three, which is just beginning, has not yet been decided. In this round
Japan has set out to dominate in key high-tech industries (computers, industrial
robotics, and telecommunications). Round four is not far off, and in that time
interval, world control of aerospace production will be determined.

THE STRATEGIC BALANCE OF POWER

Five sets of factors will determine the overall outcome of this global battle
for industrial supremacy:

1. *Natural advantages*: the availability of relatively low cost factors of production in
   each country.
2. *Appropriate trade and investment policies*: trade (tariff-quota-other) and foreign investment (regulation of FDI) policies.
3. *Maintenance of a sound and healthy domestic economy*: policies and regulations that
   affect the efficiency of industry (tax burden, labor laws, antitrust regulation, efficient
   financial markets, control of inflation).
4. *Application of appropriate macro policies*: policies in areas of interest rates, and
   foreign exchange rates.
5. *Economic power*: leverage on world affairs enjoyed by a large nation, such as the
   United States.

In 1980 the United States was at a clear disadvantage vis-à-vis the rest of the world in three of these areas (Table 9.1). Since then the U.S. performance has improved somewhat in maintaining a sound and healthy domestic economy. Today the United States enjoys an advantage in three of these five areas. Unfortunately, the United States continues to suffer a disadvantage with respect to application of appropriate macroeconomic policies.

Chapter 8 contains specific policy recommendations, which, if followed, would give the United States an advantage in items two and four in Table 9.1. Adoption of the broad policy lines described in Chapter 8 would give the United States a clear advantage in all five sets of factors.

The United States has the ability to regain and hold the strategic balance of power and to maintain its relative leadership position in world manufacturing. The doomsayers who claim we need an industrial policy, that we must pick the industry winners and losers, have inappropriately diagnosed the problem. At present the problem consists of inappropriate macro and micro policies, and the need to reorient our trade and investment strategies and multilateral negotiations to deal more effectively with the unfair competitive practices of other nations. Implementation of policies along the lines suggested earlier in this volume will assist America in preserving the competitive spirit as well as maintain a healthy and robust manufacturing and industrial sector.

Table 9.1
Factors Determining Outcome in the Battle for Industrial Supremacy, 1980 and 1985

Factor	1980		1985
	Advantage to Rest of World	*Advantage to United States*	*Advantage to United States*
Natural Advantages	O[a]	X[b]	X
Appropriate Trade and Investment Policies	X	O	O
Maintenance of a Sound & Healthy Domestic Economy	X	O	X
Application of Appropriate Macro Policies	X	O	O
Economic Power	O	X	X
	XXX	XX	XXX

[a]Indicates disadvantage.
[b]Indicates advantage.

Bibliography ───────────────

BOOKS and MONOGRAPHS

Abernathy, William J.; Clark, Kim B.; Kantrow, Alan M. *Industrial Renaissance: Producing a Competitive Future for America*. New York: Basic Books, 1983.

American Iron and Steel Institute. *1983 Annual Statistical Report*. Washington, D.C.: American Iron and Steel Institute, 1984.

Arpan, Jeffrey F., and Ricks, David A. *Directory of Foreign Manufacturing in the United States*. 2d ed. Atlanta: College of Business Administration, Georgia State University, 1979.

Bain, Joe S. *Barriers to New Competition*. Cambridge: Harvard University Press, 1956.

Baranson, Jack. *The Japanese Challenge to U.S. Industry*. Lexington, Mass.: Lexington Books, 1981.

Bergsten, C. Fred; Horst, Thomas; and Moran, Theodore H. *American Multinationals and American Interests*. Washington, D.C.: Brookings Institute, 1978.

Bruck, N., and Lees, F.A., *Foreign Investment, Capital Controls, and the Balance of Payments*. New York: Institute of Finance, New York University, 1968.

Buckley, Peter, and Casson, Mark. *The Future of the Multinational Enterprise*. London: Macmillan, 1976.

Caves, Richard E., and Jones, Ronald W. *World Trade and Payments: An Introduction*. 4th ed. Boston: Little, Brown, 1985.

Crandall, Robert. *The U.S. Steel Industry in Recurrent Crisis*. Washington, D.C.: Brookings Institute, 1981.

Dunning, John H. *International Production and the Multinational Enterprise*. London: George Allen and Unwin, 1981.

Franko, Lawrence. *The Threat of Japanese Multinationals: How the West Can Respond*. New York: John Wiley and Sons, 1983.

Fry, Earl H. *Financial Invasion of the U.S.A.*. New York: McGraw-Hill, 1980.

Grubel, Herbert G., and Lloyd, P.J. *Intraindustry Trade*. New York: John Wiley and Sons, 1975.

Hogan, William T., S.J. *World Steel in the 1980's*. Lexington, Mass.: Lexington Books, 1983.

Hymer, Stephen A. *The International Operations of National Firms: A Study of Foreign Direct Investment*. Cambridge, Mass.: M.I.T. Press, 1976.

Khoury, Sarkis. *Transnational Mergers and Acquisitions in the United States*. Lexington Mass.: Lexington Books, 1980.

Kindleberger, Charles P. *American Business Abroad: Six Essays on Direct Investment*. New Haven, Conn.: Yale University Press, 1969.

————, ed. *The International Corporation: A Symposium*. Cambridge, Mass.: M.I.T. Press, 1970.

————, ed. *The Multinational Corporation in the 1980's*. Cambridge, Mass.: M.I.T. Press, 1983.

Knickerbocker, Fredrick. *Oligopolistic Reaction and Multinational Enterprises*. Cambridge, Mass.: Harvard Business School, Division of Research, 1973.

Krueger, Anne O. *Exchange Rate Determination*. Cambridge: Cambridge University Press, 1982.

Lamont, Douglas. *Foreign State Enterprises*. New York: Basic Books, 1979.

Lawrence, Robert Z. *Can America Compete?* Washington, D.C.: Brookings Institute, 1984.

Lindert, Peter H., and Kindleberger, Charles P. *International Economics*. 7th ed. Homewood, Illinois: Richard D. Irwin, 1982.

Lodge, George C. *The American Disease*. New York: Alfred Knopf, 1984.

Lowenfeld, Andreas. *Public Controls on International Trade*. 2d ed. San Francisco, Calif.: Mathew Bender and Company, 1983.

McKinnon, Ronald I. *An International Standard for Monetary Stabilization*. Cambridge, Mass.: M.I.T. Press, 1984.

Morton, Kathryn, and Tullock, Peter. *Trade and Developing Countries*. New York, John Wiley and Sons, 1977.

Ozawa, Tetrutomo. *Multinationals, Japanese Style*. Princeton, N.J.: Princeton University Press, 1979.

Reich, Robert B. *The Next American Frontier*. New York: New York Times Books, 1983.

Servan-Schrieber, Jean-Jacques. *The American Challenge*. New York: Atheneum, 1968.

Spero, Joan Edelman. *The Politics of International Economic Relations*. 2d ed. New York: St. Martin's Press, 1981.

Toder, Eric. *Trade Policy and the U.S. Automobile Industry*. New York: Praeger, 1978.

Waldman, Raymond J. *Direct Investment and Development in the U.S.*. Washington, D.C.: Transnational Investments Ltd., 1980.

————, and Cohn Robert A. *Business Investment in the United States*. Washington, D.C.: Bureau of National Affairs, 1984.

White, Lawrence J. *The Automobile Industry Since 1945*. Cambridge, Mass.: Harvard University Press, 1971.

CONTRIBUTIONS TO VOLUMES OR SYMPOSIA OF CONFERENCE PAPERS

Adams, Walter, and Mueller, Hans. "The Steel Industry." In *The Structure of American Industry*, Walter Adams, ed. 6th ed. New York: Macmillan, 1982.

Aliber, Robert Z. "The Theory of Foreign Direct Investment." In *The International Corporation*, Charles P. Kindleberger, ed. Cambridge, Mass.: M.I.T. Press, 1970.

Arrow, Kenneth J. "Economic Welfare and the Allocation of Resources for Invention." In *The Rate and Direction of Inventive Activity: Economic and Social Factors*. National Bureau of Economic Research. Princeton, N.J.: University Press, 1962.

Diebold, John. "The Information Technology Industries." In *Trade Policies for the 1980's*, William R. Cline, ed. Washington, D.C.: Institute for International Economics, 1983.

Foster, Richard N. "Why America's Technology Leaders Tend to Lose." In *Research and Development: Key Issues for Management*. New York: The Conference Board, 1983.

Good, Mary L. "Licensing-Technology Transfer for Profit." In *Research and Development: Key Issues for Management*. New York: The Conference Board, 1983.

Johnson, Harry G. "The Efficiency and Welfare Implications of the International Corporation." In *The International Corporation*, Charles P. Kindleberger, ed. Cambridge, Mass.: M.I.T. Press, 1970.

Keyworth, George A. "Creating a Climate for Industrial Progress," In *Research and Development: Key Issues for Management*. New York: The Conference Board, 1983.

Logue, Dennis, and Willet, Thomas. "The Effects of Exchange Rate Adjustment on International Investment." In *The Effects of Exchange Rate Adjustments*, Peter B. Clark, Dennis E. Logue, and Richard Sweeney, eds. Washington, D.C.: U.S. Department of the Treasury, 1977.

McClosky, P.F. "Joint Research Ventures." In *Research and Development: Key Issues for Management*. New York: The Conference Board, 1983.

McCulloch, Rachel, and Owen, Robert F. "Linking Negotiations on Trade and Direct Investment." In *The Multinational Corporation in the 1980's*. Charles P. Kindleberger and David B. Audretsch, eds. Cambridge, Mass.: M.I.T. Press, 1983.

McLain, David. "Foreign Direct Investment in the United States: Old Currents, 'New Waves' and the Theory of Direct Investment." In *The Multinational Corporation in the 1980's*, Charles P. Kindleberger and David B. Audretsch, eds. Cambridge, Mass.: M.I.T. Press, 1984.

McManus, John. "The Theory of the International Firm." In *The Multinational Firm and the Nation State*, Gilles Paquet, ed. Toronto: Collier-Macmillan, 1975.

Magee, Stephen P. "Information and the International Corporation: An Appropriability Theory of Foreign Direct Investment." In *The New International Economic Order*, Jagdish Bhagwati, ed. Cambridge, Mass.: M.I.T. Press, 1977.

Milberre, Egils. "The Federal Government Role and Its Programs." *Research and Development: Key Issues for Management*. New York: The Conference Board, 1983.

Safarian, A.E. "Trade Related Investment Issues." In *Trade Policy in the 1980's*, William R. Cline, ed. Washington, D.C.: Institute for International Economics, 1983.

Seabury, Paul. "Industrial Policy and National Defense." In *The Industrial Policy Debate*, Chalmers Johnson, ed. San Francisco: Institute for Contemporary Studies, 1984.

JOURNALS AND NEWSPAPERS

Agarwal, J. "Determinants of Foreign Direct Investment: A Survey." *Weltwirtschaftliches Archiv* 116, No. 4 (1980): 739–773.

Agmon, T. B., and Lessard, D. F. "Investor Recognition of Corporate International Diversification." *Journal of Finance* 33 (1977): 1049–1055.

Ajami, Riad A., and Ricks, David A. "Motives of Non-American Firms Investing in the U.S." *Journal of International Business* 12, no. 3 (Winter 1981): 25–34.

Alchian, A., and Demsetz, H. "Production, Information Costs, and Economic Organization." *American Economic Review* 62 (December, 1972): 777–795.

"America's Best Managed Factories." *Fortune* (May 28, 1984): 16–17.

Andreassen, Arthur; Saunders, Norman C.; and Su, Betty W. "Economic Outlook for the 1990's: Three Scenarios for Economic Growth." *Monthly Labor Review* 106 (November 1983): 11–23.

"Are Foreign Partners Good for U.S. Companies?" *Business Week* (May 28, 1984): 59.

Bauman, G. "Merger Theory, Property Rights and the Pattern of U.S. Direct Investment in Canada." *Weltwirtschaftliches Archiv* 7 (1975): 676–698.

Brainard, W., and Tobin, J. "Pitfalls in Financial Model Building." *American Economic Review* 58 (May 1968): 99–122.

Brodie, Fredrick A. "GM Seen Buying Stakes in 3 Companies That Make Systems to Let Machines See." *Wall Street Journal*, August 1, 1984, p. 8.

Buckley, Peter. "A Critical Review of Theories of the Multinational Enterprise." *Aussenwirtschaft* 36, Heft 1 (1981): 70–87.

Burck, Charles G. "Will Success Spoil General Motors?" *Fortune* (August 22, 1983): 94–104.

"Can Japan Ever Be More Than an Also Ran." *Business Week* (July 16, 1984): 103–104.

Caves, Richard E. "International Corporations: The Industrial Economics of Foreign Direct Investment." *Economica* 38 (February, 1971): 1–27.

Chira, Susan. "For Mazda, a U.S. Car Plant." *New York Times*, December 1, 1984. p. D1.

———. "Japan Allotments Set on Cars for U.S." *New York Times*, April 27, 1985. p. 31.

———. "Mitsubishi Motors Greets Maturity." *New York Times*, April 22, 1985. p. D8.

———. "Struggle Continues at Wheeling-Pittsburgh." *New York Times*, August 10, 1984, pp. D1 and D2.

Coase, Ronald. "The Nature of the Firm." *Economica* 4 (November 1937): 385–406.

Cuff, Daniel F. "U.S. Steel in Korean Import Plan; Pohang Will Supply Plant in California." *New York Times*, December 17, 1985, pp. D1 and D2.

"Daihatsu, King of the Japanese Minicar, Steers Its Sights Toward the U.S. Market." *Wall Street Journal*, May 31, 1984. p. 35.

"Democrats Seek Currency Intervention Policy." *New York Times*, April 25, 1985, p. D5.

Dunning, John P. "The Determinants of International Production." *Oxford Economic Papers* (January 1973).

The Economist 295 (May 4, 1985): p. 76.

The Economist 295 (May 12, 1985): p. 72.

"Even If Steel Gets Import Relief Its Anxieties Won't Go Away." *Business Week* (June 25, 1984): 29–30.

Financier (May 1984): 31–32.

Flowers, Edward B. "Oligopolistic Reactions in European and Canadian Direct Investment in the U.S." *Journal of International Business Studies* 7 (Fall/Winter 1976): 43–55.

"Foreign Capital Growth in U.S. Causes Concern." *New York Times*, March 31, 1985, pp. D1 and D2.

Franko, Lawrence G. "Multinationals: The End of U.S. Dominance." *Harvard Business Review* 56 no. 6 (1978): 93–101.

Furubotn, Erik, and Pejovich, Svetozar. "Property Rights and Economic Theory: A Survey of Recent Theory." *Journal of Economic Literature* 10 (December 1972): 1137–1162.

"GM Moves into a New Era." *Business Week* (July 16, 1984): 48–54.

"GM Pushes Big Computerization Program—Battle with Japanese Takes a High Tech Turn." *Asian Wall Street Journal*, July 10, 1984, p. 3.

Gomez-Ibanez, J. A., and Harrison, D. "Imports and the Future of the U.S. Automobile Industry." *American Economic Review* 72 (May 1982): 319–323.

Gordon, Sara L., and Lees, Francis A. "Multinational Capital Budgeting: Foreign Investment Under Subsidy." *California Management Review* 25 (Fall 1982): 22–32.

Greenhouse, Steven. "Komatsu Plans to Make Equipment in U.S. Plant." *New York Times*, February 11, 1985, pp. D1 and D14.

Harris, R. J., and Nag, A. "GM Appears to Be Leading Candidate in Competition to Buy Hughes Aircraft." *Wall Street Journal* May 8, 1985, p. 2.

Hout, Thomas M. "Trade Barriers Won't Keep Out Japan." *New York Times*, April 29, 1984, p. D1.

"How the IBM Juggernaut Will Keep Rolling." *Business Week* (July 16, 1984): 105.

Incantalupa, Tom. "Korea to Sell Cars in U.S." *Newsday* February 17, 1985, p. 110.

"The Inroads Japan Is Making in Fiber Optics." *Business Week* (May 21, 1984): 176.

"Japanese Investment in U.S. and Europe Aids Mutual Development." Keizai Koho Center, no. 15 (Japan Institute for Social and Economic Affairs), (February 1984).

"Kawasaki Steel to Acquire 25 Percent of U.S. Venture." *Wall Street Journal* (July 17, 1984), p. 2.

Kemple, F., and Lachica, Z. "Cocom Feuds Over Trade to East Bloc." *Wall Street Journal*, July 17, 1984, p. 35.

Kolhagen, Stephen. "Exchange Rate Changes, Profitability, and Foreign Direct Investment." *Southern Economic Journal* 44 (1977): 43–52.

Koten, John. "Giving Buyers Wide Choices May Be Hurting Auto Makers." *Wall Street Journal*. December 15, 1983, p. 33.

Kristof, Nicholas D. "Cash Flows Count More than Goods." *New York Times*, May 12, 1985, p. 38.

Lees, Francis A. "Mature Creditorship and the Balance of Payments." *Economic and Business Bulletin* 22, (Spring/Summer 1970): 31–35.

LeMoyne, James. "Mineba's Ball Bearing Bid." *New York Times*, July 16, 1984. p. D1.

Lewis, Paul. "Allies Curb Computers for Soviets." *New York Times*, July 17, 1984. p. D7.

Lindenberg, E.B., and Ross, S.A. "Tobin's q Ratio and Industrial Organization." *Journal of Business* 54 (1981): 1–32.

Little, Jane S. "Foreign Direct Investment in the U.S.: Recent Locational Choices of

Foreign Manufacturers." *New England Economic Review* (November/December 1980): 5–22.

———. "Location Decision of Foreign Direct Investors in the U.S." *New England Economic Review* (July/August 1978): 42–63.

McKinnon, Ronald I. "Currency Substitution and Instability in the World Dollar Standard." *American Economic Review* 72 (June 1982): 320–333.

Malcolm, Andrew H. "Canada's New Economic Clout." *New York Times Magazine*, February 17, 1985, pp. 63–65 and 69.

Mann, Catherine L. "U.S. International Transactions in 1984." *Federal Reserve Bulletin* 71 (May 1985): 277–282.

Morgan Guaranty Trust Company of New York. *World Financial Markets* (March/April 1984). pp. 1–9.

"National Steel Plan with Nippon Kokan Reflects Japan's Stagnant Home Market." *Wall Street Journal*, October 26, 1984, p. 2.

"Nippon Steel to Assist Wheeling-Pittsburgh in Constructing and Operating Rail Product Plant." *New York Times*, April 20, 1979, Section 4, pp. 5–6.

"North Korea Illegally Got Hughes Copters." *Wall Street Journal*, January 4, 1985, p. 28.

"Pan-European World Airways." *The Economist* 293 (September 22, 1984): 79.

"Reshaping the Computer Industry." *Business Week* (July 16, 1984): 84–85.

Rhys, D. G. "European Mass-Producing Car Makers and Minimum Efficient Scale." *The Journal of Industrial Economics* (June 1977): 313–319.

Riche, R. W.; Hecker, D. E.; and Burgan, J. "High Technology Today and Tomorrow: A Small Slice of the Employment Pie." *Monthly Labor Review* 106 (November 1983): 50–58.

Rohatyn, Felix. "Reconstructing America." *New York Review of Books*, March 5, 1981, p. 16.

Stopford, J.M. "German Multinationals and Foreign Direct Investment in the United States." *Management International Review* 20, No. 1 (1980): 7–15.

Tobin, J. "A General Equilibrium Approach to Monetary Theory" *Journal of Money, Credit and Banking* 1 (February 1969): 15–29.

Vernon, Raymond. "International Investment and International Trade in the Product Cycle." *Quarterly Journal of Economics* 80 (May 1966): 190–207.

———. "The Product Cycle Hypothesis in a New International Environment." *Oxford Bulletin on Economics and Statistics* 40 (1979): 255–267.

Williams, Winston. "The Shrinking of the Steel Industry." *New York Times*, September 23, 1984, p. D4.

Wilson, Marilyn. "How the Japanese Run U.S. Subsidiaries." *Dun's Business Month* (October 1983): 32–40.

Wynter, Leon E. "Congress Is Debating Federal Role in Setting Technological Priorities." *Wall Street Journal*, August 1, 1984, p. 1.

Young, Stepen, and Hood, Neil. "Recent Patterns of Foreign Direct Investment by British Multinational Enterprises in the United States." *National Westminster Bank Quarterly Review* (May 1980): 20–32.

Zschau, Ed and Ritter, Don. "Encourage Innovation Instead of Industrial Lemons." *Wall Street Journal, August 1, 1984, p. 24.*

OTHER PAPERS AND PUBLICATIONS

Chrysler Corporation, *Annual Report for 1982*.

Marcus, Peter F., and Kirisis, Karlis M. (World Steel Dynamics of Payne-Webber), "Steel's Survival Challenge." Paper presented at the Warren, Ohio, Area Chamber of Commerce, March 21, 1985.

Mueller, Hans. "Trends in Steel Production and Trade." Paper presented at the Annual Meeting of the Eastern Economics Association, New York City, March 1984.

INTERNATIONAL ORGANIZATIONS

International Monetary Fund. *IMF Survey*. December 9, 1985.

———. *1984 World Economic Outlook*. Washington D.C.: 1984.

Organization of Economic Co-operation and Development (OECD) . *Job Losses in Major Industries*. Paris: 1983.

———. *Long-Term Outlook for the World Automobile Industry*. Paris: 1983. OECD.

United Nations, Centre on Transnational Corporations. *Salient Features and Trends in Foreign Direct Investment*. New York: 1983.

———. *Transnational Corporations in the International Auto Industry* (ST/CTC/38), 1983.

GOVERNMENT DOCUMENTS

Canada, Foreign Investment Review Agency, Policy, Research and Communications Branch. *Barriers to Foreign Investment in the United States*. 1982.

U.S. Congress, Congressional Budget Office. *The Effects of Import Quotas on the Steel Industry*. Washington, D.C., July 1984.

U.S. Congress. House of Representatives. Subcommittee on Commerce, Transportation and Tourism of the Committee on Energy and Commerce. *Fair Practices in Automotive Products Act* 97th Cong. 2d sess. Hearings held on March 2, 1982. Washington D.C.: Government Printing Office, 1983. Statement of Howard D. Samuel cited.

———. Subcommittee on Economic Stabilization of the Committee on Banking, Finance and Urban Affairs. *Status of the Economy*. 98th Cong. 1st Sess. Hearings held on May 26, 1983. Washington D.C.: Government Printing Office. Statement of Leon Taub cited.

———. Subcommittee on Economic Stabilization of the Committee on Banking, Finance and Urban Affairs. *To Determine the Impact of Foreign Sourcing on Industry and Communities*. 97th Cong., 1st Sess. Washington D.C.: Government Printing Office, 1981. Statement of James E. Harbour cited, 1983.

———. Subcommittee on Investigations and Oversight of the Committee on Science and Technology. *Possible U.S. Responses Using Research Joint Ventures*. 98th Cong. 1st Sess. Hearings held on June 29–30, 1983. Washington D.C.: Government Printing Office, 1984.

———. Subcommittee on Oversight and Investigation of the Committee on Energy and Commerce. *Capital Formation and Industrial Policy* (Part 3). 97th Cong. 2d Sess.

Hearings held on April 23, 1982. Washington D.C.: Government Printing Office, 1982. Statement of Joel Hirschman cited.

———. Subcommittee on Science, Research and Technology of the Committee on Science and Technology. *Research and Development: Joint Ventures*. Hearings held on July 12, 1983. Washington D.C.: Government Printing Office. Statements of Doug Walgren and Ronald Myrick cited.

———. Subcommittee on Trade of the Committee of Ways and Means. *Domestic Content Legislation and the U.S. Automobile Industry*. Analysis of H.R. 5133. Hearings held on August 16, 1982. Washington D.C.: Government Printing Office, 1983.

———. *Fair Practices and Procedures in Automotive Products Act of 1983*. Hearings of September-October 1982. Report 98–287, Part 1. Washington D.C.: Government Printing Office, 1983.

———. Subcommittee on Transportation, Aviation and Materials of the Committee on Science and Technology. *Materials Research and Development Policy*. 98th Cong., 1st Sess. Hearings held on May 15–16, 1983. Washington D.C.: Government Printing Office, 1984.

———. Office of Technology Assessment. *Technology and Steel Industry Competitiveness*. Washington D.C.: Government Printing Office, 1980.

———. *U.S. Industrial Competitiveness: A Comparison of Steel, Electronics and Automobiles*. Washington D.C.: Government Printing Office, 1981.

U.S. Congress. Senate. Subcommittee on International Trade of the Committee on Finance. *Issues Relating to the Domestic Auto Industry*. 96th Cong., 1st Sess. Hearings held on January 14–15, 1981. Washington D.C.: Government Printing Office, 1983.

———. Subcommittee on International Economic Policy of the Committee on Foreign Relations. *U.S. Policy Toward International Investment*. 97th Cong., 1st Sess. Hearings held on July 30, September 28, and October 28, 1981. Washington D.C.: Government Printing Office, 1982. Items cited include statements or evidence by C. Fred Bergsten, pp. 1–18; Alan W. Wolff on behalf of the Labor-Industry Coalition for International Trade (LICIT), pp. 27–83; Gary Clyde Hufbauer, pp. 143–159; Harvey E. Bale, pp. 180–190; Raymond J. Waldman, pp. 190–219; and Robert D. Hormats, pp. 224–239.

U.S. Congressional Research Service. Dick Nanto, *Automobile Domestic Content Requirements*. Issue Brief Number 1B82056. Washington D.C.: Library of Congress, August 18, 1983.

———. Dick Nanto, *Automobiles Imported from Japan*. Issue Brief Number 1B80030, Washington D.C.: Library of Congress, August, 2, 1983.

U.S. Department of Commerce. *Foreign Direct Investment in the United States*. Vols. 1 and 5, April 1976.

———. *State Government Conducted International Trade and Business Development Programs*. Washington D.C.: Government Printing Office, June 1977.

———. Bureau of Economic Analysis. *Survey of Current Business*. Various issues.

———. Bureau of Industrial Economics. *1983 U.S. Industrial Outlook*. Washington D.C.: 1984.

———. *1984 U.S. Industrial Outlook*. Washington D.C.: 1985.

———. International Trade Administration. *Direct Investment in the United States by Foreign Government-Owned Companies, 1974–1981*. Washington D.C.: Government Printing Office, March 1983.

————. *International Direct Investment: Global Trends and the U.S. Role.* Washington D.C.: Government Printing Office, 1984.

U.S. Federal Trade Commission. *The United States Steel Industry and Its International Rivals: Trends and Factors Determining International Competitiveness.* Washington D.C.: Government Printing Office, 1977.

U.S. International Trade Commission. *Carbon and Certain Steel Products.* Vol. 1. Washington, D.C.: 1984.

————. *Motor Vehicles and Certain Chassis and Bodies Thereof.* Washington, D.C.: December 1980.

The U.S. Auto Industry, U.S. Factory Sales, Retail Sales, Imports, Exports, Apparent Consumption, 1964–1982. USITC Publication 1419. Washington, D.C.: August 1983.

U.S. President's Commission on Industrial Competitiveness. *Global Competition—The New Reality.* Vol 2, January 1985.

Index

oriented, 202–3; U.S., 6, 21, 100, 195–225, 241, 255
Foreign Investment Review Agency, 234, 235
Foreign Investment Study Act (1974), 231
Foreign-owned affiliates, 34–35, 45, 72–73, 218–24; import dependence, 35, 45; investment per worker, 34; performance, 218–24
Foreign producers, unfair advantages to, 6–7
Foreign review Agency, proposal for a (U.S.), 224, 256
France, 3, 8, 19, 51, 73
Franko, Lawrence, 70, 76
Fraser, Donald, 119
Free trade, 224; in automobiles, 157
Fujitsu, 76, 210, 211
Furubotn, Erik, 53

GATT for Investment, 254, 255, 257
General Agreement on Tariffs and Trade (GATT), 178, 235, 237
General Electric, 211, 217
General Motors, 76, 106, 121, 162, 167, 179, 184, 203, 206, 213, 214
General Motors Fanuc, 210
German investors, 70, 74, 79
Global cartels, 20
Global competition, 6, 197, 216, 265
Goodrich Co., B. F., 70, 205
Government intervention, 33, 48, 53, 54, 85, 88
Great Depression, 241
Greenfield investments, in steel, 77, 114
Gross domestic fixed capital formation, 54, 60, 61, 62, 73, 78
Gross product, 72–73
Grubel, Herbert, 164–65, 239

Harris, 217
Harvard School of Business Administration, 48
High technology, 197, 198, 203–18, 224; and anti-trust modifications, 215; and Co-ordination Committee for Multilateral Export Controls, 208–9; export

controls on, 200, 215; flexible technology transfer policy, 215; foreign direct investment in, 198, 203–18, 224; government-sponsored research in, 208, 215; industries, 4, 206, 210, 224, 245, 266; joint pooling of research in, 215, 216, 217; and patent laws strengthening of, 215; productive techniques, 206, 208; sectors, 206; and tax policy, 208, 215; U.S. Congress, hearings on collective research, 216
Honda Motors, 70, 76, 108, 113, 135, 179
Honeywell, 212, 217
House Committee on Energy and Commerce, 172
Hufbauer, Gary, 253
Hughes Aircraft, 206
Hymer, Stephen, 47–48
Hyundai, 195

Immature creditor, 43–45
Immature debtor, 44–45
Imperfect competition, 47, 48
Import competition, 121, 136
Import penetration, 4; automobiles, 137, 197
Import quotas, steel, 102
Import relief, steel, 83
Incentives for FDI, 54, 68, 69, 79, 138; state and local, 69, 79
Income from FDI, 65–67, 218
Income shifts, to Japan, 155
Indicative planning, 6
Industrial base, 4, 198, 265; and defense needs, 198–203; dependence on government, 4–5; and domestic content, 178; employment, 4; and import competition, 178, 200; and industrial policy, 199; old and obsolete, 4, 200; shifting, 241
Industrial organization theory of FDI, 47, 48, 52, 55, 67, 72–73
Industrial policy, 5, 86–87, 172, 241, 255, 267
Industrial robots, 184, 206, 210
Information, investment in, 53, 212, 213
Innovation, 70, 77, 79, 199, 215

About the Authors

SARA L. GORDON is Associate Professor of Economics at St. John's University, Jamaica, New York. She contributed a chapter to *Commodity Exports and African Development* and her articles have appeared in *California Management Review*, *Industrial Development*, and *National Development*.

FRANCIS A. LEES is Professor of Economics and Finance at St. John's University, Jamaica, New York. His earlier works include *International Lending: Risks and Euromarkets*, *Economic and Political Development of the Sudan*, and *Foreign Banking and Investment in the U.S.*, as well as numerous articles in journals such as the *California Management Review*, *The Economic Journal*, and the *Columbia Journal of World Business*.